MYANMAR'S 'ROHINGYA' CONFLICT

ANTHONY WARE
COSTAS LAOUTIDES

Myanmar's 'Rohingya' Conflict

OXFORD
UNIVERSITY PRESS

OXFORD

UNIVERSITY PRESS

Oxford University Press is a department of the
University of Oxford. It furthers the University's objective
of excellence in research, scholarship, and education
by publishing worldwide.

Oxford   New York

Auckland   Cape Town   Dar es Salaam   Hong Kong   Karachi
Kuala Lumpur   Madrid   Melbourne   Mexico City   Nairobi
New Delhi   Shanghai   Taipei   Toronto

With offices in

Argentina   Austria   Brazil   Chile   Czech Republic   France   Greece
Guatemala   Hungary   Italy   Japan   Poland   Portugal   Singapore
South Korea   Switzerland   Thailand   Turkey   Ukraine   Vietnam

Oxford is a registered trade mark of Oxford University Press
in the UK and certain other countries.

Published in the United States of America by
Oxford University Press
198 Madison Avenue, New York, NY 10016

Library of Congress Cataloging-in-Publication Data is available
Anthony Ware and Costas Laoutides.
Myanmar's 'Rohingya' Conflict.
ISBN: 9780190928865

Printed in India on acid-free paper

CONTENTS

CONTENTS

MAPS, FIGURES AND TABLES

Maps

Figures

Tables

ACKNOWLEDGEMENTS

We would like to express our sincere gratitude to a large number of people who have supported and aided us in this work. In particular, we would like to start by thanking our many informants, 'Rohingya', Rakhine, Burman, Hindu, and international, and from civil society, political parties, the bureaucracy, the military, academia, and the diplomatic service. Thank you for your generosity, sharing time and perspectives. Some of you were hesitant to speak about such a difficult topic as this. We appreciate your deep concerns, given that it is such an explosive issue inside Myanmar, and that it is extremely personal to many of you. We appreciate that wrong words, or something taken out of context, may have serious consequences for individuals, communities, careers, international relations, the government, or the economy. We may not always agree, but we deeply appreciate your time sharing your perspective with us. Thank you for taking the risk and speaking with us. Thank you too, to our many friends in Myanmar, on all sides of this conflict, for the many informal conversations over the past few years. The analysis of ideas and concepts in this work are our own, and we apologize in advance to anyone who is disappointed, even upset, with any of our comments, use of language, analysis, or conclusions. We have tried to faithfully reflect your voices in our text first, even if we then go on to critique and disagree. A special thank you to those who have read and provided feedback on drafts or sections of this work, especially the two anonymous reviewers arranged by the publishers, and Martin Smith, Dr Jacques Leider, Dr Peter Thein Nyunt, and Dr Vicki-Ann Ware. Thank you for your comments, which have

ACKNOWLEDGEMENTS

helped us greatly in correcting and refining the text. Any mistakes, errors, omissions, or misunderstandings in the book are ours alone, but we are very grateful for your help in spotting issues along the way. Thank you to our two local NGO partners, who have provided us deep insights into local ethnic Rakhine, minorities' and sometimes Muslim perspectives: the Sittwe-based Community Development Education, and the Socio-Economic Development Institute. Thank you in particular to Kyaw Soe and Soe Lunn. Thank you to Christopher Lamb, the board and members of the Australia Myanmar Institute, for brokering contacts and helping us gain access to various officials and key contacts. Thank you likewise to Ronan Lee and David Mathieson for offering numerous contacts. Thank you to the Gerda Henkel Foundation, for providing a research grant for our work (AZ 12/KF/16). This is only the beginning of the findings and results of your funding. Thank you likewise to GraceWorks Myanmar for grant funding to explore the conflict dynamics in Rakhine State, in order to provide strategic advice on conflict-sensitive development approaches in parts of that state. Thank you to the Alfred Deakin Institute, for research funding which got us started on this project and for the strongly supportive research environment they provided along the way. A huge thank you to Jon de Peyer and Michael Dwyer at Hurst Publishers, who believed in us and have shown great patience and forbearance in the preparation of this manuscript. And finally, thank you to our wives and families for putting up with weeks and weeks apart, our evenings, weekends, and holidays glued to a computer screen, and endless conversations about this material. Thank you.

FOREWORD

Derek Mitchell

(*Former US Ambassador to Myanmar*)

Myanmar will confound and frustrate even its most ardent admirers and supporters. After decades as one of the world's leading liberal causes, Myanmar's evolution in recent years from an opaque, repressive state to a more open and reform-minded nascent democracy became one of the era's few 'good news' stories.

The world looked on with awe and delight as thousands of political prisoners rejoined their families, the media and civil society were substantially liberalized, and serious peace talks were undertaken to end Myanmar's decades-long civil war. Myanmar's people even had their 'inked finger' moment in November 2015, when they took part in the country's first credible and representative national election since 1990. A landslide victory for the opposition National League for Democracy party led to the ascension of democracy icon Aung San Suu Kyi to (civilian) leadership. Hope reigned supreme as fifty years of military domination appeared to succumb—finally—to people power.

Those who were watching the country up close, however, understood the limitations of that euphoric moment. An election cannot make a half-century of institutional degradation and underdevelopment disappear overnight. Fear, mistrust, and insecurity remained pervasive throughout the country. Military violence continued to rage, particularly in the north in Kachin State and in northern Shan State. A deeply flawed constitution remained unamended.

And those of us on the ground recognized the ticking time bomb that existed in northern Rakhine State.

Amidst the many positive developments in Myanmar since 2011, deteriorating conditions in Rakhine State stood out in stark relief. Eruption of communal violence in June 2012 occurred just a month before I arrived in Yangon as the first US ambassador to the country in twenty-two years, and about nine months after I began serving as US special envoy. My task as envoy had been to test whether 'principled engagement', not just isolation and sanctions, may serve as a lever for democratic reform in Myanmar. The Rohingya question had always been on the agenda, but its unique complexity and sensitivity amidst so many other priorities required that it be of lesser immediate concern.

That changed after June 2012, and then even more profoundly after the second round of violence against Muslim communities in Rakhine State in October 2012. From that point, with more than 100,000 Rohingya (and Muslim Kaman) languishing precariously in open-air pens, with limited freedom of movement, access to livelihoods, health care and educational facilities, and ability to defend themselves against potential violence, the Rakhine issue rose to the top of our agenda.

My colleagues and I travelled to Rakhine State as much as if not more than to any other area of the country outside the central Bamar areas of Yangon and Nay Pyi Taw. We spent countless hours in conversation with official and unofficial representatives on all sides of the issue to help find a way out of the impasse. We learned early about the many obstacles to a quick or easy solution: the troubled legacies of history and inter-communal friction—not just between Rakhine and Rohingya, but between the Rakhine and Burman—that dated back centuries; the prevalent narratives of victimization and fear of the other; the multiple agendas—some evident, some perhaps not—within each camp.

We also found few in Myanmar, certainly no political leader seeking popular support in a nascent democracy, willing to stand up for the rights of what were generally considered to be an alien population at best, and a profound national security threat at worst. That also included many (though certainly not all) religious leaders, and former political prisoners who themselves had been imprisoned for protesting against violations of their human rights and dignity just a few years before.

As a result, the situation stagnated, conditions on the ground steadily deteriorated, human traffickers and corrupt officials swarmed with opportunity, and helplessness and hopelessness took root. My colleagues and I failed to induce Nay Pyi Taw to act with urgency. We failed to convince the Myanmar government that time was not on its side, and that failure to be proactive in addressing underlying issues of the conflict, such as citizenship, access to livelihoods, and rule of law, would eventually take a toll on the country's security, stability, and national reputation.

And we ultimately failed to prevent expansion of the violence. The attacks by Rohingya militants against security forces along the border in northern Rakhine State in October 2016 and August 2017, the excessively violent response by Myanmar security forces, and the massive human exodus that has played out on the front pages of newspapers around the world since have only deepened the impasse. In the process, the Rohingya issue has become an international cause célèbre, the defining issue of Myanmar, exacerbating divisions not only between the Rohingya and other Myanmar populations, but between the Myanmar people and the global community.

Many in Myanmar wonder why outsiders care so uniquely about the Rohingya when so many others in the country have suffered, and continue to suffer, similar trauma and abuse inside the country. It is a reasonable question. One critical reason is that the Rohingya are stateless, unspoken for, and unprotected by any government. The same advocates around the world who spoke up for human rights and justice in Myanmar during its period of military dictatorship feel they must likewise speak out and protect these uniquely disadvantaged people in turn.

But if moral outrage may be a necessary response, it is insufficient to the task. If we want to truly help alleviate the suffering and help solve the impasse, we all must make a more honest and sincere effort to understand the situation in its full complexity and nuance. The foundation of Myanmar's mistrust of the international community and failure to heed pleas for a more humane response to the Rohingya crisis is a belief that we on the outside, fuelled by the media and other interested commentators, do not understand the issue's complexities, that we have a simplistic, one-sided view of the problem.

They are not entirely wrong.

For that reason, books such as this one are a profound public service. Some matters related to the Rohingya are straightforward, some are not. Nothing about the humanitarian tragedy and requirement to address the sustained suffering is complex. But the underlying dynamics are. And they require serious attention if we are truly to help the Rohingya people find justice and dignity, rather than simply grandstand in their name.

THE VEXED QUESTION OF NAMES

Deciding what name to use to discuss the Muslims of northern Rakhine State is a very vexed issue.

The name 'Rohingya' has become one of the most controversial words in Myanmar politics today. Most of the Muslims in question claim the right to self-identification, as 'Rohingya'. Shouldn't that settle the matter? Yet the name 'Rohingya' is so heavily contested and so highly controversial inside Myanmar that it has become a key conflict factor. To most people across the country, the name represents an extremely dangerous political cause. Many are deeply angered by the use of the name, seeing it as unqualified support or naïve complicity in a political assault on the sovereignty and territorial integrity of the nation. On the other hand, avoiding the name is seen by others as representing complicity in human rights violations, if not crimes against humanity. Use or avoid—either choice is polarizing.

This book aims to provide as reasoned and evidence-based an analysis as is possible, while causing minimal offence. We realize that is nigh impossible, but we hope not to prejudice our readers before we start. So, how do we resolve this tension?

The first thing to note is that this conundrum is not unique. Conflict routinely involves attempts to control perceptions of identity, of oneself and 'the Other'. Names are often hotly contested. For example, many Serbs do not accept the name 'Kosovar' for the residents of Kosovo, referring to them as 'Albanians'. This relates to the national Serbian narrative that locates Kosovo as the cradle of Serbian nationalism, and to the fact that Albanians migrated to the region between the late seventeenth and mid-eighteenth centuries, in response to the Ottoman–Habsburg wars. Names imply legitimacy to inhabit territory, and that is what drives many conflicts. For the same reason, many Israelis do not accept the name 'Palestinian', but call Israeli citizens of that descent 'Israeli Arabs'. So, conflicts routinely try to control names, where they may be linked to legitimacy to reside in or self-govern territory, making them very political.

So, what should we call the Muslims of northern Rakhine State in a book of this nature?

Most Muslims claim 'Rohingya' as their ethnicity. Many claim this as a 'right to self-identification' (e.g. Ullah 2017), as an ethnic group long established in Myanmar. However, there is no internationally recognized 'right to self-identification' in any human rights instrument, although one is sometimes derived from the non-discrimination principle manifest in several international instruments, such as the 'right to self-determination' or the Declaration on the Rights of Indigenous Peoples. However, both revolve around the definition of 'a people', which has been restricted in UN practice to apply only to former colonies and cases of foreign occupation, not minorities within former colonies or other nation-states. Any right to self-determination for minority groups is an evolving debate in international law. Likewise, the Muslims do not meet the delineation of indigeneity used in the Declaration, which has fairly strict criteria designed for application only in the context of settler societies. Furthermore, while international law does not prohibit any group from self-naming, there are many international disputes where names cause offence or are used to make false claims about ancestry or territory, as above.

The key issue is that the term 'Rohingya' is widely perceived by most people inside Myanmar not to represent an ethnic identity, or even a cultural practice, but to be a gambit by a recent mixed-origin migrant group for greater political rights by claiming indigeneity under Myanmar law—and through that, to claim territory and self-governance. The name 'Rohingya' is thus widely perceived as a means to prosecute a set of political claims which, in their entirety, are deemed by many in Myanmar to be a threat to national cohesion and territorial integrity.

That makes use of the name 'Rohingya' exceedingly inflammatory to a large number of people in the country. It is why not only local

Rakhine Buddhists, the Tatmadaw (Burmese military), and former regime officials all reject the name, but so too do the democratic government of Nobel Peace Prize laureate Aung San Suu Kyi and many ethnic-minority civil-society groups. The statement is often made that 'there are no Rohingya in Myanmar'. This does not deny the existence of the people themselves, but claims that they do not comprise an 'ethnicity' who are 'indigenous' to Myanmar, with the group rights that would imply.

Inside Myanmar, the people are often called 'Bengali'—or worse, *kala*. The latter literally means 'foreigner' or 'stranger', particularly of South Asian origin, but has long been seen as derogatory, with approximately the same impact as calling an Afro-American a 'nigger' (Harvey 1946). And obviously, the name 'Bengali' is used to imply they are recent, if not illegal, immigrants from Bangladesh, and thus should have only very limited claims to Myanmar citizenship.

We are not saying at this point that either set of claims is true. We simply note that use or non-use of the name is attached to conflict dynamics. Hence the difficulty in finding terminology for scholarly examination of the issues rather than advocacy.

There is evidence that the term 'Rohingya' did exist prior to Independence. It might even have been used by some as a name, although if so it appears to have been rarely used in public. However, evidence discussed later in this book suggests that it has only come into common usage since the 1950s, and has only been popularized over the last couple of decades. The evidence for these statements will be discussed later, but for these reasons, and the inflammatory way in which it is perceived, we cannot unreservedly adopt the name 'Rohingya'. Doing so would imply that we are naïve, or partial, or both.

So, what do we do instead? One option would be to follow Aung San Suu Kyi's lead. In 2016 she asked all parties to refrain from using names likely to inflame tensions—particularly 'Rohingya', *kala*, and 'Bengali'. Instead, to help defuse the situation she requested that we simply describe them as 'the Muslim community in northern Rakhine State'. While seemingly sensible and neutral, such a request cannot be divorced from the politics involved. It plays down the element of ethnicity by referring only to the religious difference, in so doing potentially excluding a priori any discussion about their possible existence and recognition as a distinct ethnic group. It also plays to an attempt by Suu Kyi and the National League for Democracy (NLD) to frame the conflict as communal, between two parties in Rakhine, in which the central government must intervene. We explore this in detail in Chapter 5, but this response by the state attempts to frame itself as an impartial, neutral external actor, only engaged in this conflict to restore law and order. This seemingly neutral request, therefore, attempts to locate the state as impartial in an asymmetrical conflict of which it is part, and endorsement of it may undermine any genuine intention to address the issue. It does not navigate a middle path of parity and fairness as much as it promotes the political agenda of one of the key actors in the conflict, which is highly problematic.

Furthermore, this option is semantically awkward. Not only is it a mouthful, but there are other Muslim groups in Rakhine State—notably the 30,000 or so Kaman Muslims. Although they are a small group and live mostly in central (not northern) Rakhine, adopting the term 'Muslims in northern Rakhine State' is thus not entirely accurate. It is also misleading in that it makes the primary identification of this group their religious belief, falsely implying that the conflict is sectarian in nature. Indeed, some of the key 'Rohingya' insurgent leaders of recent decades explicitly rejected terms such as 'Arakanese Muslim', specifically because it made their primary marker of identity religious, which they reject. This is all the more significant in a context of negative global narratives about Islam.

So options are limited. The names 'Rohingya' or 'Bengali' both inherently embody attempts to appropriate particular historical narratives into everyday naming, for political purposes, and both are seen as very provocative. Yet, avoiding them both, and referring to the 'Muslims in northern Rakhine State', is awkward and implicitly supports the narrative of the government. However, the latter at least avoids this co-option of history, and, significantly, the Advisory Commission on Rakhine State (headed by former UN Secretary-General Kofi Annan) adopted this convention (Annan et al. 2017a, 2017b)—as have several local agency reports (e.g. Aron & Gilmore 2017; CDNH 2017). In these reports 'Muslim' does not signify religion, but an identity group, and does not include the Kaman or other Muslim minorities, who are simply referred to by their ethnic names.

THE VEXED QUESTION OF NAMES

From all of this, we conclude that the term 'Muslims in northern Rakhine State' is the least-worst option, for majority use throughout the book, noting that we will carefully analyse this point further in the text. We thus adopt the following convention throughout this book:

- *Title*—As 'Rohingya' is the only name the international community knows for these people, we use this name in the book title to quickly communicate what the book is about to an international audience. The use of quotation marks should be noted: this is who they claim they are, whatever else one may think.
- *Text*—With Kofi Annan, we adopt the nomenclature 'Muslims in northern Rakhine State' for most of our own commentary, unless presenting the positions of others or 'Rohingya' is required for clarity.
- *Views of others*—When presenting the perspectives of others, we use their terminology. We thus mimic the language of others when 'Rohingya' or 'Bengali' better conveys their sentiment. This is intended to allow their voices to be heard, not to cause offence.

Again, our aim is to communicate clearly, with minimal offence, yet with clarity. We recognize that attempts at neutrality and impartiality by outsiders, regardless of intentions, may convey political benefit, especially given the significant power differentials. Nonetheless, we aim for a balanced, reasoned, analytical, and critical middle path. We acknowledge the controversy and deep political concerns. Our nomenclature is not intended to offend or to be a political statement.

For all other names—our convention is to use the names of places and groups as they were formally designated at the time being written about. Thus, we use:

- *Burma* as the name of the country when speaking about events prior to the official change of the English name in 1989—*Myanmar* for periods after this date.
- *Arakan* as the name for the kingdom, region, then state when speaking about periods prior to the official change of the English name in 1989—*Rakhine* after that date.[1]
- *Arakanese* for the local Buddhist ethnic majority in the state pre-1989—*Rakhine* after that. (This does not imply that many Muslims are not also from Rakhine state).

- *Burman* (Bamar) to refer to the majority ethnic group, and *Burmese* (or Myanmar) as inclusive of all peoples in the country, including the national language.

PART I

CONTEXT

PERSONAL JOURNEYS INTO THIS CONFLICT

Anthony: *I touched down in Sittwe, the Rakhine State capital, in late October 2012, just as the second wave of violence erupted that year. I was there to provide training for a small, unregistered civil society organization commencing community-led development projects in rural Rakhine Buddhist villages. I was not there for research or advocacy, and had not even planned to visit Muslim communities that trip. But being there as violence erupted certainly cemented their plight to me, and the importance of dealing with the conflict.*

We commenced the development project in late 2011, thus before the recent violence began. We were responding to poverty and development needs, rather than conflict issues. When we commenced, many Muslims, Rakhine and others, were living and working together fairly amicably, although the conflict definitely existed then too. Many of our project team still retain personal connections with people across the conflict divisions.

Landing in October 2012, Sittwe was almost in lockdown, with a dusk-to-dawn curfew. The city seemed quiet during the day, and life appeared to go on as if nothing were happening. But the dynamics of the conflict came home to me when I set out by bicycle on the first evening, after training, to explore the situation just before curfew. A few minutes into my ride, I rounded a corner on a residential street to be suddenly confronted by barbed-wire barricades and armed soldiers. I had arrived at the side of Aung Mingalar. As violence had swept the town three months earlier, most of Sittwe's Muslims had fled into camps to the north-west of town. The people of Aung Mingalar were among the few Muslims to stay in their homes, and their neighbourhood quickly turned into a ghetto, cordoned off by barbed wire and guarded by security forces.

So there I was, awkwardly at the edge of Aung Mingalar without purpose or authorization, shortly before curfew. Scores of Rakhine were on the street, finishing dinner and engaging in conversation or evening exercise in front of their houses. In front of me was a 20-metre no-man's land, patrolled by security, with burned houses in between. And across the way was another barbed-wire barricade, with similar numbers of Muslims on the street on the other side, also going about their evening routine. Two communal groups, who just months before had lived side by side, were now totally segregated by the military—the presence of whom both sides resented, yet relied upon. The difference was, the Rakhine were free to get on with their lives, going to school or work or markets or development project training during the day. The Muslims, on the other side of the barricade, could not leave their ghetto without pre-arranged permission and an escort. They had lost citizenship, rights, and most basic service provision. The violence had effectively imprisoned them.

Our training venue was almost right under the end of the airport runway. Planes flew in and out all day, carrying additional troops to keep the peace. We were almost deafened every time another plane landed. My Rakhine friends, who made no bones about wanting their state to be free from Burman control, were clearly strangely reassured by this inflow of troops. The irony was not lost on me!

This was before Rakhine had access to 3G phone data, so before Facebook. During one of our training days a visitor walked into the compound and pulled out a photobook. He fervently engaged the group, showing pictures said to be of Muslims disrespecting Buddha images and attacking Buddhist communities, re-telling his narrative of why to fear the Muslims. Social media before the internet! On other trips, visiting the camps for internally displaced Muslims, I have heard almost identical narrative accounts of injustice from Muslims, equally passionate and fearful as they describe discrimination and violence against them by Buddhists. It has been very rare, indeed, that I have found people talking positively about anyone from the other side, even of those who used to be friends. It has been even rarer that I have seen Muslims and ethnic Rakhine sitting together and talking amicably since 2012, although I have done so on several occasions. People on all sides are deeply traumatized by what they have experienced. And almost everyone is hearing inflammatory narratives from only one side. Segregation is almost total. Polarization of views is extreme.

One final anecdote highlights my journey into this conflict. On another occasion, after three days in Sittwe training community development facilitators, I popped out for lunch. This was in early 2014, not long before most international agency workers were evacuated because their assistance to the Muslims became construed as being partisan. An old monk in saffron robes spotted me sitting and eating in a small street-side café, and came over. Very animated, he hurled abuse at me for several minutes, his arms gesticulating wildly, while I tried to eat. My language skills were insufficient to catch every word, but his meaning was patently clear. We in the international community have clearly become a conflict actor in our own right.

Costas: *I arrived into this conflict much later, in 2014, visiting with Anthony as part of a wider pilot study on territorial separatism in Myanmar. Having studied separatist conflicts in the former Soviet Union, the former Yugoslavia, as well as in the Middle East, I was prepared to encounter the 'typical symptoms' of ethno-political conflict—but I also suspected, because of my background, that the situation is far more complex than the proclaimed linear depictions of a total clash between different collectivities.*

During my first trip to Sittwe, in 2014, I was invited to contribute to a human rights training workshop and run a few exercises with Rakhine participants. We discussed the difference between citizenship and human rights, and eventually the discussions touched the issue of the presence of Muslim communities in Rakhine—and how we can ensure the protection of human rights for all the inhabitants. Participants referred to the Muslim community using a range of names, especially kala *and 'Bengali', but what totally surprised me was younger participants openly adopting the name 'Rohingya'! So here I am, in the capital of Rakhine state, having been warned to be extremely cautious of not using the term 'Rohingya' when referring to Muslims, told it will cause offence to most Rakhine. And what I hear is Rakhine youth leaders more concerned about ensuring the human rights of all residents than being particularly bothered about the use or non-use of certain terms. This was the first, albeit informal, confirmation to me that this conflict is multi-layered, with hidden agendas and sub-groups defying the collectivization and reification driving the conflict. I immediately saw a potential not only for amplified conflict, but also for building peace in the post-transition era.*

We have subsequently observed this interchangeable use of terminology about the Muslim community in fieldwork in Rakhine villages, where the term 'Rohingya' was also employed by locals in a few villages without any prompting. Again, like the young people in Sittwe, locals in these few Rakhine villages were more interested in how to improve their well-being, their relationships with the government, and to see policy change, than in engaging in any war of names. They may not be typical, even common, but for these villagers, the coalface, so to speak, of coexistence with the other communities is an everyday practice rather than a rhetorical exercise. And it appears that they recognize many common interests, feeling forgotten, inhabiting the rural and thus more remote parts of the second most impoverished state in Myanmar.

Having said that, I am not trying to bypass the trauma all communities have endured, fuelled by narratives of hatred and enmity. The situation is dire, the recent violence and mass dislocation extreme, and the Muslims have definitely suffered the most. The isolation of refugees in Bangladesh and in segregated camps will only increase the frustration, the sense of injustice and understandable grievances they hold. A simple walk in Sittwe reveals two parallel universes: one of gradual improvement (economic and social) for the Rakhine; and one of marginalization and stagnation for the Muslims, who are entrapped in segregated communities, or forced to flee. The ongoing separation of the communities and overt control of the Muslims gradually diminishes the possibilities for reconciliation and coexistence, to the point where hope is lost.

Given the human scale and international profile of this disaster, the region, the country, and humanity cannot afford that.

1

COMPLEXITIES, MISCONCEPTIONS, AND CONTEXT

Myanmar's 'Rohingya' conflict has escalated over the last few years, to become both a massive humanitarian crisis and a significant threat to Myanmar's ongoing, fragile reforms. Mass displacement of refugees, sustained allegations of crimes against humanity, and a large-scale military intervention has propelled the conflict to centre stage. It can no longer be considered a peripheral issue. It is causing massive foreign-relations damage, robbing the country of good will just as it needs it most, and creating dangerous ire throughout much of the Muslim world. It has stoked religious nationalism, damaged social cohesion, propelled the re-emergence of both Rakhine and Muslim militancies, and shifted the balance of power between the military and the civilian government. It is likely to lead to the reimposition of international sanctions, harm international investment, and stifle the economy. This conflict, smouldering and periodically flaring for over eight decades, has erupted violently again in the last few years, wreaking havoc and endangering both Rakhine state and the country.

It is impossible to ignore the chaos of 2017–2018. Some 671,500 Muslim refugees have fled Myanmar for Bangladesh since 25 August 2017 (as of 15 March 2018; see IOM 2018). If we include those who fled prior to August, there are now 836,210 'Rohingya' Muslim refugees registered by the UNHCR in camps in Bangladesh, and the Bangladeshi Immigration and Passports Department counts a total of 1,092,136

Muslims from northern Rakhine now residing in their country. The Myanmar government acknowledges that up to 90 per cent of the Muslim population of the three northernmost townships—Maungdaw, Buthidaung, and Rathedaung—have now fled Myanmar, including virtually the entire Muslim population of southern Maungdaw—which was previously 93 per cent Muslim (Moe Myint 2018b).

This looks very much like ethnic cleansing, whether intentional or not. It is certainly one of the fastest refugee exoduses in modern times, representing over 60 per cent of the former Muslim population of the whole of Rakhine state, and resulting in the largest refugee camp in the world. This scale of human suffering is mind-numbing, and the extent of destruction vast.

Based on surveys of arriving refugees, Médecins Sans Frontières (MSF 2017) estimates that at least 6,700 'Rohingya' were killed during the violence. In just one incident, in Tula Toli village, Maungdaw, on 30 August 2017, Human Rights Watch (2017c) claim evidence that the military raped several hundred Muslims, followed by systematic killings. Several other mass graves have been identified, many more have been alleged (e.g. Klug 2018). Their satellite imagery also showed that at least 288 villages were partially or totally destroyed by October 2017 (HRW 2017a), including 62 per cent of all villages in Maungdaw. This total grew to 354 villages in mid-December (HRW 2017b). Many who did not flee arson and violence subsequently fled the loss of livelihood caused by severe new restrictions on their movement (ICG 2017). This now leaves no more than 250,000 Muslims in these three townships, and no more than 320,000 in the rest of Rakhine (more than a third of whom are in internally displaced persons' (IDP) camps around Sittwe). Many are still fleeing at the time of writing, such as 496 reported taking to 9 boats on 19 February 2018 (MoHA 2018).

At the same time, over half the non-Muslim population from the affected townships have also been displaced. Destruction and violence have affected ordinary villagers on all sides. Rakhine Buddhist and Hindu communities have also been attacked and burned, and tens of thousands have fled. The violence has been calamitous for everyone—Muslim, Buddhist, and other. The numbers and severity are definitely disproportionately skewed towards the Muslims, because of their much higher population in those townships, and as the primary targets of military action. And non-Muslims are more likely to be able to return sooner. But it is important to note that all communities in the area have been negatively impacted. The number of people killed, tortured, and raped is unknown, but accounts from all parties are horrific.

The brutal military operation that triggered this massive refugee crisis was launched in response to coordinated deadly attacks on thirty police posts and a military base in August 2017, by the militant Muslim group the Arakan Rohingya Salvation Army (ARSA). The government has declared ARSA 'terrorists'. Nonetheless, this crackdown, and the one launched after attacks in 2016, have prompted a wave of international condemnation. UN concerns culminated with the United Nations High Commissioner for Human Rights, Zeid bin Ra'ad al-Hussein, declaring in September 2017 that 'Myanmar's treatment of the Rohingya appears to be a textbook example of ethnic cleansing' (Westcott & Smith 2017). A February 2017 UN report found the 'very likely commission of crimes against humanity' by the Tatmadaw (Burmese military) (OHCHR 2017). The US Secretary of State at the time, Rex Tillerson, declared in November that the situation clearly constitutes ethnic cleansing, and British, French, and a host of other political leaders have spoken out against it. The matter has been discussed by the UN Security Council, and even Pope Francis (2017) has condemned the 'violent persecution of the Rohingya'. In early December Zeid bin Ra'ad followed up his earlier comments by indicating that it was still not possible to rule out genocide, and then led the UN Human Rights Council to condemn the probable commission of crimes against humanity by Myanmar's security forces. In February 2018 he included Rakhine State alongside Syria, Yemen, and Congo as the 'the most prolific slaughterhouses of humans in recent times' (OHCHR 2018), and has repeatedly urged the UN to create a new mechanism for criminal investigations into the perpetrators of violence against Muslims from Rakhine.

Condemnation has been widespread. Over the past few years, report after report has made scathing allegations of genocide, ethnic cleansing, and crimes against humanity (e.g. Al Jazeera 2015a, 2015b; Green et al. 2015; Yale Law School 2015; Fortify Rights 2016; Amnesty International 2017a, 2017b, 2017c; Human Rights Watch 2013, 2017a, 2017c). In

May 2015, towards the end of the term in office of former president Thein Sein and well before these latest attacks, three Nobel Peace Prize laureates declared that the 'Rohingya' faced 'nothing less than genocide' (AP 2015). Many of these reports provide substantial documentation of specific incidents. Large numbers of other academics, media, global leaders, and humanitarian organizations have expressed similar concerns. Certainly, whether intentional or not, unless the bulk of the refugees are repatriated safely soon, the end result of this crisis is highly likely to be ethnic cleansing. A million Muslims have fled Rakhine State for their lives, and unless they are brought back soon, safely and voluntarily, how else could it be described?

At this point, there is insufficient firm evidence to confirm who has committed which mass crimes, although atrocities have clearly been committed and the charges are very serious. The government and military have issued blanket denials of any wrongdoing, which is highly improbable and only reinforces a climate of impunity (ICG 2017). The only exception has been in relation to the massacre at Inn Din, southern Maungdaw Township, on 9 October 2017. The admission by the Tatmadaw of involvement only came after Reuters released a detailed investigation report, with witness statements by local Buddhists and photographic evidence (Wa Lone et al. 2018). The announcement that sixteen people, including some military officials, will be held to account (Nyan Hlaing Lynn 2018) is welcome, but very insincere given that two of the Reuters journalists involved have been charged under the Official Secrets Act for obtaining and publishing the facts around the story.

Denial of all other wrongdoing, though, is very hard to believe, especially given the Tatmadaw's brutal history and the constant testimony of those who have fled to Bangladesh. We have personally heard reliable evidence from a high-ranked Tatmadaw source and numerous credible Buddhist witnesses who claim to have first-hand knowledge of other ruthless acts against Muslims committed by the military. A massive cover-up is almost certainly being perpetrated. So while there are also witness accounts of Muslims committing violence against civilians, and it is highly likely Rakhine actors have committed atrocities too, the allegations are of such magnitude that an independent investigation is desperately needed.

Myanmar is rapidly squandering what remains of the vast good will generated by political transition, which is a real problem for navigating a path forward (ICG 2017). For decades, Aung San Suu Kyi presented herself as a champion of human rights, and the world threw accolades to strengthen her cause. The collective disappointment with her response to this situation has thus been enormous. Suu Kyi was already widely criticized for remaining silent on this issue, before inheriting power (e.g. AP 2015; Lee 2014), and criticism has mounted in the face of her failure to use her moral authority since the government's inauguration on 1 April 2016 (e.g. New York Times 2016a, 2016b; Hutt 2017). For example, Keith Harper, former US ambassador to the UN Human Rights Council, voiced concerns that,

> while Daw Suu Kyi was perfectly comfortable reaping benefits as a human rights icon for her own pro-democracy struggle, she is not prepared to display the political courage necessary to take a stand for an unpopular Muslim minority group and prevent the grave and systematic denial of their human rights. (Harper 2017; Hutt 2017)

In March 2017, the UN Rapporteur on Human Rights in Myanmar, Yanghee Lee (2017b), went so far as to suggest to the Human Rights Council that the National League for Democracy (NLD) government, not just the military, 'may be trying to expel the Rohingya population from the country'. That was five months before the recent violence, and Suu Kyi's handling of subsequent events has neither prompted peace and safety for the Muslim population nor supported their human rights. Lee has repeatedly criticized the NLD's handling of the situation, its consistent defence of military action, and its dismissal of all claims of rights abuses (Lee 2017a).

Perhaps the NLD's most positive steps to date relate to the Advisory Commission on Rakhine State, and commitments by Myanmar to accept back the refugees from Bangladesh—including promises that they could return to their own homes and land, with the government rebuilding all burned homes (RFA 2017). The Advisory Commission was set up in 2016, with Aung San Suu Kyi appointing former UN Secretary-General Kofi Annan to lead the work. It had a mandate to examine the complex long-term challenges and propose responses. The nine-person commission issued interim and final reports (Annan et al. 2017a, 2017b), which provide the best blueprint for action to date. We will return to analyse these in the final chapter, but just note for now that many of the recommendations would have been very challenging for Myanmar to implement even before the latest violence, and are currently almost impossible to imagine. Nonetheless, since receiving the recommendations on 24 August 2017, Aung San Suu Kyi and the NLD have repeatedly committed themselves to do so, as quickly as the situation allows, and appointed a number of committees to oversee the work.

However, the context and logistics suggest very slow implementation, if at all. There are real fears that insecurity or politics will prevent refugees from returning any time soon. There are also growing fears that ethnic Rakhine will move into currently unoccupied Muslim areas (Moe Myint 2017), and that other forms of land grabbing will emerge, making a return to their homes and land even harder. Such developments could also further undermine the possibility of any long-term peaceful solution.

These concerns came to a head in January 2018. Bill Richardson, a long-term confidant of Aung San Suu Kyi, resigned from the international Advisory Board to the Committee for Implementation of the Recommendations on Rakhine, formed just a month earlier. Richardson, a former US governor, congressional representative, and Clinton-era cabinet member, resigned from the Advisory Board, questioning Aung San Suu Kyi's lack of moral leadership on the issue and suggesting all she wanted from the board was to simply whitewash events and responses (Richardson 2018a; Reuters 2018). Richardson wrote:

> Aung San Suu Kyi ... has failed to show moral leadership on Rakhine and appears unwilling to listen to frank advice. Moreover, Aung San Suu Kyi's government lacks both the will and the capacity to faithfully implement the recommendations of the Kofi Annan-led Rakhine Advisory Commission ... it is becoming increasingly clear that Aung San Suu Kyi is part of the problem. (Richardson 2018b)

He went on to call for donors to withhold support for repatriation until Myanmar ensures that returns are safe, voluntary, dignified, and sustainable, and for punitive measures against Myanmar to be considered if better progress is not made soon, including sanctions.

So Myanmar's response to this conflict has been very poor, and Aung San Suu Kyi is under a deep cloud of suspicion. Having said all this, though, we also want to express serious concerns about the campaigns led by many in the international community to redress these failures. Attempting to shame Myanmar into action is counterproductive. Any sustainable outcome will rely very heavily on cooperation from both the NLD government and Tatmadaw. There is no potential alternative government with different policies, so contemplation of 'regime change' is out of the question. The NLD and/or the Tatmadaw are the only options with whom to negotiate a solution. Public shaming of the people you must later rely upon, often based on selective reports that do not acknowledge their legitimate responsibilities, fears, and constraints, does very little to win such cooperation. The situation on the ground is complex, as we will explore in the coming chapters, and the security forces had a legitimate and very serious responsibility to act to maintain law and order. They may have acted disproportionately, but they did need to act. And as for Aung San Suu Kyi and the NLD government, this conflict is the most sensitive and complex issue that they have inherited, and one that seems to have left them with few options. Blanket assertions or condemnation is most unhelpful. They may be complicit, but in many ways their hands are tied by the military's power and operational freedom, and winning their trust and cooperation is essential to any solution. Their immense challenges need to be acknowledged, including their struggles with the military and the fact the nation sits on a knife-edge of wider racial violence, even while we demand much more serious and comprehensive action.

Myanmar is at a crucial juncture. The impact of this conflict on every aspect of its domestic reform can hardly be overstated, and leadership promoting social cohesion, human rights, and law and order is currently inadequate. Myanmar faces a plethora of serious political, economic, and social challenges, but, more than any other issue, this one threatens the whole reform process. Aung San Suu Kyi and her government are locked in a power struggle with the Tatmadaw, and nowhere is this more apparent than on Rakhine policy. Suu Kyi and the NLD are likewise engaged in a struggle with Buddhist nationalists, intent on expanding the power of Buddhism over national policy at the expense of social cohesion. Further, Suu Kyi and the NLD were elected on a wave of unrealistic expectation, making them vulnerable electorally as the 2020 elections loom. Beyond this, the conflict is having a significant negative impact on foreign investment, economic development, and the wider peace process.

Our point is simply that this conflict has huge implications for Myanmar, not just the Muslims and others caught up in the brutality. In the short term, means must be found to end the destruction and violence, protect human rights, and quell the chaos. In the medium term, there must be a transparent, impartial, international investigation of the very serious allegations raised—and ways must be found to protect land and assets, de-securitize the region, and facilitate safe and voluntary return of the displaced. And in the long term, solutions must be found to address the underlying grievances, and the communities need to re-learn how to live together, side by side, peacefully. Issues of citizenship, political inclusion, representation, governance, underdevelopment, and demographic pressure must all be opened for frank discussion, then resolved.

The November 2017 announcement that voluntary refugee repatriation would begin in January 2018 was positive, but by March 2018 this remains on hold with no sign of this commencing soon. Repatriation will not be easy or quick, and many UN and international voices maintain that conditions do not yet exist for safe, voluntary return. This must change. But our point is that even if the latest violence is contained, safety is ensured, everyone returns voluntarily, and all parties commit to peace building, the grievances and fears underlying this conflict will not be resolved without significant effort and compromise. While addressing the immediate, focus must also be on the long term.

This book does not purport to have all the answers. Rather, it aims to explain and illustrate the conflict in its complexity, add a degree of nuance, and correct a range of misconceptions—primarily with international readers in mind. It seeks to illuminate the multiple dimensions and perspectives, explain the extensive role that historical narratives play, interrogate positions, and provide in-depth analysis that might help conceptualize a pathway forward. It aims to investigate the conflict dynamics in terms of intractability, security dilemma, greed, political economy, ethnic and identity grievance, territoriality, and risk of moral hazard, amongst other things. Our view throughout is towards reconciliation, rather than blame, and big-picture rather than documenting specific recent events. We seek to do this with as much academic rigour, critical thinking, and civil sobriety as possible, while remaining accessible to a wide audience.

The research for this book has come out of a combined sixteen visits to Rakhine state by the authors, between 2011 and 2018, travelling either alone or together. Most visits were of between one and three weeks' duration, with approximately equal time in Yangon during this period. Some of these visits also involved providing training to a couple of local civil society groups in development and peace-building approaches, but all involved formal interviews and informal discussions exploring the conflict and conflict dynamics. Informants came from government, political parties, local NGOs and CSOs, activists, community leaders, local media, and (occasionally) the military. The formal interviews included extended discussion with over a dozen prominent Muslim leaders in Yangon and around Sittwe who identify as 'Rohingya', and a similar number of ethnic Rakhine political party and civil society leaders. We have also conducted open community discussions in dozens of Rakhine rural villages, particularly around Kyauktaw and Mrauk-U Townships, and in Muslim IDP camps around Sittwe. We also visited Muslim, Buddhist, and Hindu villages in Maungdaw and Buthidaung Townships, prior to the recent violence. We have likewise conducted a large number of formal interviews and informal discussions with foreigners associated with international humanitarian and human rights agencies in Rakhine State and Yangon. In terms of language, neither of us is highly fluent in Burmese or Rakhine, and neither speak any Urdu or Bengali. Anthony can read and write the Burmese script (also used for Rakhine writing), and hold basic conversations in both languages. All interviews have therefore been conducted largely in English, or via an interpreter. The Burmese and Rakhine literature referred to throughout the text has sometimes been consulted to confirm key words or ascertain the meaning of very short sections, but otherwise all foreign literature referenced has been summarized to us by others.

The remainder of this introductory chapter will challenge a number of widely held misconceptions about this conflict, then outline some of the geography, history, and demography of the state, before concluding with an outline of the structure of the rest of the book.

MYANMAR'S 'ROHINGYA' CONFLICT

Addressing Misconceptions, Highlighting Complexity

Not Recent or New

There are a number of common misconceptions that we would like to deal with quickly, up front. The first is that this conflict is recent. It is not. Some portray the violence in 2012 and 2016–17 as unexpected, almost out of the blue. Certainly, there were long periods of relative calm before 2012, with many cases of good person-to-person and village-to-village relations. And there are still many examples of positive Muslim–Buddhist intercommunal relationships, economic interdependence, and even friendships between individuals. These positive links do exist, although they are now very strained, and diminished in number. Nonetheless, fear, grievance, and tension, on all sides, have resided just below the surface for decades. Thus while a recent explosion of ethno-nationalist sentiment has further polarized each population, this conflict is deeply historical.

Profound social cleavages date back more than a century, and cyclical bouts of violence have occurred every few decades since at least the Second World War. There were at least four previous mass exoduses from Arakan, in 1784, 1942, 1978, and 1991–2, with a mass exodus of Indians from the whole of Myanmar in 1962–4 also adversely affecting Arakan. Several of these were comparable in scale to that of 2017, and bear an eerie resemblance. The history is long and bloody, suggesting serious underlying issues that will not be easy to resolve—and that a sympathetic understanding of history is essential. We will discuss the 1784 events in Chapters 3 and 4, rather than go into detail here, with an assessment of the size of the refugee flow then late in Chapter 3. But let us quickly outline the other instances now.

The Second World War arrived in Arakan in 1942. Most Muslims remained loyal to the British, while the Arakanese aligned with Burman nationalists and the Japanese. As the Japanese–Burman–Arakanese forces chased an estimated 500,000 colonial officials and sympathizers out of Burma, overland through Arakan and Assam (Smith 1994), the British mobilized Muslim volunteers for intelligence and guerrilla operations, and to retain access routes back into the country (see also Murray 1949, 1980). Many historians suggest that the British would have been defeated in Arakan, and the Japanese would have reached

14

Chittagong, without Muslim help (e.g. Irwin 1946). Muslims and Rakhine were thus both mobilized during the Second World War, on opposite sides of the conflict. The violence that ensued was bloody, with horrendous massacres on both sides. The Japanese advanced to Akyab (now Sittwe) in May, but did not move north till October:

> … in the meantime, the area of mixed population was the scene of repeated large-scale massacres in which thousands of people perished or died subsequently of starvation and exposure. Eventually the two communities separated into distinct areas, the Arakanese in the south supporting the Japanese and the Chittagonians in the north supporting the British. The area was a battleground for the next two years, and was thoroughly devastated by either side [*sic*]. (Murray 1949, p. 3)

British officials in northern Arakan at the time, like Murray (1949, 1980) and Mole (2001), attest to the horrific violence resulting in almost complete segregation, as each community fled the destruction: Muslims heading north and Rakhine fleeing south. Yegar (1972) mentions 22,000 Muslims who fled to India. Yunus (1994) and Anin (2002) suggest that 100,000 fled; Jilani (1999) claims that 100,000 were killed, although these latter figures are almost certainly overinflated (Leider 2018a). Murray (1980) mentions the evacuation of 9,000 Arakanese from Maungdaw, and, drawing on Aye Chan (2005), Leider (2018a) speculates that perhaps 35,000–43,000 Rakhine were permanently displaced from northern Rakhine. These massacres and widespread acts of ethnic cleansing, perpetrated by both ethnic Rakhine and Muslims, have never been thoroughly addressed. Every bout of violence ever since has been deeply rooted in the memory of these historical injustices, the ongoing segregation, and the political implications of the withdrawal of British patronage for the Muslims at Independence. It is impossible to formulate any pathway towards long-term resolution that does not start by acknowledging this history.

Myanmar's post-Independence civil war included a Mujahid insurgency, from 1947 until 1961, but the next major mass exodus was not until after their surrender. General Ne Win took power in a *coup d'état* in 1962, and one of his deep concerns was the potential fragmentation of the state given the concessions made to various ethnic groups, including the 'Rohingya'. Indeed, forestalling acceptance of an ethnic 'Rohingya' identity was one of several key developments Ne Win was determined to achieve (Smith 2018). Under Ne Win, the military regime pursued a more ruthless policy of exclusion and assimilation across the whole country. Many ethnicities felt this as a policy of 'Burmanization', as assimilation. The Muslims in Rakhine, along with the Indians and Chinese, however, were driven to the social margins. For example, Ne Win's Burmese Way to Socialism nationalized business interests across the economy, which impacted residents of Indian origin particularly hard. As Smith (1995) suggests, some 300,000 quickly emigrated—although not as many of the Muslims from Arakan as central Burma. Nonetheless, as a major rice-growing area relying on Chettiar moneylenders and Chittagonian seasonal labour, Arakan quickly deteriorated into one of the country's poorest regions. Per capita income and literacy plummeted, to suddenly lag behind the rest of Burma, and opportunities evaporated. Asia Watch (1992) suggests that many Rakhine and Muslims began migrating into more prosperous parts of the country. When this became evident, in 1963–4, the government cracked down on the movement of Muslims from Arakan. By 1964 'the Muslims were virtually prisoners of their province, not even allowed to travel between villages within a single township' (Asia Watch 1992, p. 3).

The next exodus was in 1978, when some 200,000 Muslim refugees fled to Bangladesh. This was the result of military operations in north Arakan, codenamed Ye-The-Ha, targeting Muslim, Arakanese, and communist insurgents (Smith 1995). The operation employed the Tatmadaw's ruthless 'four cuts' counter-insurgency strategy (cut rebel access to food, funds, intelligence, and recruits) (see Smith 1999, p. 288; Selth 2002, pp. 91–2). Local villagers were relocated relentlessly, to flush out insurgent forces and their sympathizers, something that hurt all ethnicities. In tandem, however, the Tatmadaw launched a heavy-handed operation to check identity papers in the border regions, Operation Nagamin (King Dragon). Initially targeting borderlands nationally, it quickly got out of hand in Arakan, resulting in widespread reports of brutality, including rape, murder, and the destruction of homes, property, and mosques. Government officials blamed the trouble on 'armed bands of Bengalis', 'rampaging Bengali mobs', and 'wild Muslim extremists' attacking Rakhine Buddhist villages (Smith 1991, p. 241; also 1995). However, humanitarian agencies documented numerous claims of violence and abuse, including Muslims being uprooted from their villages and concentrated in fenced compounds. Muslim refugees crowded into thirteen camps in Bangladesh, administered by the UNHCR. Most were allowed to return after an international outcry, but not before further significant harm and lasting communal damage had been inflicted.

Yet another exodus occurred in 1991–2, following the rise to power of a new military faction in Yangon, after the suppression of the democracy uprising in 1988. Smith (1995) argues that the new regime's 'market-oriented' and 'open-door' economic policies added greater geo-political importance to the Bangladeshi border. In addition, the crackdown on activists saw several thousand flee to Burma's borders, including Arakan, and the ruling junta was very aware that it won almost no votes in northern Rakhine State in the abortive 1990 elections. (Yes, the Muslims had the vote in 1990, and the Muslim National Democratic Party for Human Rights dominated in northern Rakhine). All these developments brought increased pressure on northern Rakhine State.

In 1991 the Tatmadaw deployed several new regiments to Rakhine. Mro, Chin, and Rakhine populations complained of an increase in forced relocations and abuse, but the Muslims again bore the brunt (Smith 1995). Asia Watch (1992) claims that routine oppression turned to concerted brutality, with forced labour, land confiscations, destruction of mosques, rape, summary executions, and so on. Compounded by a devastating cyclone in April 1991, which the regime neither acknowledged nor provided relief towards (Maje 1991), some 260,000 Muslims quickly flowed into Bangladesh, '…in one of the greatest humanitarian emergencies' that Asia had then witnessed (Smith 1995, p. 25; see also Amnesty International 1992; Asia Watch 1992). Smith suggests that the Tatmadaw were so heavy-handed, and the crisis so serious, that a full-scale border war with Bangladesh almost erupted in late 1991. It was defused in April 1992 when the government unexpectedly called a halt to all military offensives nationally, including in Rakhine, when regime chairman General Saw Maung was replaced by General Than Shwe. Over 200,000 Muslims were again repatriated during 1993–4, although some 50,000 remained in Bangladesh as refugees. And again, just as in 1978 and 2017, the government claimed that the main problems were insurgent activities and illegal immigration, not its military activities.

So in other words, this conflict has a very long history, with multiple violent episodes and several previous mass refugee crises. Some have been communal, but most involved insurgency and army brutality. This suggests that a solution will not be quick or easy, and that a good knowledge of the deeply historical grievances and narratives is essential to understanding the contemporary dynamics.

Not Merely Oppression of a Minority

A second common misconception we would like to deal with quickly, up front, is that this conflict is solely about oppression and brutality towards a despised and vulnerable ethno-religious minority: the 'Rohingya'. While this is certainly one major dimension of the conflict, the situation is far more complex than simple victimization based on religious and cultural difference. We caution against overly simplistic representations. Too much international commentary is reductionist, flattening what is a multi-polar conflict with complex socio-political dynamics, and ignoring the legitimate grievances and real existential fears of multiple actors.

Not only have Muslims clashed with security forces in multiple rounds of insurgency and violent crackdowns, but Muslims and Rakhine have also been involved numerous times in communal violence. Likewise, Rakhine nationalist politicians struggle desperately for autonomy, while other Rakhine elements clash violently with the security forces. Certainly, significant violence has been perpetrated against the Muslims, by both local Rakhine and the Tatmadaw, and they have long been the group most marginalized and heavily impacted by the conflict. Nonetheless, Muslims have also perpetrated significant violence against both Rakhine and Burmans; significant violence has also been perpetrated between Rakhine and Burman, without involving the Muslims. This is thus a multi-polar conflict, in which at least three groups react defensively, out of deeply compelling existential fears.

Chapter 2 unpacks these multiple dimensions in some detail, along with the complexity of interests and fears. For now, perhaps we can simply illustrate this by noting that the 2017 violence and resulting refugee crisis was triggered by an attack launched by Muslim militants against security posts—not initially by an army offensive. The much-criticized Tatmadaw 'area clearance operations' were a dramatic over-reaction, but were their response to coordinated attacks by Muslims, which they chose to perceive as Islamic terrorism.

Complicating this picture, despite many reports of apparent collusion between Rakhine nationalist militia and the Tatmadaw against the Muslims, there is very deep anger—even open violence—between ethnic Rakhine groups and representatives of the Burman-led state. For example, at the same time as violence was causing Muslims to flee to Bangladesh, the Rakhine nationalist insurgent group the Arakan Army was involved in armed engagements with the Tatmadaw. In just one example, in early November 2017, only 50 kilometres from Maungdaw, eleven Tatmadaw soldiers were killed and fourteen wounded in a single attack on a supply boat on the Kaladan River (Lawi Weng & Htet Naing Zaw 2017). This is one example of almost a hundred engagements in the first three months after the August 2017 violence began between the Tatmadaw and Muslims. This does not preclude the possibility of collusion between other Rakhine militia and the Tatmadaw; it just illustrates a far more complex set of dynamics.

One final example further illustrates the depth of Rakhine conflict with the state: the deadly crackdown on Rakhine protesters in Mrauk-U in January 2018, and subsequent bombings in Sittwe. On 16 January, a crowd of 5,000 ethnic Rakhine gathered in the ancient capital of Mrauk-U, to commemorate the 223rd anniversary of that kingdom's defeat by Burman forces and Rakhine's forced integration into the kingdom that became modern Burma. The state authorities denied permission for the event, which had been requested under the guise of a 'literary talk' on the history (despite it having taken place every year previously). Two popular Rakhine nationalist organizers were arrested even as the crowd gathered: Dr Aye Maung and Wai Hin Aung. Both had given fiery speeches in the weeks prior to this event, praising the Arakan Army, calling for Rakhine independence, and urging the Rakhine people to mobilize. Shortly after 10 p.m., police opened fire on the crowd with live ammunition. Hospital staff reported nine civilian protesters dead and nineteen injured, several in a critical condition. Some twenty police were also injured. Two weeks later the

Mrauk-U township administrator (who had been transferred to Sittwe) was assassinated. The government claim that two of those arrested for this act have ties to the Arakan Army (DVB 2018). Apparently also connected, less than six weeks after the deadly attacks on the Rakhine civilians, three bombs were detonated in Sittwe: outside the home of the Rakhine State Secretary, the land office, and a court. Three other bombs were found undetonated. There was only one injury, but several Rakhine nationalists were subsequently arrested.

The deep-seated resentment, even seething anger, of a growing proportion of the ethnic Rakhine community towards the security forces and Burman-led state is thus palpable, and escalating. A large number of Rakhine feel extremely threatened, even existentially so, by the state. Tensions are often high with security forces and non-Rakhine administrative officials, who many perceive as representing a Burman colonial or occupying force.

Key actors involved in this conflict, therefore, if we define conflict as both violent and non-violent, thus include:

1. 'Rohingya' Muslims—who seek citizenship, human rights, basic services, and recognition as an indigenous national race. While most are peace-loving and have shown great forbearance under prolonged discrimination, some have turned to violence—as the ARSA attacks demonstrate. The fact that ARSA attacks primarily targeted security outposts, at least in the initial planned attacks, highlights the fact that they see their fight as primarily against the state.

2. Rakhine (Buddhists)—the local ethnic majority, who have long-running political and armed struggles for autonomy against the state. They seek greater control over governance, as well as having deep existential fears of being overwhelmed by a Muslim horde from over the border, if they are not vigilant. Their territorial claims overlap with those of the Muslims, pitting the two against each other, but their main fight (politically and militarily) has long been against Burman domination.

3. Tatmadaw—the Burman-dominated military, whose cause is summed up in their Three Main National Causes (Minye Kaungbon 1994). Articulated in 1989, but drawing on mythology from the formation of the Tatmadaw during the Second World War and earlier history, these are: non-disintegration of the Union; non-disin-

tegration of national (*taing-yin-tha*, see below) solidarity; and the perpetuation of sovereignty. They thus interpret any claims of autonomy, by either Rakhine or the Muslims, as a threat to national unity, sovereignty, and territorial integrity, particularly any claims by those not considered *taing-yin-tha* (e.g. the 'Rohingya').

4. NLD government—which is locked in a power struggle with the military, especially in Rakhine State. The military controls the three security ministries overseeing defence, the police, and the border regions, without government oversight. Thus, most key portfolios affecting Rakhine State are beyond government control. NLD reform ambitions go well beyond Rakhine issues, and all require military cooperation, adding to the complexity for the NLD in formulating Rakhine policy. The NLD also performed very poorly in Rakhine State in the 1990, 2010, and 2015 elections, so its legitimacy is contested on all sides. Thus while the NLD does not perpetrate physical violence in Rakhine State, neither is it the neutral mediator it would like to be. Its policies and practices make it an actor in the conflict, one way or another, and at the moment its role does not appear to be positive.

5. International community—which has effectively become a fifth actor in the conflict, weaponizing public shaming and often politicizing humanitarian action. We are seen as highly partisan, trumpeting one particular cause while missing other vital perspectives and the nuances of complexity. We are widely perceived as naïve at best, if not aggressively partisan.

Not about a Denial of Citizenship and Statelessness

A third major misconception we want to address up front is citizenship. This conflict is not about the denial of citizenship per se, nor is it a bigoted attempt at physical expulsion of the 'Rohingya ethnic minority' from the country. Rather, at its heart, this is a struggle over whether the Muslims constitute an indigenous 'national race' within the Myanmar polity or are a disparate group of immigrants now seeking group political rights. Some do want them expelled, but overall the conflict is primarily about the extent of inclusion in or exclusion from Myanmar polity, and their statelessness and disenfranchisement are almost by-products of how they pursue, and where they stand in, this central dispute.

Citizenship is undoubtedly one of the more contentious issues right across Myanmar today, not just in relation to the Rakhine conflict (Walton 2018). The vast majority of the Muslims in northern Rakhine state do not have citizenship. That is undeniable. However, this is more the result of decades of discriminatory practices than of law, and the fault lies in implementation rather than policy (see Tonkin 2018 for details). On paper, at least, Myanmar has always had pathways that should have given even any colonial-era migrants residency or citizenship. The various constitutions and laws differ in detail, but all have provided ways for migrants to become Myanmar citizens. Moreover, rather than deny citizenship en masse, as many commentators often suggest, both the Thein Sein and Aung San Suu Kyi governments have actively attempted to implement document-verification processes designed (at least on paper) to deliver citizenship to all who are eligible. The problem is that this has been opposed by some local Rakhine groups, and most of the Muslim population have actively resisted this pathway. The Muslim community, including activists and prominent authors, denounced it, arguing that the process delegitimizes Muslim claims to full citizenship. It is thus not that they are blocked from being citizens as much as that they are being blocked from becoming citizens with full political rights.

Absolutely central to this conflict is this question of whether 'Rohingya' can be regarded as a Burmese *taing-yin-tha*. This term, most commonly translated as 'national race' (MLC 2014), literally means something like 'offspring of the land'—hence its meaning is akin to 'indigenous' (Thawnghmung 2016; Walton 2013; Taylor 2015). *Taing-yin-tha* are defined as ethnic races settled in the Union as their permanent home before the British arrived, the date being set as pre-1823 CE. However, as TNI (2014) and Smith (2018) point out, the terms *taing-yin-tha* and *lu-myo* (commonly translated as 'race', 'kinds of people') have complex meanings, and are politically controversial even inside the country. Furthermore, as Cheesman (2017) has clearly shown, the meaning of *taing-yin-tha* has changed significantly within the Myanmar polity since Independence, from a politically insignificant concept a century ago to the defining criterion for membership in

Myanmar's political community today (see also Crouch 2016). The term has become enmeshed with programmes of nationalization, domination of ethnic ambitions of autonomy, and the exclusion of aliens, since a speech by General Ne Win in 1964, shortly after seizing power.

The term draws on an idea of a mythical past, before colonialism, in which all the races of Myanmar were united and engaged together in resistance against the colonizer. It is in this context that the second of the Three Main National Causes is significant; the nation (particularly the Tatmadaw) must fight against the disintegration of *taing-yin-tha* solidarity. The vision is of a Burman-led polity comprised of all *taing-yin-tha* in political community (Houtman 1999). The concept, and hence the terminology, is deeply problematic, ideological, and imaginary, however, and imposes categories of identity rejected by many of Myanmar's ethnic nationalities (Kyed & Gravers 2018).

In adopting this ideology, Cheesman (2017) argues, *taing-yin-tha* indigeneity has come to surpass citizenship as the pre-eminent condition for membership in Myanmar's political community. Migrants and their descendants can become citizens, even under the much-touted 1982 Citizenship Law (still in effect), just without the privileges or position granted to *taing-yin-tha*. Indeed, General Ne Win's express vision of the law was that within two generations all descendants of migrants would become full citizens (South & Lall 2018). Many Chinese and Indian migrants have become citizens that way, and are relatively accepted in Myanmar society—but they are not *taing-yin-tha*, so have only limited rights in terms of governance. Limited citizenship is highly problematic. Myanmar has conflated two different approaches to citizenship, and operationalized it to exclude particular groups. This idea has become so embedded in policy that the preamble of the 2008 constitution now defines the political community in Myanmar not as an aggregation of citizens, but of *taing-yin-tha*, thereby elevating *taing-yin-tha* membership above citizenship.

The point—and the problem—is that the government's list of 135 *taing-yin-tha* does not include 'Rohingya'. Thus, more than this conflict being about citizenship per se, it is about whether the Muslims can claim citizenship as *taing-yin-tha*, with all the additional rights that confers. As Cheesman (2017, p. 474) puts it: 'Those people who accept that they are "Bengali" are entitled to present their credentials for citizenship on a case-by-case basis. But any assertions of a collective right to political membership by virtue of being *taing-yin-tha* will not be tolerated.' The Kofi Annan-led Rakhine Advisory Commission report (Annan et al. 2017b, p. 30) describes this as being a 'hierarchy of different types of citizenship', between those who are national races and those who are not, with differing rights and with discrimination in how citizenship passes to the next generation. Annan describes the process of gradual disenfranchisement of the Muslim population through such laws. The issue is thus that the prioritization of *taing-yin-tha* marginalizes groups, particularly the Muslims of northern Rakhine.

The issue for most Muslims is that gaining citizenship by identifying themselves as 'Bengali' would leave them with few protections, and possibly still no citizenship. Most have rejected this pathway: indeed, between 7 June 2016 and 3 January 2018, just 9,173 out of over a million Muslims accepted this option, to adopt the label 'Bengali' and apply for a national verification card. Of these, only a very small proportion have been granted citizenship, and this small handful of people continue to have their movements restricted and face many forms of discrimination.

The frequent claims that the 'Rohingya' have been stateless since the 1982 Citizenship Law stripped it from them are an oversimplification. The 1982 law, which privileged *taing-yin-tha* for the first time, did not include 'Rohingya'. Nonetheless, on paper it still did allow those who were already citizens to retain that citizenship, and it created pathways even for new migrants to attain citizenship. The problem was discriminatory processes, supposedly (but not really) based on that law, rather than discrimination inherent to the law itself—and the Muslims' unwillingness to accept a 'Bengali' identity that would forfeit claims to *taing-yin-tha* political rights.

Taing-yin-tha status is important. It is linked to governance over territory, for example. The largest *taing-yin-tha* have all been granted states within the Union (Mon, Karen, Karenni, Shan, Kachin, Chin and Rakhine States), and the 2008 constitution makes any *taing-yin-tha* who constitute a majority in two adjacent townships potentially eligible for a 'self-administered zone' (Thawnghmung 2016). The Wa, Pa-laung, Danu, Pa-o, Naga, and Kokang already have such zones. The achievement of, or prevention of 'Rohingya' from becoming, a self-administered zone is perhaps the central issue in this conflict, and until this is resolved or reframed, a lasting solution may well be impossible.

This conflict therefore revolves not around citizenship per se, but whether history shows that the 'Rohingya' are indigenous, with rights not only to citizenship but also to territory and governance. It is a question of collective rights, rather than just individual civil–political rights. This is why historical narratives about when the 'Rohingya' arrived in Arakan, the make-up of the Mrauk-U kingdom, whether they are a distinct ethnicity or descendants of assorted colonial-era immigrants, how long the name 'Rohingya' has been used for self-identification, etc., are so central—and are so vehemently fought over.

These three misconceptions—about its deeply historical, multi-polar, and ethnic–political nature—sum up why much international commentary about this conflict misses the mark. It also shows why it is not likely to be resolved easily, nor in the foreseeable future. The issues are complex, and enmeshed with Myanmar's political system and nationalist ideology. Any solution that moves beyond the suppression of violence and resettlement, to contemplate an enduring, tolerant, consociational political arrangement that addresses underlying griev-ances will not emerge without significant reformulation of Myanmar's political community, and that will be incredibly difficult to achieve. Moreover, such a peace cannot be achieved while the Muslims from northern Rakhine state are excluded from the national political dia-logue process currently renegotiating federalism, citizenship, and what it means to be diverse members of one state. Such renegotiation of federalism, citizenship, and thus democracy aims to be transformative of the relationships between peoples and between peoples and the state (Walton 2018). Unfortunately, most actors remain adamant about their exclusion of the Muslims from this process.

Rakhine State: Geography, History, and Demographics

A brief overview of the geography, history, and demographics of Rakhine state provides a final bit of background information useful for understanding this conflict.

Rakhine is the westernmost state in Myanmar, running along the north-west third of the country's coastline, along the Bay of Bengal.

Formally called Arakan until 1989, the state has an overall length of about 450 kilometres, but extends inland only 50–100 kilometres for most of its length, sharing a 256-kilometre border with Bangladesh. The arable land is predominantly a coastal littoral (see Map 1). Rakhine is relatively isolated from central Myanmar by a significant mountain range, nearly impassable before recent road construction, the highest point being Khonu Msung (Mount Victoria) at 3,094 metres. This geography means that historically the region was more closely connected with Bengal via maritime trade than with the Burmese kingdoms. Van Galen (2008) described this region as an 'Arakan–Bengal continuum' prior to the eighteenth century, created by trade networks, shared geography and climate, and cultural exchange. This means that Arakan and Bengal formed a region quite distinct in character and relations from the civilizations on the plains of either the Ganges or Irrawaddy River basins, despite the Arakanese sharing religion and ethnic origins with Burma.

Arakan had a long history of independence from Burma. There is evidence that Arab and Persian traders visited from at least the ninth century (Yegar 1972), perhaps earlier. Arakan was home to a series of independent city-state kingdoms prior to the fifteenth century, particularly Dhanyawadi (fourth–sixth centuries), Vesali (seventh–eleventh centuries), and Lemro (eleventh–fifteenth centuries) (Hall 1968; Singer 2008; van Galen 2008). The ethnic Rakhine (Arakanese), closely related to the Burman, began migrating to Arakan in about the ninth century, gaining control of the region from the pre-existing population from about the eleventh century (Gutman 1976), meaning that the Dhanyawadi and Vesali kingdoms pre-date the arrival of the Arakanese. Arakan suffered raids and was possibly briefly subject to Burman rulers several times, including perhaps by Anawrahta (1044–77 CE)—although accounts in the Burman and Arakanese chronicles differ by centuries, making assertions difficult to corroborate. But Arakan was largely independent of central Burma both before and after the arrival of the Arakanese, with only short periods of exception.

A strong Arakanese kingdom flourished at Mrauk-U (also known as Mrohaung, 'the old city') from 1430 until it was conquered by the Burmese in 1784. The kingdom began as a small agrarian vassal of Bengal, but grew into a significant regional power by the early seventeenth century, asserting influence across the Bay of Bengal and ruling Chittagong as a vassal state for a period (van Galen 2008). Subjects thus included Muslims as well as Buddhists, and from the fifteenth century, Muslim influence in the kingdom at Mrauk-U is abundantly evident—although proportions and location of populations are debated. The question of Muslim settlements in Arakan prior to the fifteenth century, however, is much more contested. There were, nevertheless, definitely Muslims in high positions in the royal court from the fifteenth century onwards, and most of the kings adopted Muslim as well as Buddhist titles (Gutman 1976; d'Hubert & Leider 2008; Serajuddin 1986).

We will return to discuss this further, but the most significant points for now are that the kingdom was independent of the Burmese empire for centuries, until 1784, and that there was significant Muslim influence and presence in Mrauk-U from the fifteenth century. It was then conquered by the British just forty years after the Burman subjugation, in the First Anglo-Burmese War (1824–6),[1] and was retained by the British until Independence in 1948. Arakan was thus independent of Burma for most of the past millennia, under direct Burmese rule for just forty years, then under British control for 124 years before Independence—significantly longer than most of the rest of the country. These factors all greatly impact its current politics.

Arakan has been a hotbed of both communal and separatist conflict since Independence. By this we mean that the region has a history of conflict between the local Muslim and Buddhist communities, and that each has a history of conflict with the Burman-led state. This mix of centre–periphery and intra-periphery tensions (using Gottman's 1980 terminology) is driven by acute civil, political, and economic inequalities, including horizontal inequalities between the Muslim and Buddhist communities in Rakhine, as well as between each of these and the Burman ethnic majority (as per Stewart 2000, 2008). These inequalities are multi-polar, encompassing not only different levels of poverty/development, but also inequitable relationships.

Prior to the current exodus Rakhine was home to approximately 3.2 million people. A little under 2 million are ethnic Rakhine, 1.1 million were Muslim, and the remainder are Burman, or from a diversity of very small minority groups including Chin, Mro, Daignet, Kaman, and

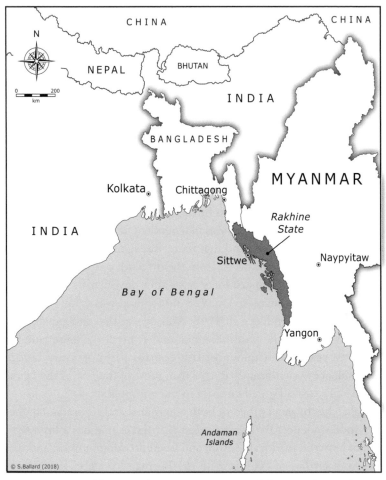

Map 1: Rakhine in relation to Myanmar and the Bay of Bengal.

Hindu (UoM 2015). (The Muslim figure is an estimate, calculated from the total number of people listed as residing in northern Rakhine State by 2014 census enumerators but not enumerated.) Many of these populations also extend across borders into Chin State, India, and Bangladesh, complicating the ethnic make-up. For example, there is a sizeable Rakhine population in Bangladesh, and the Rakhine nationalist insurgent group the Arakan Army has been organising in Paletwa Township, across the border in Chin State, rather than in Rakhine.

COMPLEXITIES, MISCONCEPTIONS, AND CONTEXT

The socio-economic dimensions of these inequalities are readily quantifiable. The fact that the Muslims were not enumerated during the 2014 census inadvertently gives a clear snapshot of the standard of living of the ethnic Rakhine, given that they constituted the vast majority of those enumerated in Rakhine State in 2014. What emerges is a compelling picture of underdevelopment in comparison to the rest of the country. Table 1 shows the average Rakhine figures for an assortment of indicators measured in the census, in comparison to national average figures, highlighting underdevelopment across all sectors.

Table 1: 2014 Census data contrasting Rakhine with the national average (UoM 2015)

Measure	Rakhine	National	Notes
improved drinking water	37.8%	69.5%	lowest in country
improved sanitation	31.8%	74.3%	less than 1/2 average
electricity for lighting	12.8%	32.4%	about a 1/3 average
mobile phone access	15.8%	35.9%	less than 1/2 average
only thatch roofing	72.5%	35.1%	more than 2x average
cook with firewood	88.9%	69.2%	
no identity papers	37.7%	27.3%	
under five mortality rate	75/1,000	72/1,000	

NB. These figures exclude the Muslims of northern Rakhine state, and thus reflect the living conditions of ethnic Rakhine.

The World Bank used this census data to create a Wealth Ranking Index (World Bank 2015) for all 330 townships in Myanmar. This ranking places over half of Rakhine's seventeen townships amongst the twenty most impoverished in the country. When the index is averaged at the state level (see Table 2), Rakhine has by far the lowest wealth rank, meaning that it is now the poorest state in Myanmar even without considering the Muslim population.

The poorest townships in Rakhine state, based on the World Bank Wealth Index, are amongst the poorest in the country: particularly, Kyauktaw, Mrauk-U, Ponnagyun, Rathedaung, Myebon, Minbya, and Pauktaw—in other words, all of central Rakhine (see Map 2). As this data considers only the non-Muslim population, the figures for the majority-Muslim townships of Maungdaw and Buthidaung are distorted by the relatively few ethnic Rakhine and Burman who live there, many with better-paid positions. Given the mobility and citizenship issues faced by the Muslims, together with poor service provision, it is almost certain they are more poor, marginal, and vulnerable than the above Rakhine figures, although no hard data exists to quantify this.

Table 2: World Bank Wealth Index for each state and region in Myanmar

Township	Wealth Index
Yangon	6.751
Nay Pyi Taw	2.106
Mandalay	0.507
Mon	0.324
Shan (South)	−0.414
Kayah	−0.504
Shan (East)	−0.630
Kayin	−0.745
Tanintharyi	−0.924
Shan (North)	−0.955
Bago	−1.079
Chin	−1.306
Sagaing	−1.534
Kachin	−1.666
Ayeyarwady	−1.840
Magway	−1.892
Rakhine	−3.431

NB. *This is an index, so values are not as important as comparison between values. The World Bank methodology is based on 5 key wealth indicators from the census data.*

The 2014 census data thus clearly shows that northern and central Rakhine has fallen significantly behind the rest of the country on almost every indicator, and that this is now the poorest part of Myanmar. Not only are the Muslims mired in poverty, but almost everyone across central and northern Rakhine State—Buddhist as well as Muslim—live in some of the worst poverty in Myanmar. It is also a region prone to extreme weather events, particularly frequent cyclones and damaging flooding. This means that the local political economy, with competition between very poor neighbouring communities over basic livelihoods, land, and services, cannot be ignored in trying to understand the dynamics of this conflict.

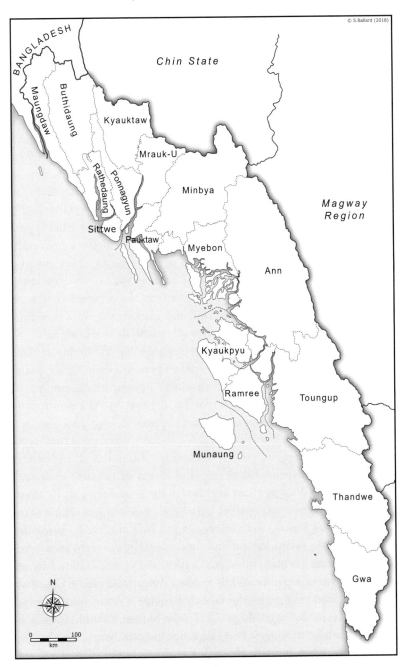

Map 2: Townships in Rakhine State, Myanmar.

Approach, Definitions, and Outline

The approach in this book is to seek to understand complexity and multiple perspectives. This endeavour is constructivist and phenomenological in nature. Constructivism holds that understanding and meaning are constructed by people as they engage with the world, and that we all interpret information we receive through classifications schemata in the mind (Gray 2009; Crotty 1998). A phenomenological approach seeks to understand and explain the internal logic of each of these perspectives before seeking to analyse—to gain understanding of people's experience of reality and prevailing social understandings, as it were, before offering critique (Titchen & Hobson 2005; Gray 2009; Denzin & Lincoln 2005). Given that most parties in this conflict appeal very strongly to historical narratives, we therefore delve significantly into their understandings of history. Yet we do not seek to document a detailed history of the 'Rohingya', or of Rakhine State or the Arakanese kingdom per se. What we seek to do is present the perspective of each side in sufficient detail to understand and explore the ways they predominantly present things, before we offer analysis and critique.

A couple of quick definitions before proceeding. We define conflict as a situation in which two or more parties perceive their values, goals, intentions, and actions as being mutually incompatible, and act in accordance with this perception (Bar-Tal 2013, p. 5). As a result, conflict encompasses much more than just physical violence, and the violence of conflict is not only physical. Violence is often structural (systematic inequalities in power, embedded in political and social structures) and psychological (e.g. the threat of physical violence) (Galtung 1969). Violence can also be latent or unintended. By these definitions, violence and conflict have been endemic in Rakhine State for a very long time—and violence is not only directed against the Muslims. While asymmetrical and fundamentally different in nature, ethnic Rakhine, Burman, other minorities, and even the state have all suffered forms of violence. While conflict can sometimes be a positive force for social change, by directly challenging a status quo or social injustice (Taylor & Moghaddam 1987), the human scale of violence in Rakhine leads us to suggest that this is not the case here.

Likewise, when we talk about peaceful resolution of conflict, and seeking solutions to issues, we recognize that any outcome is likely to remain agonistic and contested for a long time to come. Differences of opinions, competing needs and interests, and difficulties in accommodating one another will remain. What is essential, though, what we might consider to be minimal criteria for 'peaceful resolution', are a guarantee of rights and freedoms, just systems and processes for legitimate contestation and resolution of grievances, and a commitment to non-violence by all sides (Lederach 1995, 1997).

This book is divided into seven chapters, in three parts. This introductory part is concluded by Chapter 2, which illustrates the tripartite nature of this conflict by exploring the interrelated outbreaks of serious violence in Rakhine State over the past five years. These are the intercommunal violence of 2012, the 2015–16 Arakan Army armed insurgency in Rakhine State, and the 2016–17 Arakan Rohingya Salvation Army insurgency and its backlash. It concludes by discussing the significance of this conflict on Myanmar's domestic politics, economic and political transition, and international support. Part II then delves more deeply into the competing nationalistic historical narratives, and explains why these are such a key part of the 'societal psychological repertoire' used to maintain, escalate, or de-escalate what has become an 'intractable conflict' (Bar-Tal 2013). Chapters 3 and 4 articulate the competing historical narratives and representations of memory sustaining this conflict, from Muslim, Rakhine, and Burman perspectives respectively, and interrogate these narratives against the available historical record.

Part III then presents our conflict analysis, conclusions, and recommendations. Chapter 5 analyses the conflict against the idea of ethnic and demographic security dilemma, the role of the state, and the question of resources through two lenses, the greed thesis and the political economy of conflict. Ethnic and demographic security dilemmas suggest that times of political transition can facilitate heightened fears between rival ethnic or cultural groups and make them more vulnerable to extremist narratives and recourse to violence. The question of economic resources underpinning this conflict is analysed through the 'greed thesis', very popular with some international donors, showing its limitations in this particular context. We also examine the political economy argument, highlighting the interplay between the pre-existing conflict and the post-transition economic dynamics in the region.

Chapter 6 then explores the question of how much material and non-material aims are underlying drivers of this conflict, particularly issues of identity and territory. Chapter 7 concludes with a discussion of the role that the international community has played, and could play, with discussion of the Kofi Annan-led Rakhine Advisory Commission report, our concluding thoughts, and our own recommendations from the analysis in this book.

2

RECENT VIOLENCE AND SIGNIFICANCE

This conflict was propelled into international attention by communal violence in 2012, and has hardly been out of the spotlight since. Most readers know about it because of the advocacy triggered by the events of 2012, cemented by the Tatmadaw crackdowns in 2016–17. These have galvanized both transnational advocacy and local nationalist narratives.

This chapter offers a brief account of three major rounds of violence in Rakhine State over the last five years, representing what we suggest are three interconnected dimensions to the conflict. It is important to note that in presenting these three axes of conflict alongside one another, we are not implying that the human toll or impact is in anyway equivalent; it is not. The Muslims have suffered far more as a result of conflict in Rakhine State than any other party, particularly as the crisis situation that has emerged since 2012 escalated further with the mass exodus post-August 2017. We present these three accounts not to imply equivalence, but to highlight their complexity, multi-polarity, and interconnectedness. Indeed, the asymmetries of power should be apparent through the account.

These three accounts place the recent horrific events into a broader context, an understanding of which we argue is necessary to conceptualize realistic steps towards resolution. Each of these three rounds of violence involves different sets of actors. Not all are particularly well known outside Myanmar. Some have affected far fewer people. And while specific events quickly become dated, the details presented illuminate both the complexity and longer-term conflict tensions to be resolved.

Three Interconnected Conflicts, Not One

2012 Inter-Communal Conflict

Long-simmering communal tensions erupted into open violence in June 2012. This was the first serious outbreak of violence in the state in two decades, and the beginning of the current emergency situation. The proximal trigger was the brutal rape and murder of an ethnic Rakhine woman by Muslim men on 28 May, in a rural village in southern Ramree Township (ICG 2012, 2013, 2014). Significantly, this occurred in southern central Rakhine, where Muslims are in the minority, and not in the north, where they are a majority. Communal tensions had been high for months, escalating ever since the military-backed Union Solidarity and Development Party (USDP) made promises to woo the Muslim vote in the 2010 election campaign, trying to lock out the local Rakhine nationalist party. (In many regards, this was the real trigger for the 2012 violence.)

According to state media (NLM 2012b), local Burmese police quickly detained three suspects in the rape case, all Muslims, just two days after the attack. State media referred to them as 'Bengali'. With local passions so high, the police hastily transferred them to Kyaukphyu, the state's second-largest town, some 70-odd kilometres to the north, to await trial. That afternoon a Rakhine mob besieged the local police station, demanding that the police hand over the suspects. The police refused 'mob justice', and in the end had to fire shots into the air to disperse the crowd. This confrontation escalated tensions, and triggered the further distribution of inflammatory anti-Muslim leaflets.

Three days later another Rakhine mob attacked and murdered Muslims in nearby Toungup Township. State media reported (NLM 2012a) that a Rakhine group was distributing leaflets displaying a photo of the murdered woman's corpse, and warning of a risk that Muslims would assault Rakhine women. Word spread quickly of a group of Muslims on a bus nearby. An angry mob quickly besieged the bus, dragging ten men off, killing them, and destroying the bus. The murdered Muslims were not actually 'Rohingya', and not even from Rakhine, but were Muslim visitors from central Myanmar. The government maintains that they were a proselytizing group who had been exhorting local Muslims to build a controversial mosque in Rathedaung Township, in northern Rakhine State, and offering financial support (UoM 2013). Other reports describe the group as pilgrims who had visited an old mosque in Thandwe. Perhaps both are true. Either way, the attack ignited Muslim fears and ire.

Rumours and accusations swirled on both sides. On 5 June Muslims protested outside the Bengali Sunni Jamae Mosque in central Yangon, near the Sule Pagoda, demanding that the Rakhine murderers of the Muslim men be brought to justice just as quickly as the Muslim rapists (Ei Ei Toe Lwin 2012; Ko Pauk 2012; DVB 2012a). Concerned at the potential for serious escalation, on 6 June the military-backed USDP government announced a full investigation—and, in a move breaking with decades of authoritarian practice, openly declared the investigators' names and mandate on the front page of the state-run *New Light of Myanmar* (ICG 2012). This pre-emptive action largely calmed the escalation in Yangon. The situation in Rakhine State, however, continued to deteriorate.

Seven people were killed in communal violence in central Rakhine the next day, with seventeen injured and over five hundred houses destroyed (UoM 2013). Violence spread quickly. The following day, 8 June, violence erupted in the north, in Muslim-majority Maungdaw. Around 1 p.m., after Friday prayers at a local mosque in the northern end of town, a Muslim crowd began throwing stones at government buildings and Buddhist-run businesses (Reuters 2012; DVB 2012a; Nyein Nyein 2012; BBC 2012). Police fired warning shots to disperse the crowd, and at some point several were killed. The crowd scattered, but some set fire to homes of local ethnic Rakhine—who launched reprisal attacks on Muslim villages. Violence quickly snowballed across large parts of the state, including attacks by the two communities against one another.

Analysis of the government response was contradictory: the government was either too slow to respond, was powerless, or overreacted. Public use of the derogatory term *kala* by at least one official did not help (DVB 2012b). On 10 June Rakhine Buddhists gathered at the

Shwedagon Pagoda in Yangon demanding that all 'Bengalis' 'be removed' from the country (AFP 2012a, 2012b). The government imposed a state of emergency that same day, calling the military into six of Rakhine's seventeen townships, with a curfew, a ban on unauthorized meetings, and significant new troop deployments. This was eventually sufficient to restore a semblance of order—but not before 98 people had been killed and 5,338 homes destroyed (UoM 2013). According to official government figures, two-thirds of those killed were Muslim, and 80 per cent of the homes destroyed were owned by Muslims. The vast majority of the 75,000 IDPs were 'Rohingya'.

The state of emergency provided calm for a few months, but only by suppressing violence, not addressing grievances or resolving issues. Tensions simmered, and isolated incidents continued. In a bungled attempt at requesting assistance, on 11 July President Thein Sein aggravated tensions by asking the UN High Commissioner for Refugees to put displaced Muslims into 'refugee camps'. In a statement posted on the government website the next day (subsequently removed: see Vandenbrink 2012), the President—who otherwise achieved many very positive social, economic, and political changes in Myanmar—said:

> We will take care of our own ethnic nationalities, but Rohingya who came to Burma illegally are not of our ethnic nationalities and we cannot accept them here. ... The solution to this problem is that they can be settled in refugee camps managed by UNHCR, and UNHCR provides for them. If there are countries that would accept them, they could be sent there.

Interestingly, given the sustained criticism Aung San Suu Kyi has faced over her silence about the human rights of the Muslim community in Rakhine State (e.g. AP 2015; Lee 2014; Green 2013; Green et al. 2015), at that time she did show some support. She expressed concern at the handling of the situation, in particular the failure of authorities to dampen anti-Muslim sentiment after the woman was attacked (Ei Ei Toe Lwin 2012), and followed this public comment by inviting Muslim leaders to NLD headquarters in Yangon to express her condolences. In public comments, she said that there was an urgent need for justice and proper law enforcement nationally, and she called on Buddhists to 'have sympathy for minorities' (AFP 2012c; Mizzima 2012). Alluding to the Muslim community in northern Rakhine State as a legitimate 'minority' needing consideration was a significant concession, in a conflict where any official support is rare.

The mandate for the military intervention had an automatic end date of mid-October. As that date approached without official measures to address grievances, Buddhist nationalists became emboldened. On 2 September Ashin Wirathu led a march in Mandalay to protest what he saw as a pro-Muslim bias by the UN Rapporteur on Human Rights in Myanmar, and to 'show solidarity and support' for demands to deport hundreds of thousands of 'Rohingya' (Ponnudurai 2012; Sithu Lwin 2012). The protest march drew some 5,000 monks, the biggest protest in the country since the Saffron Revolution in 2007, and strongly Buddhist in character. It was well publicized nationally. Wirathu had previously been imprisoned for inciting religious conflict (released in early 2012 as part of a general amnesty on political prisoners). As a result of his role in this protest, he went on to become a leader within the ultra-nationalist 969 Movement and a prominent voice connected with the Association to Protect Race and Religion (abbreviated Ma Ba Tha—now renamed Buddha Dhamma Philanthropic Foundation after bans in 2017). This was followed by a large Rakhine nationalist meeting on 25–26 September, at a Buddhist monastery in Rathedaung, 30 kilometres north of Sittwe (Narinjara 2012; ICG 2013). With around two thousand attendees, the meeting was said to be the biggest public meeting in the state since Independence. Billed by some as being 'focused on resolving the sectarian tensions between Arakanese Buddhists and Rohingya Muslims' (MPM 2012), the meeting laid out a radical nationalist manifesto that included calls for armed local militia, the removal of all 'Bengali' villages, and the reclamation of land that had been 'lost' to them (Narinjara 2012; ICG 2013). It also objected to the return of IDPs and any issuing of national identity cards to the Muslims.

The desire for ethnic cleansing is clear through all this, from many ethnic Rakhine and Buddhist nationalist organizations, as well as key government officials. Aung San Suu Kyi is about the only public figure who demonstrated any other response.

It is thus hardly surprising that, shortly after the state of emergency ended, a second wave of violence erupted. Attacks commenced on 21 October, in multiple areas across Rakhine. Unlike the first round of violence, these appeared to be well planned and coordinated, targeting Muslims (ICG 2013). Buddhist-monk-led religious nationalism was implicated in reports by international observers, but no culprits were positively identified. The security services, while perhaps not without some blame, were not implicated in any reports. Official government figures put the combined toll from the two attacks at 192 dead, 265 injured, 8,614 homes destroyed, and almost 2,000 public buildings razed, with violence in 11 of the 17 townships (UoM 2013). The number of IDPs swelled to 140,000, the vast majority Muslim, although around 20,000 Rakhine and numerous Kaman were also displaced (UNOCHA 2013). So while many Rakhine were impacted by the violence too, the official government report shows that 86 per cent of the houses destroyed and people displaced were Muslim (UoM 2013).

Displaced Muslims were confined in IDP camps, often within walking distance of their previous homes (Slim 2014). The military response resulted in far stricter segregation of Muslim and Buddhist communities than had previously existed, implemented by placing far more stringent travel restrictions on the Muslims. Even before the 2012 violence, Muslims were virtually confined to village tracts, needing to apply for a pass even to visit a neighbouring village, and had no permission to travel or relocate outside Rakhine. This situation was described by some as an 'open prison' even before the 2012 violence (Lewa 2009; Siddiqui 2008). After 2012 travel restrictions became even more severe, with segregation enforced to such an extent that access to health, education, markets, and other services became highly restricted. These restrictions on mobility reinforced conflict dynamics, preventing Muslims who might relocate from doing so, exacerbating Muslim grievances, and conveniently isolating the situation in Rakhine State where the national government could portray it as a local issue requiring its intervention to resolve—as if the state were a neutral actor. It clearly is not, given the decades of state-sanctioned discrimination and disenfranchisement.

We will explore the Kofi Annan-led Rakhine Advisory Commission recommendations (Annan et al. 2017a, 2017b) in the Conclusion, but central to these were that the government should remove all restrictions on movement in Rakhine State, particularly those on the Muslim community, and especially those denying equal access to healthcare and education—regardless of citizenship. This conflict will not be resolved while movement is restricted, the people segregated, and half the Muslim population now in Bangladesh.

2015–2016 Arakan Army (AA) Insurgency

The preceding discussion illustrates one dimension of this conflict, between Rakhine and Muslim nationalists in northern Rakhine State. This dimension is the dominant narrative inside Myanmar, and is fairly well recognized internationally. To more thoroughly locate our analysis within the wider complexity of interconnected factors, we now also look at two additional, concurrent conflicts. Both are either widely overlooked or conflated into the above. Equally important to the overall conflict context, Rakhine and Muslim communities both have a long history of struggle against the Burmese state. These parallel centre–periphery struggles include both violent and non-violent dimensions. This section explores recent violence between the ethnic Rakhine Arakan Army (AA) insurgency and the security forces. The following section outlines the violence involving the Arakan Rohingya Salvation Army (ARSA) militants.

Armed violence erupted in Rakhine State between the AA and Tatmadaw forces in March 2015. The AA had been founded in April 2009, to fight for self-determination for the Rakhine people (BNI 2017), but were based in Kachin territory until 2015, training and fighting with the Kachin Independence Army (KIA). Closely allied with the KIA, the AA has fought alongside them since conflict resumed in Kachin State in 2011, and is a member of the Northern Alliance coalition. The Northern Alliance also includes the Myanmar National Democratic Alliance Army (MNDAA), the Ta-ang National Liberation Army (TNLA), and claims strong ties to the Chinese-backed United Wa State Army (UWSA), although this is a little overstated. Interestingly, the Northern Alliance's most recent (English-language) press releases talk of armed engagement with the Tatmadaw in both northern Burma and Arakan, highlighting how Rakhine State is being drawn back into the centre of country's long-running civil wars, in a way that remains separate from the 'Rohingya' conflict. Being based on the other side of the country, the government has till now seen the AA as lacking legitimacy as an ethnic insurgent group. The AA were formed, however, on the back of a number of other Rakhine ethnic armed groups that did operate in Rakhine State over the decades, including most recently the Arakan Liberation Army (ALA), and their engagements in Rakhine over the last few years expand on this history. Rakhine insurgency and armed struggle against the state is nothing new.

Reports indicate that the AA began moving forces to Rakhine in 2014. Their first attacks in Rakhine State were on 29 March 2015. An AA unit attacked Tatmadaw outposts in Paletwa Township, southern Chin State, across the border in the north of Kyauktaw Township, Rakhine, gaining control of at least one military camp (BNI 2017; MPM 2016). Further clashes in April, in Kyauktaw and Maungdaw Townships, forced an estimated 540 Rakhine villagers to flee (Ye Mon 2015). Minor confrontations continued until a major flare-up in December 2015, in Kyauktaw and Mrauk-U Townships. AA reports, which may be exaggerated, claimed that twenty-one government soldiers were killed, including a battalion commander, and thirty were injured in attacks that forced hundreds more civilians to flee (MPM 2016).

The AA clashed with military forces at least fifteen times between 28 December 2015 and 4 January 2016 alone (GNLM 2016a), highlighting their strategic capability. Reports claim that thirty government soldiers were killed in just one of those AA attacks, in Buthidaung on 4 March. This prompted major military 'area clearance operations' to remove them (BNI 2017). In all, there are reports of between seventy and eighty armed clashes during the first half of 2016, in northern parts of Kyauktaw, Ponnagyun, Rathedaung and Mrauk-U Townships, with many dozens of Tatmadaw casualties. Estimates of the number of Rakhine villagers displaced by the fighting range up to 2,000 people (Nyan Lynn Aung 2016; Mratt Kyaw Thu 2016; Htet Kaung Linn 2016), noting that most of the fighting occurred in remote areas. The AA has repeatedly accused the military of using civilians as human shields, forcing villagers to flee.

The 2016 Tatmadaw crackdown was partially successful. AA attacks subsided for almost a year, with several arrests. Many AA apparently retreated back to Kachin State (Burma Times 2016; Htet Kaung Linn 2016). However, the AA action was successful in having its inclusion in national political dialogue debated by the national parliament (GNLM

2016b; Swan Ye Htut 2016). While they were not included, this seems to have been a key aim of the AA's action in Rakhine State: to become accepted as an 'ethnic armed group' representing the grievances of a *taing-yin-tha*, and hence gaining a seat in national political dialogue talks. The Tatmadaw have repeatedly blocked NLD attempts to include them in talks, despite the AA repeatedly seeking dialogue (e.g. Wa Lone & Thu Thu Aung 2016; also Htet Kaung Linn 2016). Perhaps this rebuff is partly behind the increasing recurrence of AA attacks in Rakhine during 2017 and 2018.

While 2015–16 was the first outbreak of AA activities in Rakhine State, and they are a relatively new force, these attacks must be seen in the context of a much longer history of Rakhine nationalist armed struggle against what is perceived as Burman domination. It could be said that this struggle dates to at least the conquest of Arakan by Burman rulers in 1784 (see Chapter 4), but even since Independence there has been a large number of armed nationalist Rakhine groups—the AA is simply the most recent of many (Smith 1994, 2007; Lintner 1999; South 2008; BNI 2017). The Arakan People's Liberation Party (APLP), for example, was founded in 1945 by a nationalist Arakanese monk, and resorted to armed struggle from 1946 until their surrender in 1958. Rakhine nationalist ambition was also an important aspect of the 'red flag' Communist Party of Burma (CPB) rebellion in Rakhine State after Independence. A pro-Marxist Arakan National Liberation Party (ANLP) was formed in June 1960 by former APLP activists, and in 1962 an armed Communist Party of Arakan (CPA) was established by 'red flag' CPB defectors. Subsequently, the Arakan Liberation Party (ALP) was founded in 1967, and members trained with the Karen National Union in south-east Burma before seeking to establish itself in the Rakhine State borderlands. An Arakan Independence Organisation (AIO) was also formed in 1970 by Arakanese students from Rangoon University, who trained with the Kachin Independence Organization (KIO) in north-east Burma, but then—like the ALP—suffered heavy losses during an attempt to set up bases along the borders with Bangladesh and India. Much diminished in strength, in 1988 the remaining leaders of the ANLP, CPA, ALP, and AIO forces joined in a National United Front (subsequently Party) of Arakan (NUPA). The ALP, however, soon broke away, later signing a ceasefire in April 2012.

As well as opening offices in the towns, the ALP still apparently maintains four small bases in the remote Burma–Bangladesh–India border area. Meanwhile the NUPA leadership have struggled on and, in an Arakan National Council (ANC) alliance, are seeking inclusion in nationwide peace talks with the government. Both the ALP and NUPA/ANC have become very small powers in military terms. However, the arrest of a senior ANC leader in relation to the three bombs detonated in Sittwe in February 2018 may signal some attempt to change that perception.

This history demonstrates that while the AA is a relatively new group, it continues a long history of armed Rakhine struggle against the Burman-led state. The AA is also growing in significance. It now has an estimated three thousand well-trained and battle-hardened soldiers in Kachin State (BNI 2017) and is seeking to expand its operations throughout the tri-border region between India, Bangladesh, and Rakhine State. Furthermore, the government believes that the AA was operating in Rakhine State out of an ALA base near the Bangladesh–India–Myanmar border (GNLM 2016f), suggesting new alliances. As yet, while agreeing to peace negotiations with ALP and ANC representatives, the Tatmadaw and government have rejected direct peace talks with the AA, but all of these factors raise the importance of this insurgency.

What is particularly significant about the AA attacks (and those of Rakhine insurgency before them), is that their struggle has been entirely directed against government forces and institutions. No attacks have perpetrated violence against the Muslims. Indeed, even the villagers displaced by the violence have all been Rakhine, as the Tatmadaw clearance operations sought to isolate the AA from its local supporters. This conflict is thus about the power relationships between the ethnic Rakhine and the Burman-led state/military/majority. In unison with most other ethnic nationalities in Myanmar, the AA complain of systematic discrimination against ethnic Rakhine by state agencies and institutions—an institutionalized Burman privilege that Walton (2013) describes as similar to Whiteness—and the neglect of Rakhine development needs apart from resource exploitation. The AA seeks Rakhine control of Rakhine State's political and economic future, without Burman domination. It thus seeks some form of self-rule, usually expressed as being within a federal union.

RECENT VIOLENCE AND SIGNIFICANCE

The AA cause is thus not the removal of the Muslims from Rakhine, and is not inherently related in any way to the Muslim issue. The AA has gone to great pains to make this point. For example, an official AA statement in 2014, issued in response to a *Foreign Policy Magazine* article which accused them of an anti-Muslim agenda, read:

> The author demonized and accused the Arakan Army as [an] armed gang against Muslims. AA is not a safe haven for the extremists to do as they pleased [*sic*]. Nor do we intend to harm any innocent people or groups against humanity. We are highly disciplined with morals and strongly committed to freedom, justice, human rights and dignity. The Arakan Army was only established to strive for our right to self-determination and equality which no honest man shall lose in his/her life. More importantly, AA is not a religion based armed group which is only formed with Buddhists but people with other religious faiths are also allowed to join AA in order to share our cause. This alone proves our belief in religious diversity and our desire to create an open society where basic human rights are guaranteed. (AA 2014)

Lest the AA agenda be seen as a fringe or secondary issue in comparison to the Muslim issue, the seething animosity, if not anger, that many Rakhine hold towards the military and the Burman-led state must be noted. A powerful example in early 2018 was the defiance of the state by a large Rakhine crowd in Mrauk-U, which led to security forces open firing and killing nine civilian protesters and injuring nineteen others. This incident has already been noted. The crowd was gathered on the 223rd anniversary of defeat of the Arakanese kingdom by Burman forces, to express to the military and the government their strongly separatist sentiment. The denial of permission for the event, the killing of unarmed civilians by security forces, and the subsequent assassination of the township administrator who authorized the crackdown, followed by bombings at symbolic locations in Sittwe, all highlight the depth of conflict tension between large sections of the Rakhine community and the Burman-led state.

The extensive support by Rakhine people for the Arakan National Party (ANP), and the connections between the ANP and AA, is another significant example. The ANP is a political party, and has a commitment to working within the system, formally espousing non-violent political means. It has not been involved in armed violence, at least directly. However, it prosecutes a similar Rakhine nationalist agenda vis-à-vis the Burman-led state. The Speaker of the Rakhine State parliament, U San Kyaw Hla, an ANP MP, is the father-in-law of Brigadier General Tun Myat Naing, chief of the AA (Mratt Kyaw Thu & Gleeson 2016). ANP MPs were at the forefront of the push to have the AA included in political dialogue talks (Sithu Aung Myint 2016; Swan Ye Htut 2016). And one ANP MP, Sein Wai Aung, even prefaced remarks on that discussion in the national parliament by controversially referring to the AA as 'Rakhine's Tatmadaw'. Clearly, many in the ANP have a strong connection and affinity towards the AA and its aims.

Highlighting the strength of support for this cause, the ANP is currently the third-largest party in both houses of the national parliament—despite being a single-ethnic party. The ANP was formed out of a merger of the Rakhine Nationalities Development Party (RNDP) and the Arakan League for Democracy (ALD)—the ALD won the third-largest vote nationally in the abortive 1990 elections (the most of any ethnic party), and the RNDP won the fourth-largest bloc in 2010, across both houses of parliament. (The ALD, like the NLD, chose not to compete in the 2010 elections). Nationalist parties have had similar results at the state level: the ANP holds the majority of elected seats in the Rakhine parliament since 2015, and Rakhine is the only state or regional parliament whose largest party has not been the national governing party after either 2010 or 2015.

In other words—and this is the key point—ethnic Rakhine voters (particularly in north and central Rakhine) have demonstrated very strong aspirations for autonomy, and deep distrust of Burman leadership at all three of the last elections (1990, 2010, 2015), and have not shown disapproval of AA links. This is far stronger electoral support for ethnic autonomy than any other ethnic minority has demonstrated. Clearly, most ethnic Rakhine do not trust Burman-led or multi-ethnic parties to look after their interests, and want more control of their governance and economy. That this sentiment is stronger in Rakhine State than amongst the Kachin, Shan, or Karen nationalities is very significant. And this long-term power struggle with the Burman-led state is both independent of, yet intertwined with, their competition with the Muslims.

The key difference between the AA and ANP, apart from the recourse to arms, is that the AA has refrained from any anti-Muslim positions. Many in the ANP have vocally opposed all moves to verify documents, grant citizenship, or otherwise expand the rights of the Muslim community. Nonetheless, the ANP has repeatedly issued statements calling for the rule of law and opposing violence against Muslims (Ei Ei Toe Lwin 2012). The ANP's strident nationalism has definitely hurt the rights of the Muslim population, and undoubtedly enabled violence against them, even endorsed sentiments that lay behind some embracing an ethnic cleansing agenda. But most in the ANP are not extremists in themselves. Formally they advocate non-violence (as opposed to some Burman Ma Ba Tha Buddhist nationalists). So while there are some in their midst who could be considered extremist, there are deep sensitivities around Muslim issues, and some tension within the party on this issue, their primary struggle has clearly long been to wrest political and economic control over their state from Nay Pyi Taw, rather than directed towards the Muslims.

The key point of this section is that, while some ethnic Rakhine nationalists have indeed perpetrated violence against Muslims, particularly during the communal violence of 2012, the AA attacks and the ANP/Rakhine political party track-record demonstrate that Rakhine nationalism is more strongly directed against ending Burman domination than against the Muslims. Clearly though, these two issues cannot be resolved independently.

2016–2017 Arakan Rohingya Salvation Army

This chapter has now explored two major axes of this conflict—the Muslim–Rakhine and the Rakhine–Burman dimensions. We now turn to the third major axis, between the Muslims and the Burman-led state. This is well illustrated by the attacks in 2016 and 2017 by the new militant group, the Arakan Rohingya Salvation Army (ARSA).

It is important to note from the outset that, notwithstanding populist views in Myanmar to the contrary, the Muslims of northern Rakhine State have never previously been a particularly violently or religiously radicalized population (Selth 2003, 2004, 2013; Yegar 1972, 2002; Horsey 2016). This is in the face of decades of marginalization and despite the deep fears of Rakhine and other Burmese ethnicities. These fears, it must be noted, closely parallel exaggerated global narratives about Islamic extremism. However, since the 2012 violence, most Muslims in northern Rakhine State have now been either detained in squalid IDP camps or restricted to their village tracts, often under curfew and patrolled by a heightened security presence, and their livelihood options and access to services severely diminished. This on the back of decades of systemic discrimination, restricted mobility, and limited service access. As a result, a growing sense of despair has permeated the Muslim community. This desperation has allowed a growing number to justify recourse to violence.

This said, there have been seven decades of armed insurgency by small groups of Muslims, against Burman domination, along similar lines to the ethnic nationalist insurgencies of the Rakhine and many other ethnic minorities (Smith 1999, 2018; Lintner 1999). The Mujahid rebellion of 1947–61 was the largest, and must be seen in the context of nationwide civil war, not as an indicator of inherent Islamist tendencies. Their political demands centred on northern Arakan, where Muslim communities were a majority. After the surrender of the remaining Mujahids in a 1961 peace agreement with the U Nu government, armed opposition revived following General Ne Win's 1962 military coup. The Rohingya Independence (later Patriotic) Front (RPF) formed the following year, with the explicit objective of promoting an 'ethnic' rather than 'religious' identity for the political rights of Muslim communities in Arakan (Smith 1999, 2018). This, perhaps, is one key reason for the popularization of the name 'Rohingya'. The Rohingya Liberation Party was likewise formed in 1972, by former Mujahid leader Zaffar Kawal. By the late 1970s militants had been pushed back to the Bangladesh borderlands by counter-insurgency offensives and the 1978 Operation Nagamin. The Rohingya Solidarity Organization (RSO), a more radical breakaway group, was formed in 1982 by Muhammed Yunus, and became the most influential and extreme 'Rohingya' faction. An Arakan Liberation Organisation was also briefly active in the mid-1980s, promoting an 'Arakanese Muslim' rather than 'Rohingya' identity for local communities. As the RPF declined, the more moderate Arakan Rohingya Islamic Front (ARIF) was founded in 1986 by Nurul Islam, the former RPF Vice-Chairman. In 1998 the Arakan Rohingya National Organization (ARNO) was formed by a merger of ARIF and two RSO factions (ARNO 2007).

Since that time ARNO has become the main political voice for 'Rohingya' rights internationally. Until the 2016 emergence of ARSA, remaining RSO elements were considered the most militant force still in the field. Armed activities, however, were rare.

The point of this is to highlight the fact Muslim insurgency against Burman domination has been ongoing since Independence, even if not hugely popular, and had a relatively similar history, motives, strategy, and degree of success to that of the ethnic Rakhine insurgencies—and other insurgencies across Myanmar. It is most significant that all were primarily or solely engaged in attacks on military and strategic targets. None ever gained significant popular support in terms of mass recruitment or resourcing, nor strategic impact, at least after the Mujahid rebellion failed, and none ever posed a serious military threat. Concentrated around the Bangladesh border, over recent decades these groups have been more involved in publicity and occasional attacks than seeking to build up a 'liberated area' or parallel government. And none was Islamist, as we know that terminology today. Indeed, RPF leaders were long insistent on using the name 'Rohingya' rather than 'Arakanese Muslims', as they claimed an ethnic rather than religious identity and struggle.

As with the AA insurgency, it is highly significant that the formally planned and executed ARSA attacks in October 2016 and August 2017 were both—at least the initial attacks—exclusively directed against the state security apparatus. There is evidence of summary execution of potential civilian informants before the attacks, both Muslim and non-Muslim (ICG 2017), which is deeply concerning, and violence against civilians certainly spiralled after the August 2017 attacks, but it appears that the formally planned and executed attacks targeted state security posts, not local non-Muslim communities. The strategic logic of these attacks conforms to secessionist goals, which we argue is their primary motivation, although the change of tactics does suggest international links.

The October 2016 attack has been well documented by the ICG (2016), and much of what follows is drawn from that report. On 9 October a group initially calling itself Harakah al-Yaqin ('faith movement' in Arabic), subsequently renamed ARSA, launched deadly attacks on three border-guard police posts in Maungdaw and Rathedaung

Townships in north-west Rakhine (ICG 2016; Horsey 2016; GNLM 2016d; Nay Yi 2016). The border-guard police are a military-trained force tasked with maintaining security in unstable borderlands across the country, mainly operating checkpoints. This was the beginning of attacks that appear to have ambitiously (and naïvely) aimed to take over and gain independence for the north-west of the state. In the early hours some 400-odd Muslims launched the coordinated, simultaneous attacks in Maungdaw and Rathedaung Townships, mostly armed with knives and slingshots. The assailants seized 67 military weapons and 10,930 rounds of ammunition (UoM 2017i). The incidents involved sophisticated multi-phase tactics, including an improvised explosive device (IED) and an ambush to delay reinforcements (ICG 2016). These attacks were a major escalation of a conflict that had seen little sign of organized Muslim recourse to armed violence for at least two decades. This attack was followed by clashes with security forces, who fought to regain control. These clashes resulted in the deaths of at least ten police and seven soldiers, one a senior ranking army officer (UoM 2017i).

Concerningly, immediately after the initial attack a series of at least eleven videos was uploaded to social media calling for other 'Rohingya' to join the jihad to liberate northern Rakhine State, and appealing for foreign support, weapons, and fighters.[1] The main speaker in the videos, Ata Ullah, has been identified as the son of a Muslim from northern Rakhine State who was born in Karachi, and grew up in Mecca. He disappeared from Saudi Arabia after the 2012 communal violence. The Myanmar authorities claim that there is evidence he spent six months training with the Pakistan Taliban (GNLM 2016c), and there are unconfirmed reports that he received insurgency training in several other countries. Recruitment, training, and planning apparently began shortly after the 2012 communal violence, and was funded by a cadre of the 'Rohingya' diaspora in Saudi Arabia, most of whom fled there during the 1950s civil war in Myanmar (i.e. they are not refugees from recent anti-Muslim action). Active recruitment of local leaders in Rakhine State began in 2013, and covert training of villagers in 2014 (ICG 2016).

Given that this violence was planned and instigated in the wake of Muslim–Rakhine communal violence in 2012, it is significant that these initial attacks only targeted the state security apparatus. Thus while civilian informants were executed before the attacks, and violence against civilians spiralled out of control after the August 2017 attacks, it does not appear as if non-Muslim communities, leadership, or institutions were the target of pre-planned attacks. It should be noted that, unlike the Tatmadaw and AA, ARSA is not a highly trained and disciplined force with a central command, but a loose collection of cells consisting of villagers who have only been given some very basic training. Violence against civilians after the initial attacks, therefore, could as easily be the result of a lack of discipline and of a command structure as of orders or plans. Understanding the targets and command structure is thus central to a robust analysis of this aspect of the conflict.

Government press releases and ICG research suggest that ARSA's 2016 plan was to take complete control of Maungdaw Township, cut off communications with Buthidaung to the east, and establish a defendable, liberated area similar to the areas controlled by some of the larger ethnic armed groups in Myanmar's northern and eastern borderlands (ICG 2016). From this very ambitious initial goal, the aim was apparently to gain control of Buthidaung and parts of Rathedaung, giving it complete control of the Bangladeshi border and allowing it to guarantee the freedom of most of the 'Rohingya' population in Myanmar. However, this plan was hastily altered when two senior leaders left and two informers were captured.

This attack plan properly frames the subsequent 2017 ARSA attacks, as well as the 'area clearance operations', the chaos, and the mass exodus. The 2016 attack aims and approach appear to be classic ethnic insurgency in scope and execution. And despite their rhetoric of jihad, their initial name, meaning 'faith movement', and appeals for foreign support ARSA does not appear to have (yet) adopted the language or aims of global Islamic extremism—just some of their organizational and tactical strategies.

ARSA consolidated its authority in Muslim villages during the months following the 2016 attacks, preparing for a larger 2017 attack (ICG 2017). The extensive Tatmadaw 'area clearance operations' aided recruitment into village-level cells, led by respected local leaders, including clerics. ARSA also killed dozens of suspected Muslim informers with links to the authorities, and ramped up training and IED production. A series of incidents during May–August 2017 put security forces and Rakhine villagers on edge. Several foreigners were identified as involved, raising fears of international Islamist involvement. The first known ARSA killing of non-Muslim civilians was in June, when four Rakhine villagers came across bomb-making material while foraging in northern Maungdaw. The authorities were apparently aware of these developments, and deployed 500 additional troops in early August. The Tatmadaw Commander-in-Chief, Senior General Min Aung Hlaing (2017a, 2017b), has confirmed that the army launched area clearance operations before the second attack, allowing ARSA to claim that their subsequent attacks were in defence of Muslim communities suffering increasing atrocities at the hands of security forces—i.e. provoked, not unprovoked attacks. On 16 August ARSA uploaded a video warning the Tatmadaw to stop its brutality against Muslim civilians (ARSA 2017f). After the August attacks ARSA claimed that it was fighting only to end military attacks on Muslim civilians, and prevent the military from jeopardizing implementation of the Annan recommendations (ARSA 2017b, 2017d, 2017e).

The second ARSA attack came just after midnight on 25 August 2017, and is well documented in ICG (2017). On 22 August the Advisory Commission on Rakhine State, headed by former UN Secretary-General Kofi Annan, handed its final report to the Myanmar president, U Htin Kyaw (Annan et al. 2017b). The report was made public at a press conference the evening of 24 August. Hours later, just after midnight, ARSA launched a series of coordinated, deadly attacks, targeting thirty border-guard posts across Maungdaw and a Tatmadaw base in Rathedaung Township—with human wave attacks involving hundreds of people, mostly untrained local villagers armed with farm tools. It appears that their strategy was to incite a general uprising among the population. Such a strategy, however, is a very perilous one, with high risks for the vulnerable populations in Rakhine, as we discuss in the last part of the book.

This attack conformed closely to the intelligence above, the attack plan strongly suggesting an aim to liberate Maungdaw as a bold separatist act. However, the timing, immediately after the release of the Annan report, does raise eyebrows. Annan's recommendations constitute the best proposals towards peace yet drawn up. The timing can hardly be coincidental; clearly, someone is attempting to thwart implementation—but who? The government claims that ARSA launched the attacks to prevent the recommendations being implemented. ARSA argues that it was trying to prevent the military jeopardizing implementation of the recommendations (see ARSA 2017d, 2017b). ARSA blamed the military for all civilian destruction, and even initially invited the Rakhine people to join with it in opposing the oppressive Tatmadaw (ARSA 2017a),[2] although the sincerity of this has been questioned, and it has been implicated in attacks on civilians.

On 28 August Ata Ullah issued a WhatsApp audio message instructing his followers to burn down Rakhine Buddhist villages—in direct contradiction to their repeatedly stated policy to refrain from attacking non-security targets. This was probably because non-Muslim militias were believed to be helping the Tatmadaw burn villages during clearance operations. The ICG reports that only three non-Muslim villages are known to have been burned by Muslims as a result, although it is possible that some ARSA recruits engaged in further ethnic cleansing efforts after the initial attacks, to drive collaborating non-Muslim minorities out of the territory they were attempting to capture. Moreover, ARSA declared a unilateral ceasefire in September, and appears to have carried out no further attacks from then until January 2018, undermining the idea that it planned rolling attacks on non-Muslims. This, however, is in contrast to what the ICG suggest was widespread, systematic, and pre-planned burning of villages by the military, border-guard, and Rakhine militias (ICG 2017), leading to the mass displacement of Muslims we have seen.

It is unfortunate that they quickly labelled ARSA as terrorists (e.g. UoM 2017e, 2017d). Before that point, attack planning appeared to conform to a separatist agenda rather than what we would usually define as terrorism. Senior General Min Aung Hlaing (2017a, 2017b) estimated that there were around 4,000 attackers, with up to 10,000 recruited to ARSA. The government strongly disputes claims the military committed atrocities, but this label, and these numbers, have allowed the military and government to defend violence against *any* Muslims in northern Rakhine State as a legitimate response to terrorism, given that so many were local villagers. This made it impossible for any high-level discussions about a ceasefire or any sort of peace accord.

The August 2017 attacks were hardly unexpected. Tensions had been escalating for months, with increasing activity by both Buddhist nationalists and Muslim insurgents. The government tried to ban Ma Ba Tha's anti-Muslim activities across the country as early as May, but faced defiance and a backlash of criticism. As this struggle raged nationally, deadly attacks increased in Rakhine State. For example, on 4 July a group of seven Muslims from an IDP camp was attacked by ethnic Rakhine at a jetty in Sittwe, resulting in the death of one Muslim and injury to the other six. They had travelled into Sittwe accompanied by police, to negotiate the purchase of a fishing boat. Conversely, several Rakhine villagers went missing in Maungdaw on 27 July, and a search team subsequently found seven hacked bodies and a suspected militant training camp in the densely forested hills near the village (Irrawaddy 2017). On 3 August six Myo villagers were killed in their fields in Maungdaw by unknown attackers, and two other women kidnapped (Min Thein Aung 2017). Tensions grew further when, on 9 August, ANP representatives asked the Tatmadaw Commander-in-Chief to create a 'No Bengali Zone' in northern Rakhine State. On 13 August a series of large-scale protests by ethnic Rakhine in fifteen of seventeen townships demanded that they be allowed to form armed militias, that the army step up efforts to eradicate militants, and that international organizations leave the region immediately. ICG (2017) documents a series of other escalations. So tensions and confrontations were escalating for some time.

Since the attacks and crackdown, of course, both al-Qaeda and the Islamic State have threatened terrorist attacks (Moore 2017; Chan 2017)—and there have been unconfirmed reports of Islamic State operatives arriving at the Myanmar–Bangladesh border area (Voice 2017). This fuels fear that the conflict will be co-opted by these groups, particularly given the requests by ARSA for support, the origins of the leader Ata Ullah, and the discovery of Pakistanis working with ARSA in Rakhine State. ARSA vehemently denies any association with either al-Qaeda or Islamic State (ARSA 2017c), and there is little confirmed evidence of more than the above, but fear runs deep.

The Tatmadaw's 'area clearance operations' in response to the 2016 attacks were harsh. Formal operations lasted five months, from 9 October 2016 until 9 February 2017, and were disproportionate in comparison with the response to the AA attacks. The litany of human rights abuse allegations discussed in Chapter 1 relates primarily to this crackdown period, although most international reports omit discussion of the initial ARSA attacks. The security forces' responsibility to bring this violence under control must be acknowledged, as well as the fact that both the military and the government deny allegations of excess. We will return to examine this claim shortly. Eventually, the five-month operation did result in 585 arrests and 69 attackers killed (UoM 2017i), 64 of whom have since been found guilty, with another 294 cases under way (Min Aung Khine 2018). In addition, 25 of the weapons were recovered (UoM 2017a). Given that all the militants' deaths were in clashes during the first few days of operations (Slodkowski 2016), one can imagine that the military's argument is that they have shown considerable restraint.

By contrast, the 'area clearance operations' after the second attacks lasted only two weeks. But they were sharp. According to the State Counsellor's Information Office, during these two weeks there were 97 engagements with ARSA, resulting in the deaths of 371 suspected militants and 13 members of the security forces (UoM 2017g). The State Counsellor's Office acknowledges 6,842 houses burned, but explicitly claims that it was ARSA torching houses, to make it look as if the military was responsible (UoM 2017f). There is little evidence to corroborate this. But it also claims that 163 civilians were killed by ARSA before the 2017 violence, for cooperating with the authorities, including 79 people killed the day before the 25 August attacks (UoM 2017b). Thus, although reports of violence, massacres, human rights abuses, and burning of villages have continued long after the 'area clearance operations' were over, it is not totally clear whether these attacks are the work of the Tatmadaw, ARSA, or Rakhine or Muslim militias. Aung San Suu Kyi puts the blame primarily on Rakhine militia (Robinson 2017), which is unlikely. Few Rakhine live in Maungdaw, and most fled quickly as the violence erupted. And if this were the case she would have to explain the military's unwillingness or inability to control the violence of anti-Muslim nationalists. Most evidence and witness accounts point to the Tatmadaw burning most villages.

Claims and counter-claims have been made over the atrocities committed against civilians. MSF (2017) estimates from surveys with refugees that between 9,430 and 13,750 Muslims died during the 31 days following the 25 August attacks, at least 6,700 due to the violence (most were shot, but also hundreds burned alive in their houses). This figure is likely to be an underestimate, as it does not account for those whose stories never left Myanmar. We have no figures about the number of Rakhine, Hindu, and other non-Muslim civilians attacked and killed, but mass graves of Hindus have been unearthed in Maungdaw, and many Rakhine claim to have been attacked. Groups ranging from Amnesty International to the Office of the High Commissioner of the United Nations Human Rights (OHCHR) claim that the security forces perpetrated widespread and systematic human rights violations, deliberately targeting the civilian populations, with little or no regard for their connection to militants. They report executions, random shootings, arbitrary detentions, rape, physical assault and beatings, torture, degrading treatment, looting and destruction of property (OHCHR 2017, p. 3; Amnesty International 2017b). Witness accounts of attacks on Hindus and Rakhine civilians describe the perpetrators as men dressed like Muslims, with their faces covered. However, many of the people we have personally heard testify do not believe they were their local Muslims, leading them to speculate that the violence was accentuated by foreign Muslim fighters. Some even suggest that some attacks were perpetrated by Tatmadaw disguised as Muslims.

Given the horrific human toll, the clear evidence and the constant documented allegations of mass atrocities, an independent investigation is vital. The three commissions launched in early 2017 by the Myanmar authorities lacked independence and therefore credibility (UoM 2017i; Kyaw Thu 2017b, 2017a). The Rakhine State Investigation Commission was a more serious attempt at an independent, balanced, credible investigation, but the outcome is far from convincing. The Myanmar government should accept the need for a wide-ranging UN investigation by respected, impartial, external figures. In the chaos and carnage, it is almost certain that the Tatmadaw, ARSA, and local militias have all perpetrated violence against civilians. The Tatmadaw has a reputation for excess, and it is hard to believe that its actions have been beyond reproach. ARSA and the Rakhine militias are not well-trained and drilled forces, and any hierarchy they may have is not necessarily in the control of people who might act on their behalf. This makes it more likely that they have acted, yet more difficult to positively identify anything as officially sanctioned by their organizational leadership.

Nonetheless, given the scale and ferocity of this violence, against groups on all sides, it is hard to conclude anything other than that all sides have perpetrated atrocities. A detailed, open, international investigation is urgently required into these crimes.

It must be noted that that Tatmadaw's quick and decisive response to both attacks has been relatively popular amongst the ethnic Rakhine and other Burmese populations, despite the human cost to the Muslim population. Why?

Take a moment to imagine how this narrative would play out if a similar attack had occurred on US soil, or in another Western country. Imagine, if you will, the response in Trump's America, or with the right wing in parts of Europe. Imagine the panic, fear, and outrage, if coordinated deadly attacks on security forces were launched by hundreds of angry Muslim youth, with evidence of sophisticated planning, IEDs, diversionary tactics, and radical jihadist social media posts—all with links to Taliban training and Saudi Arabian funding. Not to mention the deaths of police and soldiers, and the theft of military weapons. There would be very loud public cries demanding swift and decisive action to completely eradicate the threat once and for all. A massive mobilization would occur, to arrest all those responsible and recover the weapons. The security forces, having borne the brunt, might overreact. Definitely, any communities believed to be harbouring, enabling, or showing support for the attackers should expect a forceful crackdown.

It should be no surprise, then, that in Myanmar, fears of terrorism and radical Islam have provoked very much the same response. This does not excuse the violation of human rights, but it does put the military response in context. And, as already noted, the decisive response, however harsh, has been very popular domestically. And the crackdown on a threat widely perceived as external (compared with all the other insurgencies) has actually improved the prestige and popular perception of the Tatmadaw, helping re-legitimize them within the Myanmar polity.

The Tatmadaw appears to have adopted its infamous counter-insurgency four-cuts strategy, cutting off the four main sources of support for rebel groups: food, funds, intelligence, and recruits (see Smith 1991, 1999; Selth 2002). These are the same tactics used against the AA and other ethnic armed groups—the difference is that they usually adopt the approach in more sparsely populated regions, and thus the human cost is usually much lower. With a curfew in place, people were ordered not to leave their villages, and the military sealed off areas while they implemented operations in densely population Muslim areas.

These attacks were, in many ways, a self-fulfilled prophecy. Fear and suspicion prompted the state to treat the Muslims in ways that have encouraged some to radicalize, the very thing it has long dreaded.

> The fear of extinction acts like a self-fulfilling prophecy, spreading throughout the community and gaining strength from negative interpretations of each ensuing act of provocation or violence; generating a dialectic of escalating acts of violence until they reach full-blown civil conflict. (Hancock 1998, p. 13)

Yet, while there is now a very real security danger posed by ARSA, and a risk of its cause turning into a transnational Islamist threat, continued heavy-handed military responses will almost certainly backfire, and will only drive more Muslims into backing the militants (Paddock *et al.* 2017; Robinson 2016). There has already been a surge of international political support from Islamic countries that casts the 'Rohingya' as the Palestinians of South East Asia. There is also the danger of criminalization to fund further activities: a growing number of large amphetamine shipments by Muslims have been seized in both Sittwe and Maungdaw (e.g. UoM 2017h, 2017c; Aziz 2018).

In conclusion, it is important to note that planning for these violent attacks appears to have commenced in the wake of the 2012 communal violence between the Muslims and the ethnic Rakhine. Given this, it is striking that the attacks and rhetoric so directly targeted state security forces, rather than attacking Rakhine villages, leadership, or institutions. This is significant. These attacks show that many Muslims see the Burman-led state as their primary problem, more so than their ethnic Rakhine communal neighbours.

The detail in the preceding three narratives will quickly date, as the situation in Rakhine State continues to evolve. In presenting these three dimensions, we are not in any way suggesting that the three are equivalent, nor is the impact equal. The point we are making is about complexity, multi-polarity, and interconnectedness. Most commentary tends to conflate or flatten these interconnected dimensions in a manner that oversimplifies the situation, leading to unhelpful recommendations. Our aim throughout this book is to highlight the complexity and explore the multiple perspectives, to analyse with a view to reconciliation rather than apportioning blame.

What these three dimensions mean about the conflict will be examined throughout this book. The most important points to take away from this chapter are that the conflict in Rakhine State is multidimensional and complex, and that the Myanmar authorities are neither neutral actors attempting to contain a regional conflict, nor the only perpetrators of violence.

Significance of the Conflict for Myanmar

Domestic Significance

So, what does this all mean for Myanmar? We would suggest that, of all the serious political, economic, and social challenges facing Myanmar today, the 'Rohingya' conflict is *the* most sensitive and *the* most likely to derail the national reform process. Reform gained momentum after the Saffron Revolution in 2007 and Cyclone Nargis in 2008. It accelerated after the 2010 elections, when new president Thein Sein embarked on an extensive liberalization programme (see Lall 2016). Aung San Suu Kyi and the NLD government were elected in 2015 on a platform of furthering this reform. However, little momentum has been achieved in furthering the political, economic, and social reforms necessary for the transition of the country. A range of challenges now threatens to derail their ambitious plans. We argue that the 'Rohingya' conflict is the most serious of these.

Aung San Suu Kyi's NLD government is confronted by two powerful advocacy groups, both seeking to undermine its legitimacy unless their demands are met. One group, mainly anchored in domestic conservative circles and with tacit support from the Tatmadaw, portrays the government as weak in protecting Buddhism, and demands a hard-line position against the Muslims, especially in Rakhine State. Another, spearheaded by international actors, portrays the government as colluding with the military on human rights abuses, ethnic cleansing, and genocide. Both seriously challenge the government's legitimacy. Despite the NLD's efforts to move the country beyond partial democratization, we suggest that the Rakhine State conflict is so sensitive, complex, and volatile that it threatens to derail the whole transition process.

The significance of Rakhine to Myanmar's reform process can thus hardly be overstated. The narratives, discourses, and fears bring together the explosive mix of politics, religion, and ethnicity, co-opting global narratives about terrorism and security. The 'Rakhine issue', as it is often euphemistically called, is deeply political, extremely emotive, and highly volatile—all the more so given the extent to which Myanmar has enshrined ethnicity and indigeneity into politics, and used religion as a marker of nationalism and a purveyor of political legitimacy. Every decision, action (or inaction), and statement the government and Tatmadaw make on Rakhine is watched exceedingly closely, right across Myanmar as well as internationally. We identify four key risks.

The greatest (perhaps the only) beneficiary of the recent conflict in Rakhine State has been the Tatmadaw. Under the flawed 2008 constitution, the military controls the three ministries responsible for security—Defence, Border Affairs, and Home Affairs. As a result, the Tatmadaw has effective political control of most key matters in Rakhine State. It is not popular in any other armed conflict in Myanmar, all of which are clearly civil and involve the military fighting against citizens of the country. However, by dealing decisively with what is popularly perceived as a threat 'external' to the nation, the Tatmadaw has enhanced its legitimacy as the protector of the state. This is significant at a time when the NLD government is trying to limit the political powers of the Tatmadaw and recast its place in society. Rakhine is thus one of the main battlegrounds in the power struggle between Aung San Suu Kyi's government and the military. The wrong response to Rakhine could weaken its ability to confront the military or scrutinize its actions on other matters. It could even potentially backfire into a justification to expand military political power.

A second danger posed by the Rakhine State conflict is further damage to already fragile national social cohesion. The authorities were shocked at the rapid spread of sentiment and violence across the country after the 2012 violence in Rakhine State (ICG 2013). Anti-Muslim violence quickly spread to Meiktila in central Myanmar. March 2013 saw two days of rioting by a thousand-strong mob, including by monks in robes, and left at least forty-four dead (including twenty students and several teachers from a Muslim school), thousands injured, and several thousand rendered homeless (PHR 2013; Ei Ei Toe Lwin 2013). Police appeared either complicit, or lacking the ability to stop the violence. In the first half of 2013 alone there were also smaller outbreaks of anti-Muslim violence, for example in Yangon region, Bago, the Kachin jade-mining town of Hpakant, Sagaing Region in the north, and Lashio in the north-east (ICG 2013). Four small non-lethal bombings in Yangon in late 2016, near markets and government offices, and a fifth found at Yangon airport, also appear related to Rakhine. Furthermore, the growing power of ultra-nationalist groups such as the Ma Ba Tha, and the growing religious dimension of these ultra-nationalists, is largely the result of Rakhine State conflict dynamics.

One recent survey has suggested that religion is a more important aspect of identity in Myanmar than even ethnicity (Welsh & Huang 2016),[3] suggesting that the social divisions in Myanmar may be even more pronounced between religious identities than ethnic ones. Schissler et al. (2015), likewise, find concern about religious conflict to be significant right across Myanmar. Certainly, Christian and other minorities also feel under threat, not just Muslims, with this sentiment of religious division being quite pronounced in the Kachin conflict, for example. But most importantly for our case, both sets of research suggest that the Muslim–Buddhist divide is the deepest in Myanmar society. Schissler et al. found evidence that Muslims are widely perceived as a threat, right across the country, being viewed as violent, untrustworthy, and extremist. Islam is thus widely seen to pose an existential threat to Buddhism, as well as to the nation in the sense of being overrun by migrants. Given such views, and the degree of polarization caused by the Rakhine State conflict, this conflict runs the risk of inflaming religious and race-based rhetoric across the country, with a worrying potential for violence. There is a real danger of social cohesion deteriorating much further, and Muslims being targeted nationally, if these divisions are co-opted into political campaigning around the 2020 elections. Either way, the conflict risks further damaging social cohesion in an already deeply divided country, widening ethnic and religious schisms and making ongoing governance reform even more difficult.

A third risk posed by the Rakhine State conflict is to the peace and political dialogue process. Aung San Suu Kyi has repeatedly declared that peace and reconciliation is her government's top priority (e.g. Lun Min Mang 2015; NLD 2015; GNLM 2016e). Violent conflict has plagued the borderlands since Independence, and claimed an estimated million lives (Smith 1991; Steinberg 2006). Eight ethnic armed groups signed a Nationwide Ceasefire Agreement on 31 March 2015, but the remainder of the twenty-one recognized ethnic armed groups either abstained or were banned due to ongoing fighting. The process has now moved on to a national-level political dialogue phase, with the first 21st-Century Panglong Conference (as the political dialogue process has been called) meetings held in August 2016 and May 2017. Further meetings and working-group sessions are scheduled until the end of 2019, despite the fact that some ethnic armed groups are excluded, including the AA and ARSA. The military have angrily threatened to 'eliminate' the AA entirely (Ye Mon & Thu Thu Aung 2016; Gerin 2016), and ARSA has ominously pledged to fight 'until the last drop of blood' (Sakhawat 2017). Some argue (e.g. BNI 2017) that the peace process has already slowed under the NLD, as the previous military-backed USDP government had more incentive to compromise because they derived legitimacy from progress, and the new NLD peace team are less experienced. With this level of fragility and attacks on social cohesion, Rakhine issues risk harming the national peace process.

A final domestic risk posed by the Rakhine State conflict is to the electoral fortunes of the NLD. The risk is that electoral politics may overwhelm the actions required to resolve the underlying issues. The NLD swept to power in 2015, riding a wave of popular support—support that remained high for twenty-five years after their 1990 election victory. Ethnic-minority parties made the greatest gains in the April 2017 by-elections, pointing to the re-emergence of ethnic distrust as a political force. The Rakhine State conflict is the issue most likely to impact electoral popularity and undermine social cohesion, meaning that electoral politics cannot be discounted as a motivation for any decisions about Rakhine. Certainly, since coming to power, NLD key figures have all routinely avoided any comment, discussion, or interviews about Rakhine. There is a fear among many of Myanmar's political leaders that, in an overwhelmingly Buddhist and deeply anti-Muslim country, any concessions about any Muslim cause is political suicide (Robinson 2016). And, as in the West, policies to 'crack down' on 'illegals' or 'improve border security' are electorally popular. All of this makes it profoundly difficult for a government in a relatively weak position to implement the sort of actions required to resolve the underlying drivers of conflict in Rakhine State.

International Significance

The conflict in Rakhine State not only poses a significant domestic risk, but also a risk to Myanmar's international reputation and relationships. Mounting criticism of Aung San Suu Kyi over her response to this conflict has already been noted. There are questions over whether her rhetoric about human rights and democratic values was merely instrumental, to win power, rather than being core personal and party beliefs (e.g. Harper 2017; Hutt 2017). It is thus an indicator of the extent of democratization, economic liberalization, security-sector reform, balance of power between the government and military, and hence how much constructive international engagement to expect from Myanmar in the coming years.

This issue has already significantly strained relationships with Myanmar's Asian neighbours. As their lives have become increasingly fragile, marginal, and insecure, many Muslims have unsurprisingly made the decision to flee. As we have noted, almost 885,000 refugees have fled to Bangladesh since August 2017, on top of an estimated 199,500 between June 2012 and August 2017 (IOM 2018; UNHCR 2017; OHCHR 2017; OCHA Myanmar 2017), and an estimated 200,000 living in that country prior to that (UNHCR 2016). The Bangladeshi immigration department recognizes 1.07 million now residing in their country (IOM 2018), and this is only those officially recognized. Hosting over a million refugees is a huge impost on any neighbour, and Bangladesh's (and Myanmar's) response has included plans to strengthen and complete a 170-kilometre border fence between the two countries, to prevent further irregular movement of people (Htet Naing Zaw 2018; VOA 2018). Thailand, Malaysia, Indonesia, and Pakistan have also all felt the impact of large numbers of refugees from this conflict. In 2015 an estimated 25,000 took to the

Bay of Bengal in rickety boats, prompting regional angst over people smuggling and informal migration (BNI 2017). Many ended up stranded in Thailand and Malaysia as smuggling operations were targeted, an incident which attracted a lot of regional consternation. The total number of 'Rohingya' refugees in the Asia-Pacific region was already 420,000 before the latest exodus (UNHCR 2017), on top of those in Bangladesh. A further 400,000 'Rohingya' are said to live in the Middle East (mostly Saudi Arabia), plus 200,000 in Pakistan (UNHCR 2011), from the Second World War, Independence, civil war, and Ne Win exoduses. These numbers are huge, suggesting that perhaps 2 million Muslims have now been displaced from northern Rakhine State, over several decades. This places a significant encumbrance on regional relations, and UN sources now believe the return of at least half of these people to be virtually impossible: names have been struck from official household surveys, and property and records have been destroyed.

Already, governments and civil society in several of Myanmar's Islamic neighbours have mounted a growing number of protests. For example, in June 2015 in Aceh in Indonesia, the Coalition for Caring for Rohingya sent a petition urging Indonesia to act decisively against the Myanmar government's role in the crisis (Romah 2015). In November 2016 around 5,000 Bangladeshi Muslims demonstrated in Dhaka, calling for an end to violence against the 'Rohingya' (CNA 2016). There were also smaller protests in Jakarta, Kuala Lumpur, and Bangkok. But perhaps the harshest fallout has been with Malaysia. A war of words erupted between Putrajaya and Nay Pyi Taw in early December 2016, ending with the Malaysian foreign ministry issuing a statement accusing Myanmar of engaging in 'ethnic cleansing' of its 'Rohingya' Muslims, and claiming the the 'spillover effect [will] affect the safety, security and standing of Malaysia' (The Star 2016). The next day Prime Minister Najib Abdul Razak and Deputy Prime Minister Datuk Seri Dr Ahmad Zahid Hamidi participated in a solidarity march in Kuala Lumpur, with the deputy prime minister urging action against Myanmar by the International Court of Justice. Such protests and voices are extraordinary in a region where leaders rarely criticize each other and countries largely mind their own business.

The fifty-six-member Organization of Islamic Cooperation (OIC) has held a number of meetings on the 'Crisis Situation Facing the

Rohingya in Myanmar', including emergency meetings in Geneva and Brussels (OIC 2016). In January 2017 Malaysia hosted an OIC Extraordinary Session, convened to discuss the situation in northern Rakhine State. As a prelude to the meeting, Malaysian Prime Minister Najib Razak called the military action in Rakhine State 'genocide', and challenged Aung San Suu Kyi saying, 'Does she really have a Nobel Peace Prize?' Critics argue that Prime Minister Razak was seeking to distract attention from embezzlement allegations as much as to address Myanmar. Nonetheless, the OIC meeting final communiqué expressed 'grave concerns' over the handling of the violence, and demanded that security forces act in accordance with the rule of law and that perpetrators of abuse be brought to justice (OIC 2017).

In other words, of all the conflicts that have raged in Myanmar for decades, and of all the issues currently facing the country, the Rakhine State conflict has the greatest potential to damage the international and regional standing of Aung San Suu Kyi, the NLD government, and Myanmar (Robinson 2016). The international damage is already significant as far as ASEAN, other regional neighbours, and the broader international community are concerned. The conflict has the potential to further strain relations dramatically, and poses a significant danger of totally derailing Myanmar's reforms. Only by exploring and interrogating the competing perspectives in depth, and analysing from new perspectives, can we hope to arrive at conceptualization that points to solutions.

PART II

HISTORICAL NARRATIVES, REPRESENTATION, AND COLLECTIVE MEMORY

HISTORY AND MEMORY OF CONFLICT

One of the more striking experiences in conducting field research in Rakhine State is that key informants regularly insist on presenting lengthy historical narratives before engaging in any other discussion. This is particularly true when meeting Rohingya key informants for the first time. Our experience has been that, on sitting down to discuss the conflict, most Rohingya leaders (in particular) launch into a well-rehearsed narrative of what they claim as the history of their people, spanning several centuries, culminating in their personal history of hardship and struggle. This narration was almost universal, and could last up to an hour. Many Rakhine and Burman key informants also do something similar, although not usually quite as detailed and lengthy, but still insisting on articulating their historical narrative up front as the basis of their position.

We were initially frustrated at this practice, and tried to circumvent it by communicating our familiarity with the historical background at the start of interviews, as well as the number of visits we had made to Rakhine State, the amount of time we had spent researching the issues, the range of interviews already conducted, the extent of our community fieldwork, etc. We were surprised, however, to find that this made little if any difference—most informants still proceeded with just as lengthy a narrative before allowing us to ask interview questions.

Perhaps this practice is, in part, a result of informants becoming accustomed to the flood of journalists and others seeking out their stories. Perhaps it is a concerted effort to capitalize on the attention, to promote their perspective to an international audience, to mobilize transnational advocacy, or to counter what they see as unfair or biased accounts. However, the nature, frequency, and length of these rehearsals have convinced us that the mobilization of historical narratives and collective memory is far more than this.

The terms 'historical narrative' and 'collective memory' are notoriously hard to define. For the purpose of this book, 'collective memory' is a representation of the past shared by members of a group (Wertsch 2008). 'Collective memory' constitutes a constructed social reality shared by group members (Bar-Tal 2014), one that coherently interrelates historical and contemporary events as an account of a community's collective experience, thereby becoming the fabric for hegemonic social beliefs (Bar-Tal 2013). The French sociologist Halbwachs (1992) argued that all remembering is shaped by collective narratives, meaning that to him personal memory only functions meaningfully within a collective or social context, and thus that collective memory is always selective based on the needs of that social context. That does not make it wrong or historically inaccurate, just always selective.

Every nation and ethnic group needs a historical narrative that tells the story of the group's past, helping shape group interpretations of social reality. Social representations of history are an essential ingredient in inventing and maintaining the 'imagined community' of nationhood (Hobsbawm 1990; Anderson 1983; Wertsch 2002). Nations and ethnicities use such narratives to propagate and justify images of themselves and the Other, and to build cultural identities from these images (Hancock 2014). This is an essential function undertaken by every nation with a sense of shared identity. While described as being historical 'fact', historical narratives can be and are continually constructed and reinvented in the present, to build group identity and cohesion, inform intergroup relations, and set the agenda for future action (Nicholson 2016; Jovchelovitch 2012). This construction and reconstruction need not be non-factual, but at a minimum the process revolves around deliberate selection, inclusion, and exclusion of material.

Historical narratives create diachronic links between historical and present events, influencing perspectives and strategies for future action and change (Liu & Hilton 2005). Representation of historical events thus allows the shaping of social realities in ways that serve to position the interests of the group in the present, and for the future (Psaltis 2016). Historical narratives re-invent history as a useful resource for building inter-group solidarity, defending identity, and maintaining social cohesion, in order to transform, stabilize, and give resilience to specific social representations (Jovchelovitch 2012). As Jovchelovitch (2012, p. 441) puts it, '[what] we feel, perceive, think and talk about in the present can only come into being through the stories we choose to remember and the manner in which we tell them'. Rehearsals of nationalist historical narratives are therefore 'acts of positioning' (Brescó 2016), something every nation and ethnic group does.

There has been a lot of research in recent decades around the role of historical narratives, representation, and collective memory in what Kriesberg (1993; also Kriesberg et al. 1989) and Bar-Tal (2013) call 'intractable conflicts'. Intractable conflicts are characterized by being protracted, violent, and total (in the sense of projecting a perceived existential threat that endangers everything), with a widespread perception that the issues are irreconcilable (Kriesberg 1993, 1998; Rouhana & Bar-Tal 1998; Bar-Tal 2013). Actors see everything in zero-sum terms.

According to this research, intractability is closely interlinked with an irreconcilable clash of historical narratives, particularly those by which the different group identities are defined (Rouhana & Bar-Tal 1998). Within intractable conflict, historical narratives about one's own group and that of 'the other' amplify the sense of existential threat. Intractability is rooted in and characterized by a 'stalemate of stories' (Hammack 2010), with the clash of narratives describing the heart of the factors reproducing the sense of existential threat (Bar-Tal 2007). Unsurprisingly, by definition, the collective memory narratives from different sides of an intractable conflict differ dramatically. Indeed, contradictory collective memories and struggle over the historicity of the representations made by the other side are key aspects of intractability (Bar-Tal 2014). This proliferation of polarized collective-memory narratives has been well documented in intractable conflict (e.g. Hammack 2010). Research has also shown that groups immersed in intractable conflicts place considerable value on extensive propagation and defence of their historical narrative—largely to convince the international community that the other party's past (and current) actions are unjust, immoral, and violate human rights principles (Baram & Klar 2016; Bar-Tal 2007, 2014).

Bar-Tal (1998, 2001, 2003, 2007, 2013, 2014) has been a leading scholar of intractable conflict for decades. While his research has primarily focused on Israel–Palestine, not Myanmar, his work makes extensive reference to a range of other conflicts, including Sri Lanka, Chechnya, Kashmir, and the Middle East. This suggests that his ideas have widespread applicability. His analysis is that societies embroiled in intractable conflict develop a 'sociopsychological infrastructure', through which the psychological needs of most society members are still able to be met, despite the conflict, and gives groups tools with which to withstand their rival(s). People living within an intractable conflict must cope with the serious stress of unending vulnerability, uncertainty, and fear. These socio-psychological tools are a means of coping with a never-ending sense of existential threat.

Bar-Tal suggests that while this socio-psychological infrastructure helps people cope with the harsh psychological conditions of intractable conflict, the prolonged nature of intractable conflict makes this infrastructure 'hegemonic, rigid, and resistant to change as long as the intractable conflict continues' (Bar-Tal 2007, p. 1430). The stressful, threatening conditions lead to a 'cognitive freezing' in which society members commit themselves to certain beliefs, and refrain from critically challenging them or listening to any account that differs from them, selecting and elaborating information only consistent with their already-held belief (Rouhana & Bar-Tal 1998). This ends up fuelling the continuation of conflict, becoming part of the vicious cycle of intractability, one of the things making resolution seem so impossible. Thus, intractability is rooted in and characterized by the 'stalemate of stories', and irreconcilable accounts of history are part of what perpetuates that intractability.

Intractable conflicts are especially difficult to resolve precisely because the intense socio-psychological dynamics institutionalize collective memories and emotional orientations on all sides. In most cases, the social representations of collective memory function as an obstacle and barrier to peace 'because they crystallize a self-righteous and ethnocentric narrative that hides, not only own misdeeds and deficiencies, but also blocks information about the humanness of the rival, and especially about his just needs and goals' (Bar-Tal 2014, p. 18).

Myanmar's Rakhine State conflict fits the description of an intractable conflict perfectly, particularly in terms of this 'stalemate of stories'. The irreconcilable clash of historical narratives and collective memory in Rakhine State is played out in a daily struggle to propagate competing versions of history. As Leider expresses it:

> History counts for Buddhists and Muslims alike, and it is a field where battles are fought to establish the credibility of ethno-religious narratives. In the eyes of both communities, "history" does not only define their acclaimed cultural, religious and ethnic identity, but also establishes their rights to claim the land as their own ... Muslim Rohingya and Buddhist Rakhine, unlike other ethnic groups in Myanmar, have been known for creating historical societies and are keen on organizing historical seminars to convey their political points rather than, say, publishing legal reports or human-rights briefings ... Remarkably, the international community has totally ignored this historical and cultural debate since the 1950s. (Leider 2015, pp. 165–6)

This second part of this book thus presents a summary of the historical narratives of each of the protagonists, as they present them, identifying some of the more central texts or proponents of each, but also interrogating the historicity of key aspects of their story. Complicating efforts, however, are what Leider (2005, p. 48) calls the 'confusion and the false certainties that reign in the field of Rakhine history', due to the poor state of archaeology in Rakhine State, superficial and uncritical treatment of the sources by most writers for more than a century—and now the emergence of these powerful, polarized, historical narratives.

Chapter 3 presents a sketch of the Rohingya 'Origin' narrative, from *their* sources and using *their own* terminology as much as possible (i.e. phenomenologically), with a discussion about those sources and interrogation of aspects of the narrative. Chapter 4 is similar, presenting then interrogating what we define as the Rakhine 'Independence', the

Burman 'Unity', and the Rakhine–Burman 'Infiltration' narratives. We present these latter three narratives in a single chapter, but not to imply that they are somehow less important than the Rohingya narrative (which has a whole chapter of its own). We do so simply because four separate iterations through similar history, from different perspectives, would be overly repetitive and is unnecessary. The narratives can be presented and critiqued far more succinctly in second and subsequent overviews of history.

It is impossible to question every aspect of each story, and beyond the scope of this book to compile an accurate, full history of the region out of the quagmire. But key points of history and narratives are discussed in detail. We agree with Leider (2018b) that detailed historical study is one important, and often overlooked, component in moving towards a long-term resolution to this conflict. In this text, every attempt is made to evaluate each narrative and set of claims impartially. In challenging deeply felt beliefs of all groups, though, we recognize that no group will be entirely happy. This book does not aim to advocate for any one side in this conflict, but tries to highlight nuances and analyse complexity. In presenting narratives one after the other, the incongruities and depth of intractability should be apparent.

One last point worth emphasizing from the intractable-conflict literature is that social representations of collective memory, while presented as historical facts, remain socially constructed narratives. They are created to meet contemporary societal needs and argue a contemporary political case. They are thus not simply 'history', and are not necessarily based on thoroughly researched historiography at all. They may at times be biased, selective, distorted, or even false (Hobsbawm & Ranger 1983; Liu & Hilton 2005; Bar-Tal 2007, 2014). The temptation to credit mythology as history, or take that which was presented as speculation in an earlier century as now being established fact, is greatest when faced with what seems an existential struggle for the very survival of oneself and one's culture, identity and people—or a people with whom one feels a strong affinity. This is the nature of intractable conflict.

THE ROHINGYA 'ORIGIN' NARRATIVE

Sources and their Socio-Political Context

Numerous Rohingya advocates, most of whom (but not all) identify as Rohingya, have attempted written histories. These are all written primarily to express grievances and inherently make claims. This chapter presents an overview and critique of these histories, in the light of Bar-Tal's idea that irreconcilable historical accounts are part of what perpetuates intractable conflict. We have also conducted formal interviews or extended discussions with over a dozen prominent Rohingya leaders in Yangon and around Sittwe, most of whom gave us extended verbal recitations of their history, as mentioned in the previous section. These verbal recitations align closely with the written histories, but this chapter uses the written texts as primary and the interview discussions only to help interpret the written histories where necessary. This chapter presents a synthesized summary of the written histories, interrogating key points at periodic intervals.

In presenting and interrogating perspectives in this chapter, we seek to allow their expression of their narrative to be heard using their own terminology. We thus allow these people use the name they claim for themselves, Rohingya. This use is not intended as a political statement, but for clarity.

In terms of written text, it must be noted that Rohingya is a spoken language with no agreed written script. Even today, there are multiple proposed scripts, no popular adoption, and very high illiteracy rates. Since the colonial period, literate Rohingya have written mainly in English or Burmese. Urdu or Bengali were used during the colonial era, but English has become the preferred medium for communication, given their aim to garner international support. This chapter is therefore primarily drawn from the English-language literature.

The earliest identified Rohingya written history is Tahir's (aka Ba Tha: Tahir 1998 [1963]) *A Short History of Rohingya and Kamans of Burma*, commissioned by the United Rohingya National League. It was written in Burmese in 1963, and translated into English in 1998 by A. F. K. Jilani (see his other work below). While relatively short, this essay largely set the template for subsequent works. The scholarship of this and later sources varies greatly, with variation also in tone, style, and level of historical detail. Overall, the level of consistency is high. Notable among the subsequent English-language written Rohingya histories are the following. Many are unpublished manuscripts or self-published:

- Mohammed Yunus (1994) *A History of Arakan (Past & Present)*, a more detailed 98-page account by the founder of the insurgent group the Rohingya Solidarity Organization (RSO);

- Ahmed F. K. Jilani (1999) *The Rohingyas of Arakan: Their Quest for Justice*, a detailed 500-odd-page self-published manuscript by the translator of Tahir's *Short History*; also his (2001) *A Cultural History of Rohingya*. Jilani was a founding member of the NLD in Arakan, still active in 2010, and elected as an NLD representative for Maungdaw in the 1990 general election (Kyaw Hla 2010). He was also an executive committee member of the nationalist insurgent groups ARNO and RNO.

- Abdul Karim (2000) *The Rohingya: A Short Account of their History and Culture*, significant given that Karim is a highly regarded and well-published Bengali history professor, a former vice-chancellor of Chittagong University;

- Abu Anin (2002, a pseudonym for a Rohingya politician, according to Tonkin 2018) *Towards Understanding Arakan History: A Study on the Issue of Ethnicity in Arakan*, a widely circulated but as-yet-unpublished manuscript. There are (dubious, unverified) claims that this manuscript was reviewed by the respected Burmese history professor Than Tun (see Zul Nurain 2009).

- Mohammad Mohibullah Siddiquee (2014) *The Rohingyas of Arakan: History and Heritage*, which is largely an edited compilation of older essays and documents. The main significance of this work, apart from the collection of manuscripts itself, is that Siddiquee is an associate professor at the University of Rajshahi, Bangladesh;
- Azeem Ibrahim (2016) *The Rohingya: Inside Myanmar's Hidden Genocide*. Ibrahim is a senior fellow at a US foreign policy think-tank, a British Pakistani who studied at Cambridge University and previously held research fellowships at Harvard and then Yale Universities. His position and the profile of the publisher means that this book has had great circulation.

A representation made by the Muslim League of North Arakan in 1947, to the British Parliamentary Under-Secretary of State, for an autonomous region comprising Maungdaw and Buthidaung (Jamiatul-ulema 1947), raised the historical arguments later expanded into these narratives. The Muslim League also made a number of such representations to the Burmese government after Independence, demonstrating that the narrative in this chapter was already being articulated in shorter form at this point. More recently, a report distributed by the Muslim-led National Democratic Party for Development to national parliamentarians in 2012, entitled *In Respect of the Fact that the Muslim Inhabitants of Rakhine State are Natives by Race and Citizens of the Republic of the Union of Myanmar under Law or by Natural Birth* (NDPD 2012), covers this material in considerable depth. Khan (1992) is another useful reference, from a Bangladeshi perspective.

Beyond this list of sources, a large number of other Rohingya historical narratives displaying less original content or academic merit have been produced. These include: Ali (1967), Zaw Min Htut (2001), Siddiqui (2008), and, Bahar (2010). These have been read, but have not contributed to the synthesis in this chapter. There has also been a proliferation of brief Rohingya historical narrative contributions in conference papers, magazines articles, newspapers, or online (e.g. Islam 2011; Siddiqui 2012, 2014). Further, many other writers that have not set out primarily to document a history have nonetheless commonly drawn upon similar narratives (e.g. Islam 2007; Zarni & Cowley 2014). This absolute proliferation of histories in recent decades, particularly since the late 1990s, is a demonstration of two key points: (a) the growing importance placed on historical narratives in what has increasingly become an 'intractable conflict'; and (b) the emergence of a more educated Rohingya diaspora internationally. Again, this chapter summarizes the seven English-language Rohingya histories listed above, from Tahir to Ibrahim, presenting a synthesis of their historical narrative, and only draws on any of these other works or our interview fieldwork as indicated.

It is striking that the earliest of these Rohingya narratives, that of Tahir (aka Ba Tha), dates as recently as 1963. In his publisher's notes on the 1998 translation, Alam (1998, p. 1) claims that in 1963 this 'was the only printed history book of Rohingya by a Rohingya in Burmese'. Surprisingly, no written histories appear to exist from the colonial or pre-colonial era. Muslim poets and educated elite serving in the courts of the Mrauk-U kings during the seventeenth century wrote in Bengali (see Karim 2000; d'Hubert 2014, 2015a, 2015b). Most of these elite courtiers appear to have been attracted or brought to the court from Bengal, rather than being local Muslims. None document a Muslim history in Arakan. The famed poet Alaol, for example, perhaps the most famous pre-colonial Muslim scholar in Arakan, was born in central modern Bangladesh and brought to Mrauk-U by Portuguese corsairs. He translated and elaborated Persian works, without making reference to a local indigenous Muslim population (d'Hubert 2015a). This does not mean that no such population or identity existed at that time, but it does show that the Muslim court elite were more expatriates than local Muslim advocates, and no early Muslim histories appear to have been written.

This recent date for written historical narratives, and the number of key figures from nationalist organizations writing them, lends itself to the interpretation that these narratives are the product of the post-Independence political situation. As Anderson (1983) helpfully conceptualized in *Imagined Communities*, a shared sense of nationalist ethnic identity emerges out of particular socio-political pressures. Taken together, to us this supports the suggestion that the 'Rohingya' identity is a response to conditions that the people have faced since moves towards Independence in the early twentieth century, more than being a strong identity pre-dating this period—although Rohingya advocates would argue with that view.

The political context in which these histories were written is significant. Tahir's *Short History* was published in 1963, commissioned a year or two earlier. Important context, therefore, is that in early 1961 the democratic U Nu government decided to establish an Arakan state within the Union of Myanmar, with some devolution of power.[1] To placate the Muslims in northern Rakhine, U Nu also created the Mayu Frontier District in May 1961, encompassing Maungdaw, Buthidaung, and the western part of Rathedaung. This district was under military administration rather than being autonomous, but the Muslims were delighted, believing it a step towards greater recognition, even limited autonomy. In many ways, the surrender of the remaining Mujahid forces in 1961 was because of this major concession. According to Yunus (1994, p. 68), Anin (2002, p. 201), and other Rohingya writers, in November 1959, while trying to bring an end to the Mujahid rebellion, both U Nu and defence minister U Ba Swe ran rallies in northern Arakan offering the Rohingya full recognition as an ethnic group equal to the Shan, Kachin, Karen, and others (see also Ibrahim 2016, p. 8 and Nay San Lwin 2012). Yunus and Anin also note that during a surrender of 290 Mujahid in southern Maungdaw Township on 4 July 1961, Brigadier-General Aung Gyi, then Deputy Commander-in-Chief, used the name Rohingya and implied their equal status as one of Burma's *taing-yin-tha*. So while Ne Win's Military Council abolished the Mayu District in February 1964, after the 1962 coup, Tahir's *A Short History* was commissioned at the height of Rohingya confidence about establishing their identity within the Burmese state. It was commissioned as civil war receded, and they rode a wave of optimism about ultimately being granted recognition in Burma, even governance over northern Rakhine State. It was intended to establish their status as an indigenous race, and thus their credentials to take political control of Mayu in due course.

Chronologically, the next Rohingya history was Yunus's (1994) *History of Arakan*. Yunus was founder of the Rohingya Solidarity Organization (RSO), one of several Rohingya armed insurgent groups active at the time, thus with similar aims to Tahir. Yunus claims that he formed the RSO in 1982, in response to the infamous 1978 Operation Nagamin, so his history should be read as a response to persecution rather than optimism. Nagamin was an operation to crack down on illegal immigrants nationwide, but became largely focused on Muslims in northern Rakhine (Yegar 2002), resulting in some 200,000–250,000 Muslims fleeing into Bangladesh. While 200,000 were repatriated in July 1979, this was only after strong pressure from the UN (UNDP and UNHCR), Saudi Arabia, India, and the World Muslim League. The RSO and other Rohingya insurgent groups then became increasingly active again after the failed 1988 democracy uprising (Smith 1994), provoking renewed military operations against them in 1991–2—which once again led to over 250,000 Muslim refugees fleeing to Bangladesh, and again required intervention from the UNHCR to secure their return (Human Rights Watch 2000). Yunus's *History of Arakan* (1994) must thus be read in the context of this armed struggle to be recognized in the land.

The main rush of Rohingya histories were then written between the late 1990s and 2000s, with several more published in the wake of the 2012 violence in Rakhine State. The earlier of these should be placed in the context of the collapse of the remaining operational capability of Rohingya insurgent groups, the regime's attempts to strike peace with other ethnic armed groups while ruling out talks with the Muslims, and increasing pressure in Bangladesh to repatriate all remaining displaced Rohingya. In each case, this historical context provides a vivid backdrop to the motivation and sense of urgency behind each of these publications.

Having set the scene, this chapter will now summarize the key 'Rohingya' narrative of their origins, their representations of history, and interrogate key aspects. (The next chapter will do the same to both Rakhine and Burman narratives.)

The Rohingya 'Origin' Narrative

Rohingya historical narratives all seek to establish the Rohingya as an indigenous race, with deep historical roots in Arakan. They all date the origin of the Muslim community in northern Rakhine State to a time prior to the arrival of the ethnic Rakhine, in the ninth to tenth centuries (Gutman 1976)—thus also prior to the arrival of the Burman into Burma. Most argue that the Rohingya arrived in four waves of Muslim

migration, and intermingled with the pre-Rakhine indigenous population—who they say converted to Islam before the arrival of the
Rakhine people. Ibrahim (2016, p. 6) turns this around, suggesting that
the Rohingya are descendants of the pre-Rakhine indigenous population, who lived in Arakan three millennia before the arrival of the
Rakhine, and who later assimilated the waves of Muslim migrants.
Either way, they argue that their Rohingya ancestors lived in Arakan
continuously for millennia, and were integral to its political and socio-
economic life until its 1784 conquest by the Burmans. Various waves of
settlers have been assimilated over centuries, they argue, into a single
ethic identity with a strong historical connection to the land, and a
distinct language, culture, and history indigenous to the region.

Historically, Arakan sat at the interface between Muslim sultanates
to the west and Buddhist kingdoms to the east. There was, Rohingya
narratives suggest, a long, largely peaceful coexistence between
Muslim and Buddhist communities. They draw on the works of Gutman
(1976), Charney (1998b, 1999), and van Galen (2008) to suggest that
historically Arakan functioned more as a frontier region of India and
the Bengal region than as a frontier region of Burma, negotiating the
two worlds and acting as a conduit for medieval Muslim scholarship
into Burma. Certainly, until recent road construction Arakan was
largely isolated from Burma by mountains, making trade and political
interaction easier by sea. The Mrauk-U kingdom, they suggest, thus
functioned as much as (if not more like) an Arakanese sultanate than a
Buddhist kingdom.

According to this narrative, there were the four waves of Muslim
migration and settlement into the region (Karim 2000), which we
discuss and interrogate below.

First Wave: Arab Traders and Settlers (sixth–fourteenth centuries)

Almost all Rohingya narratives start by arguing that Arab traders
arrived in Arakan from at least the time of the founding of Vesali in 788
CE, if not earlier. Rohingya historians often cite Yule's (1882) identification of Arakan as Ptolemy's 'Argyre' (in *Geographical Tables*, dated
about 150 CE) as evidence of much earlier contact with the Middle
East (cited in Hall 1956; Gutman 1976 and others; see Singer 2008 for

a good discussion). We find this all highly speculative. Rohingya narratives also cite references by early Muslim travellers, and trade between the Middle East and what they claim was Arakan, even of Muslim settlements in that region. These include accounts by Sulymen (851 CE), Yaqubi (880 CE), Ibn al-Fakih (902 CE), Masudi (943 CE), HudulAl-Alam (982 CE), and Marvazi (1120 CE), for example (Tahir 1998 [1963]; see also Tibbetts 1979). Nonetheless, we would argue that there has been insufficient critical analysis of Arakanese historical sources to speak confidently about any of these early records. As Singer (2008, p. x) put it, history of this era is 'shrouded in what appears to be an impenetrable haze ... sabotaged by inaccurate information by native chroniclers of a later age ... [and fantasies] slavishly repeated' by some foreign writers.

The NDPD report (2012, in Thawnghmung 2016) cites evidence that 80 per cent of the scripts used in Vesali are written in the same languages used by the Rohingya today, claiming this as evidence that the Rohingya today are descendants of the people who comprised the Vesali kingdom, later converting to Islam. This is heavily debated, and it seems that none of the Rohingya historians consulted any of these texts, raising further questions about this claim.

Most Rohingya histories highlight the reference in Phayre (1844, p. 36), in which he summarizes a compilation history he commissioned from various Arakanese chronicles, mostly now lost. In this, Phayre notes that the chronicles mention Muslim settlements in Arakan dating to survivors of several ships wrecked on the coast around Ramree. According to Phayre, the manuscripts say that these Muslims were granted permanent settlement in Ramree by the first king of the Chandra dynasty at Vesali commencing 788 CE. Many Rohingya also draw on Harvey (1925), who suggested that by the thirteenth century, while the country was nominally Buddhist, Muslim settlements dotted the coastline. Others draw on Collis (1925, p. 36), who quotes an old Arakanese manuscript purporting to give an account of the Vesali kingdom as saying that Vesali 'became a noted trade port to which as many as a thousand ships came annually ... their territory extended as far north as Chittagong'. Most of these trade ships would have come from the Bay of Bengal area, they argue, perhaps a few from Persia, and thus it is reasonable to assume that most visitors were Muslim. This may be speculation, but we consider it not unreasonable to assume the presence of at least some resident Muslims from the ninth century, as Yegar (1972) also does. However, Singer (2008) notes that the archaeology shows that Vesali was clearly Hindu, not Muslim, meaning that the proportion of Muslims, if any, was minimal at best. Anin (2002) also cites Arakanese historical texts claiming that thousands of Bengali captives were brought to Arakan after a battle in the mid-1200s, two centuries before the founding of Mrauk-U, but we find no other record to corroborate this claim.

Tahir (1998 [1963]) and Yunus (1994), in particular, argue that through this sustained contact and migration, the local population pre-788 CE converted to Islam en masse. One legend they and Siddiquee (2014) all refer to—acknowledging it as legend but still questioning whether there may be some truth behind it—is referenced to an unnamed sixteenth-century author, who apparently claimed that after the battle of Karbala in present-day Iraq, in 680 CE, that Mohammad Hanif, son of Hazarat Ali (son-in-law of the Prophet Muhammad) arrived in Arakan with his army and settled near Maungdaw. He then married the indigenous queen, and all the local people converted. While we believe that this is undoubtedly mythology, with no historical support, it exemplifies the claims made about the ancient origins of their Muslim ancestors in Arakan.

As an aside, we note that such mythology is common to the ethnic Rakhine narratives too, so our mention of it here is not to highlight a lack of historicity on one side or the other. Rakhine mythology around the ancient and very sacred Mahamuni image, for example, captured by the Burman at the fall of Mrauk-U in 1784, claims that the Mahamuni was fashioned during a visit to Arakan by Gautama the Buddha in the sixth century BCE. This legend is equally mythological, and used in similar fashion to claim the ancient origins of Buddhism in Arakan. The point of our discussion at this point is simply to note that the Rohingya claim a very ancient ancestry in Arakan, not to deride them for turning to mythology for some of that.

Second Wave: Soldiers and Courtiers from the Founding of Mrauk-U (Fifteenth Century)

A second wave of migration is claimed to have come with the founding of the Mrauk-U dynasty in 1430 CE. The story is well corroborated, being related in most Arakanese chronicles (Phayre 1844; Leider & Kyaw Minn Htin 2015 lists at least six such chronicles). As such, it is heavily relied upon by virtually all Rohingya historians. As the story goes, Narameikhla (later known as Min Saw Mun)[2] became king in Arakan in around 1404, ruled for two years, and was then driven out by a Burmese-supported revolt. He fled to Bengal, to seek help to regain his throne, but found the court embroiled in chaos. Once the Bengal usurper had died, Min Saw Mun served the new Sultan, Jalauddin Muhammad Shah (the name of the Bengali ruler as identified by Habibullah 1945, not the Arakanese chronicles; also Tahir 1998 [1963]; Yunus 1994; and Siddiquee 2014). Min Saw Mun is said to have led Jalauddin's army in battle, and successfully repelled an attack by the Delhi Sultanate. He was thus accepted by the Sultan as if he were his son. Eventually, in 1430, the Sultan committed the resources necessary to restore Min Saw Mun to the Arakanese throne. The first expeditionary force, claimed in many narratives to be 20,000 strong, betrayed Min Saw Mun and the Sultan, with its general attempting to set up his own authority instead. The Sultan sent a second force, claimed to be 30,000 strong, which successfully overcame the first and restored Min Saw Mun to the throne. Min Saw Mun founded the city of Mrauk-U (Mrohaung), which flourished as the capital of Arakan for more than four centuries, adopting the Islamic title Solaiman Shah alongside his Arakanese name.

Most Rohingya historians draw two or three significant conclusions from this record (e.g. Yunus 1994, p. 6; Karim 2000, pp. 14–34; Anin 2002, p. 65). The first is, they conclude that most of these 50,000 soldiers must have stayed on in Arakan. Once defeated, the 20,000 Muslim soldiers from the first expedition could hardly return to the king they betrayed, so it is argued that they would have taken up village life in a remote corner of Arakan. They also conclude that most of the second expeditionary force could not have returned home either, because their services would have been required to stabilize the newly reinstated king, given the existence of the remnant of the first force. They thus argue for a large influx of Muslims into Arakan in 1430, who settled and remained in the kingdom.

Their second conclusion is that King Min Saw Mun converted to Islam, and that most of his court and the kings after him were Muslim—

and thus that under most Mrauk-U kings it was more a Muslim sultan-tate than a Buddhist kingdom (e.g. Yunus 1994, p. 6; Karim 2000, p. 18; Anin 2002, p. 65). Rakhine narratives obviously counter this very vehe-mently, pointing to the extensive remains of Buddhist temples, not mosques, at the site, suggesting both royal patronage and that the vast majority of their subjects were Buddhist, evidence which we will discuss in the the next chapter. But the Rohingya written histories that make this claim base it on several grounds:

1. Min Saw Mun adopted the Islamic title Solaiman Shah from the time of his return, and a large number of kings after him, over the following century or more, likewise adopted Muslim titles along-side their Arakanese Buddhist ones. This is widely attested by other historians (e.g. Hall 1968; Yegar 1972).

2. Many of the coins minted by Min Saw Mun and subsequent Mrauk-U kings included the text of the *kalima*, the Islamic declara-tion of faith. One might take on an Islamic title for expediency, they argue, but one does not publicly make the declaration of faith with-out converting. We concur that many such coins have been cata-logued (e.g. Collis 1925), and their existence is beyond dispute—although they are undated and, based on similarities with coins from Bengal, Mitchiner (2000) dates the earliest to decades after the death of the founder of Mrauk-U.

3. The Bengali Sultan, identified in Bengali literature as a convert to Islam (Karim 2000), apparently called Min Saw Mun his son and agreed to commit extremely large resources to support his restora-tion. This would not happen without either an extremely close personal connection or very significant concessions by the recipi-ent, they argue. The Mrauk-U Kingdom was clearly subject to Bengal for a century—all sides agree about that—but many Rohingya narratives argue that it went much deeper.

4. Rohingya also ask why Min Saw Mun fled west into Muslim territory in 1404, rather than east to the Mons or other Buddhist kingdoms, unless he had a closer affiliation with Muslims than Buddhists. Burman chronicles suggest that the Burmese attack at the start of his rule was instigated by disgruntled elite seeking to replace him. Yunus (1994, p. 18), for example, asks whether this was because Min Saw Mun had already converted to Islam, or at least become so friendly

with Muslims in his domain and neighbouring kingdoms that it upset the Buddhist elite. Otherwise, he could still have fled to the Mons. (To Yunus, this divide in the elite is the primal origin of Muslim–Buddhist communal tensions in Arakan—six centuries ago.)

A third claim, argued mainly by Anin (2002, p. 28), is that mass conversions of the 'natives' to Islam occurred under some of these kings (also Jilani 1999, pp. 68–70). Anin's citation for this is a more obscure Arakanese chronicle compiled in 1927 by Tha Htwan Aung, an honorary archaeological officer at the Mrauk-U Museum, which claims to be based on a royal chronicle of a Minister Wimala, which it dates to 1536, and which covers history up to 1692 CE. (Leider 2004, pp. 469–70 gives a brief description of this chronicle). Jilani does not cite a historical source.

Because of its significance to the Rohingya narrative, further examination of these events is warranted. Despite being one of the best-known and most quoted episodes of Arakanese history, attested in most Arakanese chronicles (see next chapter), recent scholarship has raised the possibility that this story may be more legend than historical fact. We will discuss the historicity of the chronicles themselves in more detail in the next chapter, but it is worth noting here that Leider & Kyaw Minn Htin (2015), in particular, find no historical evidence in inscriptions, tax documents, or political records to support the story of Min Saw Mun's exile in Bengal and reinstatement with signfiicant help by that king, nor the idea that Mrauk-U was politically dependent on Bengal from this time. Rather, they see sufficient conflicting information in the various Arakanese chronicles, reading them in the original language, and enough surprising omissions in the style, to suggest a legendary rather than literal character to these accounts. They thus raise serious doubts about the story's historicity.

The story was popularized mostly through the retelling by two of Burma's most trusted historians of the colonial era, Phayre (1844) and Harvey (1925). However, comparing the account in Phayre to the Arakanese originals, Leider and Kyaw Minn Htin find that the chronicler harmonized and rationalized versions, omitting contradictions and dropping mythological elements. Moreover, they find very similar elements in stories from Laos, Cambodia, and Malaysia, suggesting that the original story may not even have local origins. Likewise, they find nothing in the Burman or Mon chronicles of the era to suggest signficantly increased political power of Arakan at this time. Thus, while they do not dispute that the kingdom was founded at Mrauk-U at this time, or a Muslim presence in Arakan during the fifteenth century, Leider and Kyaw Minn Htin question the historicity of this particular incident. They ascribe the story to an oral tradition pre-dating the writing of royal chronicles. This challenge does, thus, raise the probability that one of the largest claimed migrations of Rohingya prior to the colonial era may be a myth. It also raises doubts about Rohingya interpretations about Muslim population size, and the degree of Islamization of the kingdom at that time, given that most Rohingya chroniclers did not consult the original Arakanese chronicles, just the English versions.

Despite these questions over the historicity of the founding story of Mrauk-U, the kingdom did grow from being a small agrarian state in the fifteenth century into a significant regional power by the early seventeenth (van Galen 2008). Even in the fifteenth century, trading networks around the Bay of Bengal were integrated into a genuine regional commercial culture, with a high degree of mobility (Chaudhuri 1985; Charney 1993, 1998b; Gommans 1995; van Galen 2008). The expansion, then disintegration, of the kingdom were closely connected to its degree of control over south-eastern Bengal, and commercial and cultural ties with Chittagong played a central role in Mrauk-U's history as a counterbalance to the growing power of the Burman court at Ava (Charney 1998b, 1998a, 1999; Leider 2002). Indeed, Phayre (1844) notes epigraphical evidence that the first Arakanese king to defeat a Chittagong ruler was in 953 CE, and suggests a number of such incursions. By the seventeenth century, Mrauk-U asserted influence across the Bay of Bengal (Charney 1998b; van Galen 2008), to the extent that Bengali chronicles regularly discussed Arakan (Bhattacharya 1927; Khan 1937). The Portuguese Augustinian friar Manrique wrote in 1649 that Chittagong was 'the masterkey to the Arakanese Empire', highlighting the close connections and Mrauk-U's ability to control large parts of south-eastern Bengal (Manrique 1927; van Galen 2008).

Thus, regardless of the historicity of the Min Saw Mun story, Muslim influence at Mrauk-U must be noted, almost certainly involving a resident Muslim population in the city and kingdom. The extent, and the history, around this, however, requres further study. It is, nonetheless, widely attested that the Mrauk-U royal court attracted Muslim scholars and officials, including highly ranked Muslim ministers, courtiers, physicians, soldiers, merchants, traders, and labourers (Karim 2000; d'Hubert 2014). Rohingya sources claim that mosques began to dot the countryside; the remains of some can be clearly demonstrated today. Be that as it may, Persian was adopted by the court for official and diplomatic purposes (as was the practice around the Bay of Bengal). Thus while the official royal chronicles were written in Arakanese, most other surviving court literature is in Persian. Islamic literature was clearly studied and patronized at the royal court, and Bengali literature flourished (d'Hubert 2014; d'Hubert & Leider 2008).

None of this, however, is evidence of conversion. Adoption of titles and coinage could just have easily been to ensure their acceptability in trade, and is not sufficient in itself to demonstrate a declaration of faith. Importantly, the kings also drew on Buddhist sources of political legitimacy, for example portraying themselves as heirs to the legendary Buddhist kings (van Galen 2008). Rather, all of this demonstrates what Charney (1999, p. 399) describes as 'the Arakanese royal court's long-term indifference to religious identities', rather than evidence of conversion. We suggest that the Mrauk-U court at that time practised a degree of cosmopolitanism. Either way, a Muslim population clearly existed at Mrauk-U, and it appears to have maintained a distinct heritage and identity within the Buddhist-majority environment, with no evidence of significant inter-communal tension (Charney 1999).

Third Wave: Slaves Brought to Mrauk-U by Portuguese Corsairs (17th Century)

In the Rohingya tradition the third (and, we suggest, largest) wave of Muslim migration was due to Portuguese slave trading, which in time was perpetrated in conjunction with the Mrauk-U kings. As the power of the Mughals grew, Mrauk-U came to rely increasingly on Portuguese mercenaries for security and expansion (van Galen 2008). Bengal had long enjoyed support from the Portuguese, but when it fell to the Mughals in 1567, many Portuguese shifted allegiance to Mrauk-U (van Galen 2008). However, the Portuguese never fully submitted to Arakanese control; along with offering their services to Arakan, they maintained their own commercial and piracy activities. Their shift in allegiance and base of operations, therefore, also brought an explosion in slave trading. All Rohingya written histories discuss the large number of Muslims brought into the kingdom as slaves. Some (e.g. Anin 2002; Yunus 1994) are happy to identify the Portuguese as the main perpetrators of the trade, suggesting that the Arakanese only sometimes collaborated.

Rohingya narrators emphasize the impact of slave capture, transport, and resettlement on a massive scale. For this they rely largely on the record of the main independent source from the period, the account of Friar Sebastien Manrique (1927). Himself Portuguese, Manrique was in Arakan from 1629 to 1637, and claims to have witnessed 18,000 captives brought to the Arakan capital during that time, all from Bengal and north India (thus almost all Muslim). Some slaves were kept by the Portuguese and some sold to the Dutch, but Manrique testified that a considerable number of Muslim captives were taken into the king's service or forced to settle in villages as agricultural labourers. Colonial-era authorities do note the depopulation of large areas of coastal and riverine Bengal due to the trade, with raids carried out as far away as Dhaka (e.g. Hall 1956). Gutman (1976) attests that as many as 42,000 slaves were delivered to Chittagong between 1621 and 1627 by the Portuguese. In one single incident in 1638, when the governor of Chittagong fled after leading a failed rebellion, some 10,000 slaves were said to have escaped (Ali 1967). Neither of these accounts were in Arakan, but they both highlight the scale of the regional trade. Van Galen, the most reliable reference on this topic due to his detailed study of the Dutch records, suggests that the Arakanese king captured no less than 30,000 Bengali slaves in raids during 1623 alone, 10,000 more in 1624–5, then sacked Dhaka in 1626 and led that population away as slaves too (van Galen 2008, pp. 123–5). While many were sold, many others were put to work around Mrauk-U—and this trade continued for generations, from the late sixteenth to mid-eighteenth centuries. Harvey (1925, p. 143) claims that in the month of February 1727 alone, for example, a century after the reports above, the Portuguese delivered 1,800 captives from southern Bengal to Mrauk-U.

Thus, non-Rohingya sources attest to the scale of this forced migration of Muslims into Arakan. Highlighting the scale of this 'wave' of forced migration, many Rohingya narratives argue that the name Kaladan—given to the Kaladan River and the region encompassing much of Mrauk-U and Kyauktaw Townships today—means 'dwelling of foreigners', given because of the largescale resettlement of *kala*—foreign, dark-skinned Muslim captives—into the region.

Fourth Wave: The Entourage of the Mughal Emperor's Son Shah Shuja (17th Century)

The final wave of Muslims into Arakan prior to the colonial era, according to Rohingya written histories, was during the time the Mughal Emperor's son Shah Shuja sought refuge in Arakan. According to Rohingya sources, Shuja became the governor of Bengal in 1639 under the authority of his father, the Mughal Emperor Shah Jahan. However, when the Emperor fell seriously ill in 1657, his brother seized the throne, defeating Shuja at Dhaka in 1660 to conquer Bengal. After the defeat, Shuja fled with his family, treasures, and an army of 3,000 to Mrauk-U. His arrival is attested in Rakhine records. The Rohingya narratives record that the Arakanese king granted him asylum, and the promise of ships to travel on to Mecca. After a time, however, Shuja led an unsuccessful revolt. Arakanese and Rohingya accounts differ as to whether this was an attempt to claim the Arakanese throne, or a defence against the Arakanese king's attempts to gain Shuja's daughter and considerable treasure for himself. Either way, the coup attempt failed and many of Shah Shuja's forces and family were massacred. The ultimate fate of Shuja is still debated (e.g. Khan 1966), but Rohingya narratives argue that at least another several thousand Muslims entered and remained in the kingdom through these events. Van Galen (2008) corroborates the story, although not the numbers.

Drawing on Harvey (1925), Rohingya authors agree with Rakhine and Burman historians that Shuja's men became the Kaman, a group accepted after Independence as an indigenous *taing-yin-tha* ethnic Muslim group in Rakhine State. They use this acceptance to argue that, by implication, the Rohingya should thus also be accepted on the same terms, having been present from an even earlier date. After 1661 the Mrauk-U kings retained Shujah's forces, experienced archers, in the palace guard. Anin (2002) suggests that they were merged with an earlier unit of Muslims already in the king's guard, while Harvey says their numbers were strengthened by additional Muslim recruits from upper India (Afghanistan?). Either way, they remained in royal service until 1692, when they burnt the palace and went on to ravage the country for twenty years, until they were subdued and banished to Ramree Island. From that point, they have grown in number into the people now recognized as the indigenous ethnic Kaman Muslims.

Going further, some Rohingya narratives argue that in defending himself against the treachery of the Arakanese king, Shah Shuja called on the assistance of Muslims of slave origin. They thus suggest that the massacre of 1661, as Shuja fell, was the first round of communal violence between Muslims and Arakanese, as the palace turned on Muslims more generally (e.g. Anin 2002).

It is noteworthy that this incident was a significant contributing factor in the decline and eventual fall of Mrauk-U, resulting as it did in the Portuguese and Dutch leaving Arakan and realigning with the Mughals, who quickly captured Chittagong—in the process leaving Mrauk-U significantly weakened. Some Rohingya attribute this weakening of the kingdom in no small part to the loss of social cohesion after communal violence between Muslims and the Arakanese.

Thus, to establish themselves as a *taing-yin-tha* with deep historical roots in Arakan, Rohingya historians narrate the arrival of four waves of Muslim settlers into Arakan over almost a millennium, concurrent with, if not commencing prior to, the arrival of the Arakanese, and the assimilation of this population with the existing indigenous people, building to a sizeable population before the arrival of the Burmans and British. This is significant because, as we have already noted, under Burmese law and constitution, being *taing-yin-tha* offers automatic citizenship plus potential self-governance of territory. Being *taing-yin-tha* is defined as having a history and culture established in Burma before the arrival of the British, which they date as pre-1823. This is why Rohingya narratives all place great emphasis on explaining their pre-1823 origins in significant detail, with often comparatively limited comment or discussion on the colonial or post-Independence periods. Their ancestors, they argue, became a single ethnic group over many centuries, with a distinct language, culture, and history indigenous to the region. Tahir (1998 [1963], pp. 19, 23), for example, makes this explicit, arguing that the Rohingya 'have lived for many centuries within well-defined geographical boundaries which demarcate their "Traditional Homeland" … [with] millennia old history'. If this point was established in Burmese eyes, it would significantly change the power dynamics in the region. However, the above only points to the slave population (the third wave) having any real evidence in support of establishing their credentials as ancestors to the Rohingya.

Etymology of Names

In making their case for such ancient origins and a significant historical Muslim population in Arakan, Rohingya historical narratives also place great emphasis on the etymology of local names. It would be almost inconceivable for so many of their ancestors to have lived so long in Arakan without having influenced the naming of places. They insist, for example, that the name 'Arakan' itself is of Arabic or Persian origin, derived from the word *al-rukn*, the word for the five pillars of Islam (in both languages) and thus meaning 'land of Islam' or 'land of peace' (e.g. in Yunus 1994; Anin 2002; Alam 2000, 2014). This is hotly disputed by Rakhine accounts, which find Arakanese origins for these names. However, Tahir (1998 [1963], p. 5) suggests that this name was used to refer to the land by Arab–Persian geographers and travellers from the fourteenth to seventeenth centuries, as well as in medieval Bengali literature. Likewise, the names Roang/Rohang/Roshang are said to be other older names for Arakan, corruptions of the Arabic term *rahm*, meaning 'blessing, mercy', and thus meaning 'land of God's blessing'. Again, they suggest that these names were widely used by Muslim traders from as early as the eighth to twelfth centuries, including by traders who used the route over the Arakan mountains to travel to Burma and then China. Rakhine nationalists strenuously dispute this argument, pointing to Arakanese origins of the name.

Beyond this, Rohingya historians routinely claim that many other place names bear names of Muslim origin. For example, Anin (2002) claims the names Akyab (the old name for Sittwe, the state capital), Kaladan River, Naf River, Kalapanzan Creek in Buthidaung Township, and Ramree Island are examples of names derived from Persian or Arabic words, and adopted via local Muslim populations by the

Arakanese kings after 1430 CE, when Persian became the court language. Again, Rakhine nationalist advocates deny each of these, and claim that most names in even Muslim-majority areas such as most of Maungdaw are of Rakhine derivation (e.g. RNDP 2012). Most of these arguments are speculative, and hard to substantiate either way.

Even more important to their cause is establishing the antiquity of their ethnic name, 'Rohingya'. Rakhine narratives (see Chapter 4) argue that this name is an invention from the 1950s. In response, Rohingya point to mention of what appears to be the same name in Francis Buchanan's *A Comparative Vocabulary of Some of the Languages Spoken in the Burma Empire* (1799). This reference is one of the historical sources most frequently cited by Rohingya advocates as they argue for indigenous race classification. Buchanan accompanied Major Symes on a diplomatic mission to the Kingdom of Ava in 1795, as a doctor and naturalist. Having arrived in Bengal in 1794, and having worked on ships in Bengal in the region prior to that, he had presumably acquired some proficiency in a range of local languages. The Burmese capital itself had moved to nearby Amarapura, and the mission was not granted an audience to see the king. Nonetheless, the report by Major Symes was the most significant advance in British understanding of Burma in fifty years, and the most influential piece of writing dominating Western views until the 1850s (Leider 2017b). Based for nine months in nearby Ava, where most of the population resided, Buchanan compiled a comparative vocabulary of some of the languages spoken in the kingdom, as represented at the capital. Given that Mrauk-U had been conquered by the Burman only a few years earlier, in 1784, and a large number of captives taken back to Ava, he naturally met a number of people from Arakan.

In the course of this mammoth effort, Buchanan apparently met one or two representatives from each of three groups, who all said they were from Arakan (in addition to meeting ethnic Arakanese representatives). The exact wording in his text (with modernized spelling), so heavily relied upon, reads:

> I shall now add three dialects, spoken in the Burma Empire, but evidently derived from the language of the Hindu nation. The first is that spoken by the Mohammedans, who have long settled in Arakan, and who call themselves *Rooinga*, or natives of Arakan. (Buchanan 1799, p. 237)

This, he contrasted with Hindus from Arakan who called themselves 'Rossawn', who he said 'by the real natives of Arakan are called *kulaw Yakain*, or stranger Arakan', and a group whose religion he did not identify but said came from 'the frontiers of *Bengal*', who he said called themselves 'Banga'. Buchanan then offered a side-by-side comparison of a fifty-word vocabulary from each of the three languages, noting without particular comment a high number of Rossawn and Banga words derived from Hindustani compared to the significantly more distinct Rooinga.

The Rohingya widely see this entry by Buchanan as incontrovertible evidence that a population of Muslims self-identifying as Rohingya lived in Arakan prior to the Burman conquest of 1784, with a distinct language and identity. Again, this is important because it would demonstrate irrefutably that they are an indigenous race according to Burmese definitions. There is, however, considerable debate from Rakhine and Burman historians, and some international commentators (e.g. Tonkin 2014a, 2014b, 2018; Leider 2014, 2015), who argue that what Buchanan recorded was that they called themselves 'natives of Arakan' using their pronunciation of the name 'Rakhine'. Tonkin (2014a) refers, for example, to Buchanan's 1798 *Account of a Journey in South East Bengal* (van Schendel 1992), noting that he said the Bengali variously called Arakan by names including 'Rossawn, Rohhawn, Roang, Reng or Rung', and that in his voluminous other journals and writing Buchanan never again referred to Arakanese Muslims as 'Rooinga'. The etymology and historical reference argument is, therefore, strongly fought on both sides, with very inconclusive evidence.

Assessment of the Pre-Colonial Muslim Population

According to the Rohingya, a considerable Muslim minority developed in Arakan before the British took control. Some, they suggest, were descended from Vesali and Mrauk-U migrant traders and courtesans, some the descendants of the original indigenous race, converted and assimilated, while most were descendants of slaves. Based on documents from the period, Charney (1999, p. 165) estimates that at least 60,000 Muslims were living in northern Arakan by the end of the seventeenth century, thus suggesting that they may have constituted as much as

30 per cent of the northern Arakan population. Many Rohingya advocates take this estimate, together with the 30 per cent estimate of Paton (1826), to argue that the pre-1823 Rohingya population was significant, and that the population size has remained fairly stable in percentage terms over the last two centuries. However, the significantly more statistically robust first full colonial census, in 1872, reported that just 21 per cent of the population of northern Arakan were Muslim (Duncan 1875), and this was after five decades of British-sponsored labour migration to open rice agriculture in the region. It is also noteworthy to observe that the thrust of Paton's report was to argue that there was a lot of vacant or under-utilized agricultural land in northern Rakhine State, and thus recommend extensive British sponsorship of Chittagonian farmer immigration. Thus, in our estimation (see Chapter 5 for details), it is more reasonable to assume that 10–13 per cent of the population of Arakan were Muslims in 1823. We will return to the question of mass immigration during the colonial era in the next chapter, because this is so central to the Burman–Rakhine 'Infiltration' historical narrative about the conflict. For now, we just note that Tahir (1998 [1963]) and other Rohingya historians conveniently ignore other competing population figures documenting a rapidly growing population, and many other reports devoted to colonial agricultural expansion on a very large scale, mostly involving imported labour and capital. This dispute over hard-to-defend figures is unfortunate, because even if we accept the lower figure of 10–13 per cent, it still means that at least some of the ancestors of a very significant portion of the Rohingya population today pre-dated 1823.

One other thing is worth mentioning here, about language. The lack of an agreed written script, with very few Rohingya literate in their own language, corroborates the idea of slave or agricultural labourer origins, and militates against their more fanciful ideas of being descended from kings and the court elites of Vesali and Mrauk-U. The Mrauk-U court adopted Persian, and wrote poetry in Bengali. The lack of a written script amongst the Rohingya today suggests a discontinuity with these earlier elites. It is reported that Rohingya was first written with a version of the Arabic alphabet during the nineteenth century, with other attempts using Arabic, Urdu, and Latin scripts during the twentieth century (Ager 2017).

Origins of the Contemporary Conflict: Burman, British, Second World War, and Independence

Given that the definition of *taing-yin-tha* revolves around being a people with a history and culture established in Burma before the arrival of the British, thus pre-1823, Rohingya historical narratives place considerably less emphasis on events after the arrival of the British. Their argument is primarily that they qualify as *taing-yin-tha*, and therefore must be admitted to the political community of Myanmar with full citizenship and political rights. The coverage of history subsequent to the Mrauk-U era, where it is given in any detail, is written to explain how the relatively harmonious, even cosmopolitan, Arakan they portray has devolved into such horrific conflict. As per Bar-Tal (2013) and our earlier discussion, this narrative also serves to highlight to the international community the human rights abuses perpetrated against them, as part of the standard mobilization of historical narratives around an intractable conflict.

Most Rohingya written histories make three key points in their coverage of post-Mrauk-U history, namely:

a) they argue that the Burmans, since their invasion of Arakan in 1784, have targeted and persecuted Muslims in particular, and are the main instigator of communal tensions;

b) they dispute the idea that most Rohingya are descended from colonial-era immigrant agricultural labourers, arguing that these labourers were seasonal and only marginally increased the pre-existing Muslim population; and

c) they point to the violence of the Second World War and the civil war at Independence as the real origins of the powerful collective memories and grievances underlying the conflict.

We will now briefly consider each of these in turn, without attempting to address every event covered in the narratives.

As already noted, Anin (2002) proposes that the first round of communal violence between Rohingya ancestors and the Arakanese was in the massacre of Shah Shuja in 1661. The Muslim League (Jamiatul-ulema 1947) dates the first communal violence to suppression of the Kaman Muslim archers in 1710. However, most other Rohingya written histories place the blame for the contemporary conflict squarely on the ethnic Burman state. Most argue that while ethnic Rakhine ultra-nationalists are emboldened by the Burmans, it is the Burman state that has been the main culprit, instigating conflict and violence ever since the Burman King Bodawphaya invaded and plundered Arakan in 1784, deporting most of the royal court (including the Muslim elite) back to central Burma—plus a significant portion of the general population as labourers. They argue that the Burman conquest was the major turning point in communal relations. Between the battle and its aftermath, almost everything materially and culturally Islamic was razed to the ground, they say, as the Burman occupiers set about driving out the Muslims and erasing as much Muslim history in Arakan as possible (e.g. see Yunus 1994; Alam 2000; Jilani 2001). Many point to Harvey (1947, pp. 154–5), who says that while Arakan had never been populous, it now became a desert, of ghost towns and fields overgrown by jungle. Burman treatment of the entire population was so harsh that by 1799, according to one Rakhine historian (Aye Chan 2005, p. 398), as many as 35,000 people fled Arakan into British-held Chittagong to escape the 'ruthless oppression'.

Charney (1999) corroborates this, estimating that 20–25 per cent of the population of Arakan, Buddhist and Muslim, took refuge across the Naf River, in British Bengal, while many others fled east. This was a historical flow of refugees on a scale similar to recent events, and, interestingly, the perpetrators were the invading Burman army. But at that time, Muslim and Arakanese both fled into what is now Bangladesh. Nonetheless, Rohingya historians argue that Muslims were targeted more ruthlessly than the Arakanese. Ibrahim (2016, p. 25), for example, claims that one of the key motivations for the Burman invasion was to ensure the Buddhist purity of Arakan, the gateway of Buddhism into Myanmar, and reduce dangerous ties to the Muslim sultanates to the west. Certainly, the expansionist Konbaung dynasty appealed heavily to Buddhist forms of legitimacy (Koenig 1990), and their relocation to Amarapura of the sacred Arakanese Mahamuni image (claimed to have been fashioned in the presence of the Buddha in the sixth century BCE) only strengthens this view. Charney (1999) offers conjecture along the same lines, that perhaps the surprisingly low percentage of Muslims found in Arakan at the commencement of British rule (he puts the figure at 20 per cent, compared with his estimate of 30 per cent before the invasion) was due to so many more Muslims than Arakanese having been taken back to central Burma as captives, and fleeing to Bengal.

The ethnic Rakhine are at least as aggrieved by the conquest of Mrauk-U as are the Rohingya, something which will be discussed further in the next chapter. To the Rohingya historians, however, ever since this conquest the Burmans have continually sought to push the Muslims out, deliberately distort historical records to obfuscate Muslim history, and instigate communal strife. 'Arakan has always been a country with two nations within one geographic entity', argues Tahir (1998 [1963], p. 19), and the two peoples largely coexisted peacefully prior to the 1784 Burman conquest. Most Rohingya historians agree. For example, Yunus, in the preface to his *A History of Arakan* (1994, p. 4), claims: 'There is not the slightest doubt that those who occupied Arakan [the Burman] and wished to colonise it forever are deliberately distorting the historical facts ... to mislead and divide the two sister communities of Arakan.'

The royal library at Mrauk-U was burned by Burman forces in 1784, another grievance shared by most Rakhine. Many of Arakan's historical works did not survive. Of what did remain, many portions were carried off, allowing Rohingya historians to question the authenticity of the manuscripts in circulation ever since then. Alam (2000, p. 81) goes so far as to argue that after the conquest the Burmans appointed U Kala to re-write Muslims out of Arakanese history—although, as we will see in the next chapter, U Kala died fifty years before the invasion, and this reference appears to confuse U Kala's compilation of the Burman *Maha Yazawin* (Great Royal Chronicle) with later events (see also Lieberman 1986). Nonetheless, Rohingya narratives all argue that deliberate Burman destruction of their heritage and place in history after 1784 allowed persecution to continue and accelerate after Independence, and eventually turn the majority of the Arakanese population against them.

Charney (1999) certainly supports part of this contention, suggesting that part of the Burman colonizing project to subdue Arakan involved bringing Arakanese history under Burman authority. This included destroying Arakan's history, as contained in its *pesa* (palm-leaf) chronicles, and instilling new myths or reconfiguring older ones to

portray the unification of the Arakanese and Burman peoples, to legitimize the Burman annexation of Arakan. Phayre (1844) concurs that
'the ancient chronicles were sought after with avidity, and destroyed or
carried away, in the hope apparently of eradicating the national feeling', although he concludes that this was futile, as enough survived to
inhibit this. Nonetheless, it seems clear that the Burmans did at least
try to re-write Arakanese history. Whether this succeeded, and whether
this included a writing out of Muslim history, is not as clear.

From this point, Rohingya authors routinely blame the Burmans for
instigating communal tensions and directly discriminating against the
Rohingya. Yunus (1994, p. 6) concedes that 'an internecine feud'
between Muslims and the Rakhine enabled the Burmans to legitimize
their occupation of Arakan. Yunus argues that ever since, the Burmans
have resorted to ethnic cleansing of the Rohingya, out of fear of
Arakan's historical ties to Bengal being repeated. Jilani (preface, Tahir
1998 [1963]) also blames the British for making things worse, by intro-
ducing concepts of race and playing divide and rule in Arakan.
Nonetheless, they all suggest that Burman ethno-nationalism, often
displayed as a Buddhist nationalism, is primary. They blame the
Burmans for instigating horrific communal violence during the Second
World War, and Burman chauvinism and discrimination for provoking
the post-Independence civil war. Most of all, they blame Ne Win for
stripping the Rohingya of their rights and propagating narratives of
them as illegal migrants—arguing that they are victims of military
politics, 'scapegoated' (as Jilani 1999, put it) every time the military
needs relief from other domestic pressures.

Returning to the historical narrative, Arakan became part of British
India through the First Anglo-Burmese war (1824–6), just forty years
after the Burman invasion, and was thus under colonial rule for longer
than most of Burma, some 124 years. According to Rohingya historians, the arrival of the British facilitated the return of the large number
of Muslim refugee families who had fled the harsh Burman occupation.
Having sheltered in Chittagong, they argue, these people seized the
opportunity to return quickly after the war—as of course did large
numbers of Rakhine.

In some ways supporting this narrative, Charney (1999) argues that
this early colonial period was the point at which religious communal-

ism developed, both Buddhist and Muslim. He ascribes this to competition between returnees and migrants, from Bengal and other parts of Burma, as the region was rapidly repopulated in the absence of the traditional patron–client structures and established rural gentry. In its place, he suggests, people constructed new communal identities around religious leaders and spaces. The Rakhine advocate Aye Chan (2005) adds that the British administration granted ninety-nine-year leases to newly immigrated Bengali migrants, and thus that there were cases of Arakanese peasants returning to find Muslims occupying the land that they formerly owned through inheritance. Based on these assessments, we suggest that the emergence of the modern Rakhine Buddhist and Rohingya identities occurred concurrently and interdependently from the start of the colonial era, such that 'one cannot talk of the emergence of [Rakhine or Rohingya] without the other' (Charney 1999, p. 13). This rising sense of nationalism on both sides, we suggest, throughout the colonial period, led to a growing sense of shared identity amongst the Muslim population in Arakan, which for many has subsequently evolved into a self-identification as a unified Rohingya ethnic group.

Burman and Rakhine narratives, as we shall explore in detail in the next chapter, claim that the Rohingya are Bengali immigrants who entered Arakan during either the colonial period or later. To counter this, Rohingya historians point to colonial records, principally the survey by Paton and Robertson (Paton 1826, p. 36), who, based on a brief survey trip round the region just after their capture of Arakan, estimated the Muslim population of Arakan to be around 30 per cent. They thus argue that there has only been a natural population growth since then, not the influx of migrants that Rakhine and Burman nationalist advocates claim. Immigrant labour in Arakan during the colonial era, they argue, was of seasonal labourers from Chittagong. Longer-term Indian migrant labourers settled in the delta region of Burma, not Arakan. We will interrogate this claim in the next chapter, but suffice it to say here that there are other census and population figures that do not sit so comfortably with this narrative, which privileges a quick estimate based on personal survey over more statistically robust formal census data collection, without justifying why. That data does clearly show a growing migrant Muslim population in Arakan throughout the colonial period.

An unprecedented process of Rohingya identity formation appears to have taken place in the push for, and aftermath of, Burma's Independence (Leider & Kyaw Minn Htin 2015; Leider 2018a). The Burman push for independence originated within the Young Men's Buddhist Association, shortly before 1920, and thus, Rohingya historians write, drew heavily on Buddhist nationalism. The Thakin Party, which emerged as leader of the nationalist Dobama Asiayone (literally 'We Burman' or 'Our Burma' Association), was thus, unsurprisingly, particularly anti-Indian/anti-Muslim, given that the British had relied so heavily on Indians (largely Muslims) in the civil service and agricultural expansionism. This nationalism played a role in fomenting the anti-Indian riots of 1930 and 1938. Then, the Burma Independence Army (BIA), formed by the Thakin at the outset of the Second World War in Burma (1942), was equally anti-Indian and anti-Muslim, they argue. The BIA has since become the Tatmadaw, and has dominated politics in the country ever since.

Rohingya narratives emphasize the minimal communal conflict in Arakan prior to the Second World War, and see the arrival of the war in Arakan in 1942 as the key turning point. Anin (2002), Yunus (1994), and Alam (2014, p. 75), for example, all argue that nationalist Arakanese were deluded by the Burman Thakin into believing that the Muslims were a serious threat to Buddhism, and plotted with them to drive the Muslims out of Rakhine. Their aim, according to Yunus (1994), had been to gain autonomy for Arakan by driving out the white *kala* (the British) and the black *kala* (the Chittagonians), initially determining that the Rohingyas and Kamans could stay unless they came to pose a threat like the Chittagonians. They argue, however, that the Burman Thakin aim was 'to divide the two sister communities forever, so that it could be easier to rule a divided people and make Arakan their permanent colony' (Yunus 1994, p. 56).

The Rohingya–Rakhine massacres and ethnic cleansing during the Second World War has already been noted. Rohingya historians claim that thousands of Muslim villages were destroyed, driving the majority of Muslims living south of the Kaladan River northward. They claim that over 100,000 Rohingya were killed by Rakhine and Burman forces, with many more than that dislocated (e.g. Yunus 1994, pp. 56–8), although this figure is undoubtedly overinflated (Leider

2018a)—and they conveniently omit to mention reciprocal massacres, and the mass relocation of Rakhine forced south. Claims by Rakhine nationalists that they were the real victims during this period will be explored in the next chapter, but in reality both sides suffered greatly. The violence 'created wounds that never healed and cemented the division between the Buddhist and Muslim communities in northern Rakhine' (Leider 2014, p. 235). We suggest that it was these events, more than anything else, that crystallized a nationalistic sense of shared identity amongst the Muslims. It also forged a strongly nationalist Rakhine identity, and the Burman sense that the Rohingya posed a national threat. We argue that a protracted conflict (sometimes physically violent, always psychologically and structurally violent) has only intensified since then, settling into the sort of intractable conflict that Bar-Tal describes.

The worst of the Second World War onslaught was halted in the last week of April 1942, when Muslims won a decisive battle for Buthidaung, after which Maungdaw, Buthidaung, and part of Rathedaung Townships were brought under the administration of Peace Committees set up by Muslims. Relative safety was secured in those Muslim-majority areas, and it is interesting that this same area is the territory featured in all successive claims for autonomy. The decisive turning point of the war came three years later, when the BIA (and their Arakanese allies) switched sides in early 1945, on condition of early independence for the country immediately after the war. The Rohingya feel deeply betrayed by the British in the subsequent events.

The greatest question the British raised in response to demands for independence was the protection of minorities. Aung San therefore convened the instrumental Panglong Conference in February 1947, to secure the support of ethnic leaders from the frontier areas. Rohingya writers, such as Yunus (1994), complain that the Rohingya were the only major ethnic group not invited to Panglong, which is not true. The Mon and Arakanese were also not present (being from Ministerial Burma), the Wa and Nagas were not invited (being too small), and the Karen only participated as observers. But in his representation of history, Yunas directly attributes this alleged exclusion as the reason why a delegation was instead sent to Mohammad Ali Jinnah, to ask for inclusion of the region occupied by the Rohingya in East Pakistan. This was also rejected, and he expresses a feeling of betrayal at this point of his narrative, by the British, India, and Burma. This sense of betrayal is common amongst Rohingya interview informants as well as historians.

The significance of this attempt by some Rohingya to carve territory out of Burma, into East Pakistan, cannot be overstated. It has to this day been etched into the minds of Rakhine and Burman nationalists— who deeply fear that the central aim of the Rohingya movement today is to have them cede territory to Muslim control. They often cite this as proof that the Rohingya are not a Myanmar *taing-yin-tha*. No *taing-yin-tha* would ever attempt to do this.

Rohingya widely claim that they received promises from the British that they would be granted some form of autonomous governance after the war, variously described as 'partial independence' (Ibrahim 2016, p. 7) or a 'Muslim national area' (Jilani 2001, p. 89), for example. Many Muslims from northern Rakhine worked for such aims within the system. Tahir relates a conversation said to have occurred during the drafting of the 1947 constitution, around use of the term *taing-yin-tha* as a test of Burmese citizenship. Two Muslim members of the Constituent Assembly from northern Rakhine sought clarification of their status in the union (note that neither they nor anyone in the Constituent Assembly identified at that time as 'Rohingya'). In a widely quoted response, the first President of the Union of Burma, Saw Shwe Thaik, is reported to have told them:

> Muslims of Arakan certainly belong to one of the indigenous races (*taing-yin-tha*) of Burma which you represent. In fact, there are no pure indigenous races in Burma, so that if you do not belong to indigenous races of Burma, we also cannot be taken as indigenous races of Burma. (Tahir 1998 [1963], p. 25)

They did not, however, at that point seek recognition as 'Rohingya', and it was decades before Rohingya leaders sought any more formal recognition as a *taing-yin-tha* indigenous race than this.

According to the Rohingya historical narratives, many Rakhine ultra-nationalists went underground after the British return at the end of the war, then re-emerged and aligned with the communists and People's Volunteer Organization (PVO) in launching civil war in Arakan. They quickly took control of most of Arakan south of Akyab (Sittwe), claiming Rakhine autonomy more than a communist agenda.

In the same vein, and largely in response to this threat, Rohingya historians say that some of their people launched the Mujahid rebellion to protect the Muslim people, quickly taking control of Rakhine north of Akyab. Ibrahim (2016) argues that compared to the sustained revolts of other ethnic groups, this attempt to gain a degree of self-determination was minimal—but this is a huge understatement about a revolt lasting twelve years and taking a huge toll. On the back of the attempt by some Rohingya to take territory out of the union, this revolt led the military leadership (and many Rakhine) to come to see the Rohingya as a particularly serious threat to the integrity of the nation. The early 1950s thus saw large military operations in Arakan directed against the Mujahids.

In 1959, with the Mujahids largely defeated, in an attempt to quell Rohingya discontent, Prime Minister U Nu and defence minister U Ba Swe visited northern Arakan—as already noted. Rohingya leaders believe that to end the conflict they offered the Rohingya full recognition equal to the Shan, Kachin, and Karen—a promise largely seen as fulfilled by the creation of the Mayu Frontier District on 1 May 1961. (It is notable that the Mayu Frontier District comprised Maungdaw, Buthidaung, and part of the Rathedaung Townships, an area similar to that controlled by the Peace Committees during the Second World War, and the same area targeted by ARSA for independence in the recent militancy.)

Rohingya narratives also see significance in the fact that, during a Muhajid surrender ceremony in July 1961, Brigadier-General Aung Gyi used the name 'Rohingya' in a manner implying equal status as one of Burma's ethnic groups. Indeed, even General Ne Win used the name Rohingya in a 1954 speech (Thawnghmung 2016). Rohingya historians claim many other examples of widespread use of the name during the 1950s—in government reports, newspapers, documents, radio broadcasts—and the existence of high-ranking Muslims from northern Rakhine in government posts and academia. In reality, most of this usage of the name did not occur until the late 1950s, and mainly during 1960–4. Still, Rohingya historians point to this as evidence that they had become a genuine part of the Myanmar political community at that time, before the elevation of *taing-yin-tha* as the central, defining political concept. There is certainly strong evidence that the name was not, at that time, considered controversial, and was not vehemently opposed by many, if any, Burman or Rakhine nationalists.

Unfortunately, Rohingya hopes for the attainment of full political recognition were dashed after March 1962, when General Ne Win led a coup d'état. Whatever tolerance and gains had been made quickly ended. Most Muslim officers and officials in the military and bureaucracy were dismissed, forced to retire, or transferred out of Arakan. Ne Win dissolved the Mayu Frontier District, and declared the Rohingya to be aliens and foreigners (e.g. Karim 2000). All of this is widely documented by a diversity of historians. Rohingya historians take this and suggest that scapegoating, which commenced during this period, was popularized by Ne Win's regime to the point that it has been adopted as truth by a majority of Rakhine and Burman. While much more is said of the post-1962 period by some of the Rohingya writers, the die was cast. Indeed, Smith (1991, p. 194) notes some of his personal informants claiming that at that time such high levels of fear existed that an explosion of intercommunal religious violence seemed imminent, 'the likes of which Burma had never seen'.

It is worth noting again the mass exoduses to Bangladesh in 1978 and 1991–2, as discussed in the first chapter. Most Rohingya advocates point to these as evidence of official state persecution being at the core of this issue, far more than communal tensions. The citizenship provisions in the 1974 constitution, and elevation of *taing-yin-tha* status in the 1982 Citizenship Law, only put into legal effect the decrees Ne Win had issued shortly after the coup. Yunus (1994, p. 79) claims that after the passage of the 1982 law, rioting in southern Arakan, where Muslims are in the minority and thus more vulnerable, and in Akyab, saw many Muslim villages demolished or burnt in communal violence. Hill tribes, especially Buddhist groups, were resettled onto the confiscated land in an attempt to permanently change the demographic mix. This denial of rights, alienation, and discrimination, based on a distorted view of history, they argue, has continued through periods of violence and relative calm, as the primary driver of discrimination and their loss of citizenship.

Jilani (2001, p. 69) makes a concluding statement about the importance of correcting historical narratives, arguing that once a distortion of history is accepted without any strong counter-claim being promoted, it quickly becomes accepted as fact, and the basis for policy. The Rohingya therefore say that they write and continually propagate their historical narratives in an attempt to ward off the dominant exclusionary narratives about them continually promulgated by Burman and Rakhine sources. In reality, we suggest, all sides are propagating serious distortions of history. This conflict is very much a clash of historical narratives, which together sum up the entirety of the grievances and claims of all sides. In this sense, Myanmar's Rohingya conflict fits the description of intractable conflict very well.

The analysis in this chapter suggests that the Rohingya 'Origin' narrative contains enough truth to sound plausible, yet is selective enough with the evidence to be highly dubious. Fighting desperately to be accepted as a *taing-yin-tha* (national race), they present a historical account tailored to that outcome. There is good evidence of extensive engagement with Bengal and the Muslim sultanates, evidence of Muslim courtiers and slave settlements, and thus solid evidence of a certain Muslim history in Arakan. But in giving credence to legend, being selective about facts and figures, and ignoring evidence of the very large Indian migration during colonial times, aspects of their narrative remain highly questionable. They have, nonetheless, been persecuted since Independence, repeatedly targeted by the military, and now caused to flee for their lives to Bangladesh. Whatever else may be flawed in their history, the marginalization and persecution is of deep concern, and must be addressed.

Raising a final thought to which we will return, we suggest that the Rohingya are actually fighting the wrong fight. The notion of *taing-yin-tha*, and the prioritization of the political community of *taing-yin-tha* over citizenship more generally (Cheesman 2017) is, we suggest, the real problem. Or in terms used by the Advisory Commission on Rakhine State (Annan et al. 2017b), different kinds of citizenship for *taing-yin-tha* and non-*taing-yin-tha*, with different rights, is the key problem. But, as Cheesman points out, those who are subjugated can only fight for their rights within the rules dictated by the power structures by which they are held captive. Hence, the Rohingya are locked into trying to claim *taing-yin-tha* status, and make history fit their claim. As we discuss later in the book, what is really required for a long-term solution to emerge is the depoliticization of ethnicity and race in Myanmar, with a recognition of genuinely equal citizenship rights of individuals, in which citizenship follows more inclusionary models in forming the political community. With this, the Rohingya could—and should—engage with the document-verification process and accept citizenship as individuals, without needing to attempt to press historical claims to indigeneity which are questionable. And the Rakhine and Burman communities could—and should—accept a 'Rohingya' cultural identity. These, however, are challenges that the Rohingya cannot address themselves. Others, empowered rather than marginalized by the current structure, must take the lead.

4

RAKHINE–BURMAN NARRATIVES

'INDEPENDENCE', 'UNITY', 'INFILTRATION'

The previous chapter documented the Rohingya historical narrative, presenting their claims to indigeneity as expressed in the key English-language written texts, based on an argument that their forebears had lived in the land for centuries. Through this, they claim to be eligible for citizenship with equal political rights. The chapter critiqued the socio-political context within which these texts were produced, and interrogated key aspects of their narrative. This chapter seeks to do the same with three central organizing historical narratives of the ethnic Rakhine and Burmans. It outlines these historical narratives, and offers critiques of fundamental aspects of each narrative and the socio-political motivations behind production of the key texts.

We have already argued that the conflict in Myanmar's Rakhine State is multi-faceted and intractable. By nature, intractable conflicts become characterized by the stalemate of contradictory historical narratives—narratives through which grievances are articulated and people mobilized. The psychological conditions created by prolonged conflict leads to a cognitive freezing of memories, which crystallize self-righteous and ethnocentric narratives that hide not only misdeeds and deficiencies on their own side, but also information about the humanness of the rival, especially their just needs and goals (Bar-Tal 2014, p. 18). These narratives thus become obstacles to peace.

The perpetuation of contradictory historical narratives in Arakan has been facilitated by the poor state of archaeology, and a superficial and uncritical treatment of sources by most writers (for more than a century). Leider (2005, p. 48) refers to the 'confusion and the false certainties that reign in the field of Rakhine history'. Charney (2000, p. 54) bemoans the fact that 'no acceptable general survey has yet been provided for Arakanese history, and whole centuries remain unstudied'. In some ways, little has changed since. Phayre (1841, p. 681) described Arakanese history as mostly 'a tangled web of fiction'.

Despite long periods without significant physical violence, and individual cases of cooperation—and even friendship—between Rakhine, Muslims, and Burman, incompatible rival claims and unresolved grievances have chafed and festered since before Independence. As with those of the Muslims, Rakhine and Burman grievances are primarily articulated through historical narratives. Thus, while most of us from the West seek explanations for the conflict in recent history, the protagonists themselves continue to expound history to articulate their grievances and claims. To understand the issues from their perspectives, we thus need a deeper appreciation of where their views come from.

In this chapter we identify one Rakhine, one Burman, and one shared Rakhine–Burman historical narrative that sum up their grievances and claims. We describe these as:

a) the Rakhine 'Independence' narrative, which justifes demands for autonomy from Burman domination based on history;

b) the Burman 'Unity' narrative, which claims a shared ancestry and historical unity between Myanmar's national races as the basis for expectations that minorities will unite with them, to form a political community at the heart of the Union of Myanmar; and

c) the Rakhine–Burman 'Infiltration' narrative, which claims that an influx of Bengali Muslims during the colonial and post-Independence period poses an existential threat to the ethnic Rakhine, to Buddhism, and to the Myanmar nation.

We present these three narratives in a single chapter, but that is not meant to imply that they are somehow less important or historically detailed than the Rohingya narrative (which has a whole chapter of its own). We do so simply because four iterations through similar history would be unnecessarily repetitive.

In the same way that we allowed use of the name 'Rohingya' in the last chapter, so that the Muslim narrative might be heard in their own voice, we allow use of the name 'Bengali' in parts of this chapter to allow a particular Rakhine–Burman voice to be clearly heard. This is not a political statement, just a means to allow expression of their narrative using their own terminology.

The Rakhine 'Independence' Narrative

Sources and their Socio-Political Context

The most notable sources for what we term the Rakhine 'Independence' narrative are the Rakhine royal chronicles (*Razawin*). The name—from Pali *rāja-vaṃsa*, 'chronicle of kings' (Hla Pe 1985, p. 45)—would suggest that these are histories compiled progressively throughout the Mrauk-U kingdom period and earlier. However, and very significantly, all extant *Razawin* were compiled in a period commencing just before the destruction of Mrauk-U and ending shortly before the Second World War. Thus, all compilations date from the end or after the period of the kings, not during that time.

Ancient historical texts may seem to be a long way from contemporary problems in Rakhine State, but the grievances they embed into Rakhine collective memory are at the heart of contemporary problems. From a Rakhine perspective, centuries of Arakanese independence culminating in the glorious kingdom came to a tumultuous end in 1784, when the Burmese King Bodawphaya invaded. While most Rakhine today are not necessarily familiar with the text of the *Razawin*, they know the stories, and the destruction of Mrauk-U is etched deeply into their collective memory. Indeed, the destruction of Mrauk-U and the plunder of Arakan is usually top of their list of grievances against the Burman-led state today, and is used to express their contemporary fear that the army or state intend to keep oppressing the people and plundering their resources. The *Razawin* are the key originator of this collective memory, and the destruction of Mrauk-U was the key motivation behind their compilation.

No Arakanese chronicles survive from earlier times, only shorter documents and fragments. The reason commonly given for this is that the Burmans burned the royal library in 1784, and only portions escaped the indiscriminate destruction (Harvey 1925; Thant Myint-U 2006, p. 110). The Burmans certainly did inflict almost total descruction on Mrauk-U. As Phayre (1844, p. 23) notes, after the conquest 'the ancient chronicles were sought after with avidity, and destroyed or carried away, in the hope apparently of eradicating the national feeling'. This attempt to destroy their history, culture, and identity is well remembered by most Rakhine, whose response was a wave of compilation of new *Razawin*.

History is continually written, rewritten, and re-compiled. This process is always done in a manner designed to address contemporary issues and questions. The Burman kings had gained significant legitimacy from their *Maha Yazawindawgyi* chronicle, compiled by U Kala in 1724 (discussed further in the next section). Thus, establishing the historical grandeur and legitimacy of the Rakhine kingdom, by re-compiling the royal chronicles, was a means to argue their right to continue to exist. The loss of their kingdom, and depopulation of Arakan, so deeply challenged Arakanese identity that monks and historians alike began compiling histories from whatever records survived. Their success in establishing and maintaining a proud sense of independent Arakanese identity can be seen in the strong nostalgic recollection of the golden age of Mrauk-U felt today, and their stubbornly independent attitude towards Ava, Mandalay, Yangon and now Nay Pyi Taw.

Arakanese palm-leaf chronicles held in Myanmar by the National Library and Yangon University,[1] as well as those in the British Library in London[2] and the Museum of the Asiatic Society of Bengal in Calcutta, all range in date from 1775 to 1887. At least three chronicles were published in print during the mid-to-late colonial period. Unfortunately, all the Arakanese *Razawin* remain untranslated into English, so non-Burmese readers are reliant on secondary sources. Some of the more significant of these chronicles are:

1. *Rakhine Razawin Haung* (or *Min Razagri Aredaw Sadan*), compiled in 1775 when the kingdom was in disarray just before its destruction. Compiled to legitimize Arakan's continued independence as conquest appeared inevitable, and being the only chronicle surviving 1784, this is probably the template for all that follow. It was well known, even consulted by the Burmans as they compiled their

famous *Hmannan* chronicle between 1829 and 1832 (the *Glass Palace Chronicle*: see Pe Maung Tin & Luce 1923). Referred to as 'the Old Arakanese Chronicle' by many Rakhine historians, aspects of this chronicle are explained by Charney (2004) at some length.

2. *Dhanyawaddy Ayedawbon* (or *Kawitharabi Thiri-Pawara Agga-Maha-Dhammarazadiraza*), compiled in 1788 immediately after the destruction of Mrauk-U, has been available in book form since the late 1800s. It is widely cited, but significantly, this text was compiled for the conquering Burman king by one of his monks sent to bring Rakhine Buddhism into line (Leider 2005). It is significant that this manuscript is called an *ayedawbon* (memoir of royal struggles: see Hla Pe 1985; also Thaw Kaung 2000), rather than a *razawin*, and much of the text consists of ministerial speeches, making it largely a different genre.

3. Nga Mi's *Maha Razawin*. Commissioned by the Colonial District Officer, Arthur Phayre, around 1842, this chronicle aimed to harmonize the diverse, often fragmentary, accounts, and strip the supernatural and mythological from the historical. This chronicle has been highly influential. Phayre (1844) published a summary in English, and it was the basis for Harvey's (1925, 1947) histories. Leider (2005) and Zaw Lynn Aung (2009) both summarize the contents, although Leider (2005, p. 50) argues that Phayre and Harvey gave Nga Mi's account 'a credibility that it does not always deserve'.

4. *Danyawaddy Yazawinthit*, written by Rakhine monk U Pandi and published in 1910. Together with the below, this is one of the best-known Arakanese histories within Myanmar (Gutman 1976, p. iii); however, it is incomplete, and Harvey (1925, p. xix) questions its reliability, calling it 'a third-hand piece of work'.

5. *Rakhine Razawinthit* ('New Chronicle of Rakhine'), published in 1931 by the Arakanese monk Candamalalankara. In attempting to compile all prior Arakanese chronicles into a single account, rather than arriving at a single version, this chronicle often provides the reader with rival accounts. This *Razawin* is the best-known Rakhine history today, and is summarized in Leider (2005).

The historicity of these is sometimes corroborated by stone inscriptions and coinage, as elaborated by archaeologists and historians such as Harvey (1925), Collis (1925), Luce (1969, 1985), Gutman (1976),

Singer (2008), and Griffiths (2015). However, the inscription record is relatively sparse, and archaeology in the region is so poorly developed that, prior to the fifteenth century, the *Razawin* stand largely on their own merit.

The Chronicles and Rakhine Claims to Independence

The *Razawin* almost all commence with mythological accounts of the first king of humanity; various dynasties, including the Indian kings down to the Buddhist Ashoka; Rakhine's pre-Buddhist kings; the Buddha's life, including an account of a trip to Rakhine; and then the Arakanese dynasties and their exploits through to the fall of Mrauk-U. Some *Razawin* also briefly cover the Burman administration (1785–1824) and the first Anglo-Burmese War (1824–6).

What the chronicles thus do is link the Arakanese Mrauk-U kings with traditional Buddhist accounts of the origins of human society, the life of the Buddha, and the prestigious Indian Buddhist kings (Leider 2005). They identify imaginary or apocryphal geography and people from the Buddhist literature, particularly the Jataka tales, into Rakhine history. The original purpose was clearly to legitimize—almost deify— the Arakanese kings, and this practice is consistent with what the Burmans did in their chronicles. But in re-telling these stories in the *Razawin* written from 1775 onwards, the message was about the legiti- mate right of Arakan to independent political rule.

In doing so, however, the chronicles greatly exaggerate the antiquity of the Arakanese presence in Arakan (Gutman 1976). Adopting a literal reading of the lists of kings in the chronicles, Phayre (1844, p. 34) calculated a supposed unbroken line of Arakanese kings from approxi- mately 2658 BCE to the Burman conquest in 1784 CE. The *Dhanyawaddy Ayedawbon*, for example, clearly presents a picture of Arakan as an independent kingdom for at least three millennia. This is despite the fact that Mrauk-U court historians do not appear to have been able to read inscriptions from the Danyawaddy period, nor do they appear to have consulted them (Singer 2008). Instead, it is widely agreed that the Arakanese began migrating into Arakan around the ninth century, and gained control of the region in about the eleventh. The date of their migration thus sits quite late in the chronicle accounts, and raises the possibility that some Muslims were already resident in Arakan before the Rakhine arrived.

One of the most important stories in the Arakanese chronicles is that of the Mahamuni image, already alluded to briefly earlier. According to every *Razawin*, the Buddha visited Rakhine during his lifetime, and a true image, the Mahamuni image, was fashioned in his presence. The Mahamuni image is therefore considered almost unique, one of only three images fashioned on earth in the presence of the Buddha—and the only such image in Myanmar. The presence of the image was long used to underscore the importance and legitimacy of Arakan. The story positions Rakhine as the gateway through which Buddhism arrived in Burma, and maintains that Arakan prospered because of the presence of—and worship of—the Mahamuni image. In the chronicles, the fact that the founder of the first Burman empire at Pagan, King Anawrahta (*c.* 1044–77), allegedly launched a failed attempt to capture the image a millennium ago strengthens the legitimacy of Arakan as an independent political and spiritual power.

This fact, however, also makes the capture of the Mahamuni image by the invading Burmans in 1784 an even more severe attack on Rakhine identity. The conquering Burman army removed the image, supposedly back to central Burma. Despite the fact that this desecration occurred more than 230 years ago, this event is still bitterly recounted by many Rakhine today, as an example of contemporary Burman attempts to destroy their unique history, identity, and contribution to Myanmar. It has become a significant part of Rakhine collective memory, both illustrating and mobilizing deep fears of assimilation.

A literal reading of the *Razawin* is often nonsensical. For example, both Phayre (1844, p. 36) and Gutman (1976, pp. 40, 326) calculate from the internal dating that the Buddha's supposed visit to Rakhine was during the reign of a king who ascended the throne in 146–7 CE. This, of course, is some six centuries *after* the lifetime of the Buddha. Gutman (1976, p. 206) dates the actual arrival of Buddhism in Arakan to the third century, and the carving of the Mahamuni image to 454 CE (thus not in the presence of the living Buddha). And what this narrative fails to concede is that the ethnic Rakhine (Arakanese) did not begin migrating to Arakan until about the ninth century, centuries after the arrival of Buddhism in Arakan—meaning that the Arakanese inherited the

Mahamuni and Buddhism from the preceding civilization, whose iden-tity and history are even less well known. But this does not dent the importance to most Rakhine of the ideas that they have a very long history in the land, that Buddhism arrived in Burma through them, and that this history legitimizes their spiritual and political right to the land with a high degree of political autonomy.

The chronicles thus present a long history of Arakanese indepen-dence. While they recount various attacks on Arakan, including fre-quent attacks by the Pyu (fifth–ninth centuries) and many others later, the major focus is on the victories and expansion of the kingdom (Phayre 1844; Gutman 1976). They claim campaigns into Bengal, Burma, Siam, even China, as early as the tenth to eleventh centuries. By the thirteenth century they claim to have received tribute from the king of Bengal. In the early fourteenth century they claim to have briefly taken both the Mon capital of Pegu and the Burman capital at Pagan. And so on. Thus the power and independence of Arakan, even before the founding of Mrauk-U in 1430, is a recurring theme. The zenith of Arakanese power and territorial control came in the sixteenth and seventeenth centuries. By the mid-sixteenth century Mrauk-U successfully defended itself against a Burmese invasion, then occupied Chittagong for a few years, later taking full control of Chittagong for a century (Leider & Kyaw Minn Htin 2015). They thus draw from the chronicles that theirs was a mighty and prosperous kingdom until Burman domination robbed them of it.

Without wanting to rely too much more on ancient history, we do still need to briefly reconsider the Rohingya use of the story of King Min Saw Mun, founder of Mrauk-U. While the *Razawin* do document the story of the Arakanese king founding Mrauk-U, with assistance from the (Muslim) king of Bengal, which the Rohingya 'Origin' narra-tive relies upon heavily, the Arakanese accounts do so with an overall emphasis on the glories and *independence* of Arakan. The *Razawin* account presents the king as being removed from his throne by a Burman army, after one faction at the Arakanese court appealed for their intervention. In response to this incursion, the Mons also sent an army in support of Min Saw Mun's half-brother, and the Mons and Burmans struggled for possession of Arakan for two decades (Phayre 1844, pp. 44–5). Eventually, though, the chronicles say, the Mon–

Arakanese army dislodged the Burmans, and shortly thereafter the king of Bengal restored Min Saw Mun to the throne.

This restoration to the throne and the subsequent founding of Mrauk-U is best read in terms of regional political posturing, with Burmans, Mon, and Bengalis using divisions between Arakanese elites to attempt to further their own reach—yet with the eventual return of Arakanese independence and power. The point of the story thus appears to be as much about the founding of the Mrauk-U kingdom resulting from the end of the divisions among the Arakan elite as about foreign intervention or control. Supposing that religious conversion (as per the last chapter) is neither necessary nor likely, and the chronicles give no support to the idea that a large Muslim force settled permanently in Arakan due to this event. As the Bengali researcher Bhattacharya (1927) expressed it a century ago, before the current conflict narratives gained sway, the fifteenth-century Arakanese kings, 'though Buddhist in religion, became somewhat Mahomedanised in their ideas'.

It is also important to keep Leider & Kyaw Minn Htin's (2015) detailed analysis of this story in mind—that there is no corroborating historical evidence for the account in inscriptions, tax records, or political documents. There is nothing to support the idea either of the exile and restoration of the king with Bengali assistance or of a major Arakanese political dependence on Bengal at this time. Thus the historicity of even major events in the *Razawin* is called into question. The stamping of Arakanese coins with the *kalima* (the Islamic declaration of faith), and Islamic titles adopted by the kings (Collis 1925), seen by some as corroborating evidence for this story, need not imply conversion to Islam by the Mrauk-U kings, or a major resident Muslim army. Friendly relations with Islamic kingdoms are all that need be implied, particularly if the account is fictional, and the coinage only confirms is that there were significant relationships between Arakan and its Muslim neighbours, economically and perhaps politically.

Put together, the evidence suggests that the Muslim presence in Arakan at that time was probably much smaller than the accounts in the last chapter suggest, but more significant than many Rakhine today like to admit.

In this light, there remain two things in the Arakanese chronicles that are of great relevance to today. The first is actually more what is not in the chronicles: the relatively rare mention of Muslims in Arakan prior to the colonial era. Interaction with Bengal is widely mentioned, including its conquest by Mrauk-U, but mentions of Islam in the royal court are relatively rare, despite the clear evidence for it. And mention of a Muslim population living near the capital is almost non-existent. However, conquests of parts of Bengal would result in Bengali subjects, with some presumably moving closer to the Arakan capital for trade purposes, and there is strong evidence of the extensive re-settlement of Bengali slaves to agricultural regions in the Kaladan River basin (Manrique 1927; Harvey 1925; Hall 1956; Yegar 1972; Gutman 1976; Charney 1999). Somehow this is something the chronicles ignore. Perhaps this omission also helps explain how the Burmans, who historically relied on the Arakanese chronicles more than any other outside source, came to perceive all the Muslims as so definitively foreign, rather than historically local.

What this omission also highlights is that the grievance the chroniclers wrote to address, the greatest concern to Rakhine between the late eighteenth and early twentieth centuries, was Burman domination. The Muslims in Arakan during that period were apparently not a particular concern. Perhaps if Bodawphaya had not invaded Arakan, the current situation may never have evolved, although that is pure conjecture. Certainly though, Mrauk-U's cosmopolitan nature as a centre drawing courtiers and influence from Bengal and the Muslim world did not overly concern Arakanese chroniclers of this era. This strongly suggests that tensions with the Muslims, and fear of being overrun by them, dates from the late colonial or early Independence period, not the Mrauk-U period.

The second thing of great relevance in the chronicles is that the Arakanese argument for independence is based on the idea of equality between races. The 1775 *Rakhine Razawin Haung* text divides the world into 101 peoples or races, using the word *lu-myo* not *taing-yin-tha* for race (Charney 2004). Rulers of all these races were direct descendants of the legendary first king of the world. This idea of 101 races had already been circulating among the Burmese since the seventeenth century, being referenced in the *Royal Orders of Burma* as early as 1628 and 1679 (Than Tun 1983a, 1983b; Thant Myint-U 2001, p. 88).

The *Rakhine Razawin Haung* positions the Arakanese as one of seven equal Marama races, alongside the Burman and Kaman. Other *lu-myo* races include three Mon races, three Chin races, twenty-three Shan races, and so on. Importantly, it also extends this brotherhood to various Indian and Chinese races, all counted amongst the 101 *lu-myo*. The chronicle's argument is about the equality between races, not the exclusionary politics the Burmans later adopted around the idea of *taing-yin-tha*. The argument implicit in the Arakanese *Razawin* is that of equality between races and their kings, with ethnic divisions seen as being part of the natural human condition (Charney 2004). Thus, the natural order should be of equality and the independence of races. The chronicle's claim to independence was thus based on the unnaturalness of one race dominating or assimilating another.

Charney (2004) notes a very significant contrast between this argument and the counter idea in the Burman royal chronicles (which we will explore in more detail in the next section). In the Burman chronicles, the central Burmese kingdoms are said to have provided the first kings for the surrounding states, and thus it is natural for them to be gradually re-absorbed back into expanding Burman empires. In this way, the Burman chronicles give hegemony to the Burman kings, legitimizing conquest and assimilation of surrounding nations. Interestingly though, Charney suggests that to do this the Burmans define *lu-myo* (race) in non-exclusive and flexible terms. The Burman chronicles present *lu-myo* in social terms, thus able to accommodate the assimilation of diverse conquered peoples without any loss of original identity. This is a far cry from Western ideas of race, based on biological kinship, as inherited by post-colonial Burma.

The influence of this ideology is borne out in the Burman polity to this day (as discussed in the next section). Charney notes that from Bodawphaya's reign (1782–1819), court attitudes previously hostile to other races—such as the long-standing hostility towards the Mon—gave way to reconstructions highlighting the contributions other races had made to Burmese culture. It also gave way to seeking to assimilate subjugated *lu-myo* (as the Mon had been) into an overarching 'Burmanness' (Charney 2004, p. 9). This charge of 'Burmanization' has been central to the grievances of most ethnic nationalities since Independence, and a key driver of armed ethnic conflict across the country (Houtman 1999; Walton 2013). Certainly, most ethnic Rakhine today have a very deep fear of Burman assimilation, a fear that they will lose the very essence of Rakhine-ness to Burmanization. Their struggle for political autonomy is thus primarily about preserving their history, culture, and identity.

In conclusion then, we find strong evidence that historically Arakan did indeed enjoy substantial independence from central Burma. However, Rakhine nationalism tends to hark back to an idealized history to which they cannot return, and, more significantly, has lost sight of the inclusive cosmopolitanism that was one key to the strength of Mrauk-U. Furthermore, it has a tendency to exaggerate the antiquity of their claim on the land, while ignoring the substantial Muslim presence and influence in the kingdom.

The Burman 'Unity' Narrative

Sources and their Socio-Political Context

This is a good point at which to segue to the Burman 'Unity' narrative, the narrative driving the prioritization of *taing-yin-tha* over citizenship. The nation-building agenda of the Burman-led military and state has been justified for decades using this historical 'unity' narrative. For example, Senior General Than Shwe, former head of the ruling junta (1992–2011), expressed it succinctly in a speech in 1993:

> In the Union of Myanmar where national races [*taing-yin-tha*] are residing, the culture, traditions and customs, language and social systems may appear to be different, but in essence they are all based on the common blood of Union Kinship and Union Spirit like a hundred fruits from a common stem. ... There can be no doubt whatsoever of the fact that our national races have lived together unitedly in the Union of Myanmar since time immemorial. (quoted in Smith 1994, p. 18)

This nation-building narrative commonly draws on the idea that the diverse ethnic groups of Myanmar are a single family of races, one blood with a common historical origin, who lived together in unity and harmony for a very long time—until colonialism turned brother against brother. It suggests that the races have shared the same experiences, and in particular, that Second World War history and the nationalist struggle for independence should bring them together as one unified political community. Most ethnic nationalities explicitly reject this narrative, something eminently borne out by the fact that so many have resorted to armed struggle for decades. Most ethnic minorities resist both this narrative's historical premise and its centralizing implication.

This narrative, heavily promoted by General Ne Win and the Burma Socialist Programme Party (BSPP) after the 1962 coup, draws directly on eighteenth–nineteenth-century Burman chronicles. In other words, they build on a historical continuity. The two most significant Burmese chronicles documenting the history of the kingdoms in central Burma are the *Maha Yazawin* (or *Maha Yazawindawgyi*) and the *Hmannan Yazawin* (or *Hmannan Maha Yazawindawgyi* (*The Glass Palace Chronicle*, trans. Pe Maung Tin & Luce 1923). The first of these, the *Maha Yazawin*, was compiled in 1724 by U Kala, a court historian during the dying days of the Toungoo dynasty (1510–1752). The second, the *Hmannan Yazawin*, was commissioned by King Bodawphaya immediately after losing his first war with the British in 1824–6, to re-establish the legitimacy of the dynasty by drawing on traditional religious and cultural–historical criteria. The political motive of both is clear.

The name *Maha Yazawin* implies a long history covering multiple dynasties and royal cities, perhaps best translated as 'chronicle of kings in a series of royal cities' (Kirichenko 2009). In compiling his history, U Kala appears to have done something new in Burmese history: he sought to synthesize regional and foreign histories into the Burman accounts he had received (Pe Maung Tin & Luce 1923; Lieberman 2003). Perhaps this was the impact of modernity on Burmese history making; or perhaps he set out with an agenda to bring the feuding Burman, Shan, and Mon elites closer together. Either way, the impression we have from U Kala (correct or otherwise) is that it would be wrong to characterize the kingdoms in central Burma as solely or primarily Burman (as we have tended to do in the previous chapters).

According to U Kala's text, the kingdoms were never particularly constituted along ethnic lines as we know them, but built more on loyalties that transcended race. Shan and Mon interests, at least, also feature greatly throughout the histories of central Burma—or at least they do in U Kala's *Yazawin*. In one sense, we do not know enough about prior chronicling to know whether he introduced this element or whether it was always there, because most of his original sources were destroyed by a fire in Ava just twenty years after he finished. As a result, as Lieberman (2003, p. 198) notes, 'rarely has a national historiographic tradition depended so heavily on a single author as the Burmese tradition has on U Kala'. Since then, most subsequent Burmese chronicles and histories have largely reproduced his pre-1712 history verbatim, except for a few interpolations of quasi-legendary material, limited digressions on points of scholarly dispute, and a few updates of dates based on new epigraphic evidence.

If U Kala's 1724 *Maha Yazawin* synthesized Burmese history with Mon, Shan, and to some extent Arakanese accounts, drawing into the text some of that material but also reinterpreting it, then the *Hmannan Yazawin* went further. The Royal Historical Commission was charged with compiling the *Hmannan* immediately after Arakan and Mon were ceded to the British in 1824. They made extensive use of U Kala's chronicle, but also hundreds of inscriptions, older Burmese documents, local pagoda histories, regional chronicles such as the new Arakanese *Razawin*, Burmese poetical literature, and so on (Thaw Kaung 2010; Hla Pe 1985). The central aim was to legitimize the Konbaung dynasty's expansionist wars and aspirations (which had included the conquest of Arakan forty years earlier), by portraying central Burma as the centre from which other regional kingdoms originated and on which they depended.

Both these chronicles thus developed a centralizing narrative about Burman hegemony over a group of surrounding kingdoms, portrayed as sharing a common origin and history (Charney 2000, 2002, 2004). One aspect of this, as discussed above, was the framing of *lu-myo* so as to give hegemony to the central Burmese kings, legitimizing conquest. It is significant that the literati compiling the *Hmannan* consulted the *Rakhine Razawin Haung* repeatedly (Charney 2004, p. 8), yet rejected the Arakanese interpretation of the *lu-myo* as equals—presenting the counter-idea that the Burman provided the first kings for surrounding states. Charney (2002) gives the example that the founder of the second Danyawaddy dynasty in Arakan (first millennia CE) is portrayed as the son of the founder of the Tagaung kingdom in central Burma. The importance of this is elevated by the fact that it is one of Burma's most important origin myths. In this way, both U Kala's chronicle and the *Hmannan* incorporate a number of stories legitimizing a superior–inferior cultural hierarchy, and emphasize historical periods of Burman rule over surrounding kingdoms such as Arakan. Examples include neighbouring kingdoms allegedly inviting the Burman to rule their land, and a string of Burman-sponsored kings being placed on their thrones (Charney 2000, p. 55)—mostly in stark contradiction to the accounts in Arakanese and other regional historical records.

Common Ancestry, Related Peoples

The point of all this is simply that the Burmese chronicles gave hegemony to Burman rulers, legitimizing their conquests and the assimilation of other kingdoms. They did this through a historical narrative that subsequently became embedded into the modus operandi of Burman nationalism and the Burmese military/state. Central to this narrative are claims that the Burmese races share a common ancestry and historical unity, a claim used widely since Independence to convey expectations that the minority ethnic nationalities should willingly unite under Burman leadership to form a political community, the 'Union of Myanmar'.

This mythical union of the Burmese races was a theme taken up very actively by General Ne Win, after his 1962 coup. Ne Win drew very explicitly on chronicle imagery, proposing that the new socialist economy would be achieved when the various national races returned to their supposed unity prior to colonial occupation. Cheesman (2017) has documented the extent to which this dogma became embedded in Burma Socialist Programme Party publications of the 1960s–1980s, including most history texts of the period. For example, in 1967 the BSPP published a series of books exploring the economic, social, cultural, and religious commonalities of the *taing-yin-tha* (national races), imagining that:

> From the beginning they lived together in the land of this Union as kinfolk and brethren. Up until the time that the imperialists arrived in Burma, *taingyintha* lived closely with one another through weal and woe. …[Thereafter] outside instigation combined with landlordism and the evil capitalist system stirred up this country in which *taingyintha* had lived in mutual harmony through weal and woe, and the connections between *taingyintha* were broken, leading them to be ignorant of the lives of one other, and sadly, to the disintegrating of *taingyintha* unity. (BSPP 1967, pp. i–iii, cited in Cheesman 2017, p. 466)

This idea became embedded in the preamble to the 1974 constitution, which proclaimed: 'We the people ... have throughout history lived in harmony and unity....' By the 1980s it permeated all official publications (Cheesman 2017). When the new regime seized power in 1988, lacking a coherent philosophy of their own, they drew on this ideology to justify taking power. Their Three Main National Causes, plastered over every newsprint, book, and media publication for two decades, included the idea of the 'non-disintegration' of this mythical historical unity of 'national [*taing-yin-tha*] solidarity' (see Minye Kaungbon 1994 for a detailed exposition of this ideology). Indeed, this cause remains central to the Tatmadaw's mission today, and was cemented in the 2008 constitution.

Thus from the chronicles, to Ne Win, to Than Shwe, to the 1974 and 2008 constitutions, to the ideology of the Three National Causes, this myth has presented a common ancestry and shared history of the *taing-yin-tha* races, to be nurtured under Burman hegemony. A sense of common identity is essential for any successful nation-state, and attempts to forge an enduring political entity out of the diverse array of tribal and ethnic groups at Independence are admirable. However, this attempt, based on a dubious historical narrative constructed from half-truths, fails because it is both highly centralizing and inherently exclusionary.

Evidence for a common ancestry and shared history of the *taing-yin-tha* is very tenuous. As Smith (1991, 1994) has clearly articulated, Burma is one of the most ethnically diverse countries in the world, and historically the major groups are only sometimes closely related (ignoring more recent intermarriage). Waves of settlers migrated into Burma from diverse backgrounds, in different eras. Thus while Burman, Rakhine, Chin, Kachin, and Karen do belong to the Tibeto-Burman language family, for example, and therefore are almost certainly related in the distant past, that common ancestry is believed to have originated somewhere on the Himalayan plateau at least three millennia ago (Matisoff 2016). This Tibeto-Burman family also includes many other peoples in Tibet, China, India, and peninsula Asia, other races that the Burman 'Unity' narrative seeks to exclude—while the Karen, Kachin, and Chin languages are as distinct from Burmese as Burmese is from most Himalayan languages (Handel 2008). Furthermore, the Mon belongs to the Mon–Khmer family, not Tibeto-Burman, suggesting that they are descendants of a totally different South East Asian civilization. Recent scholarship also points to Shan being from the Austronesian arm of the Mon–Khmer/Austroasiatic family, thus even less related (Sagart 2005; Solnit & Li 2007). In other words, the Burmans appear to be more closely related biologically and linguistically to the Han Chinese than the Mon or Shan. Even if we go back to the time when the Mesopotamian empires flourished, before the rise of ancient Egypt, many of Myanmar's ethnic races were already separate. Any common ancestry that includes the Mon and Shan with the Burman, Rakhine, Karen, Kachin, and Chin probably dates to the Neolithic era, and includes most of contemporary Asia.

Even interpreting the narrative as liberally as possible, as a shared history beyond racial lines, commonality and unity is as much myth as anything. Clearly, many Kachin, Karen, Rakhine, and others very strongly disagree with the unity myth, claiming a largely autonomous past only periodically dominated by the expansionism of the Burman kings. Shan and Mon history may be a little more intertwined with the Burman, but their armed resistance belies the fact that they too feel that their history justifies autonomy more than common unity. Claims by most ethnic nationalities to distinct cultural, religious, ethnic, and political histories have driven decades of armed struggle for autonomy.

Similarly, not all nationalities even share recent history in the same way. For example, the BSPP claimed that 'throughout Burma's history all *taingyintha* of Burma have been united in solidarity, both in their resistance to imperialist invaders and in the defence of sovereignty and independence' (BSPP 1971, quoted in Cheesman, 2017, p. 467). But this is simply not true. Most of Burma's ethnic nationalities were on the Allied side during the Second World War, for example, when the Burman initially fought with the Japanese (Smith 1989), and the inter-ethnic armed violence around the Second World War and Independence is well documented.

The most significant problem with this 'Unity' narrative is that it is a contrivance through which political exclusion may be pursued. It redefines the political community away from the notion of citizenship, away from the 101 *lu-myo* of the chronicles (which included Indian kings), away even from the written definition of *taing-yin-tha* (which included all ethnic races settled in Burma before 1823). Instead, this narrative implies that membership in the political community requires shared Mongolian ancestry and being equally united in struggle against the British—criteria which by definition exclude the Muslims of northern Rakhine. It inherently presupposes, for example, that no Aryan race could be indigenous. And it implies the exclusion of groups that did not sufficiently side with Burman nationalists at Independence (even if that was because they feared for their safety at the hands of the military or majority).

Pre-Independence nationalism was actually a hotly contested topic. Many ethnicities had different views, and significant reservations. But this narrative glosses over these differences for some groups while marginalizing others, almost on a whim. And most specifically, it deliberately leaves no room for the inclusion of more recent migrant groups—particularly descendants of Chinese and Indians who migrated during the colonial era. Seven decades after Independence, all colonial-era migrants should have full citizenship and equal rights. Thus, any Muslims whose forbears arrived in northern Rakhine State in the colonial era or earlier should already have those rights.

Based on this narrative, Ne Win's post-1962 regime arrested and imprisoned thousands of non-*taing-yin-tha*, and forced hundreds of thousands more out of the country (Cheesman 2015; Egreteau 2015; Ho & Chua 2016). Since the 1970s it has been used primarily to exclude the Muslims of northern Rakhine State. According to Cheesman:

> Seen from inside the *taingyintha* truth regime, any claim to be Rohingya is not only to insist upon a falsehood, but also to be at once dangerous and illegal: it is an identity that is both politically and juridically unacceptable. Those people who accept that they are 'Bengali' are entitled to present their credentials for citizenship on a case-by-case basis. But any assertions of a collective right to political membership by virtue of being *taingyintha* will not be tolerated, not for any logical reason but because according to the truth regime it must be so. (Cheesman 2017, p. 474)

This narrative, despite being built on such falsehoods, allows many in Myanmar to trivialize, excuse, or even justify the horrific treatment of the people who call themselves 'Rohingya', culminating in the desperate flight across the Bangladeshi border in 2017 of over 670,000 refugees. Careful analysis of the conflict must understand how this narrative justifies and defines perception of the Burmans, and to some extent, the perceptions of nationalities in Myanmar.

The Rakhine–Burman 'Infiltration' Narrative

Sources and their Socio-Political Context

This brings us to our final historical narrative. Most authors presenting this 'Infiltration' narrative are ethnic Rakhine, but the same ideas are increasingly being adopted by Burman Buddhist nationalists. This narrative argues that there has been an 'infiltration' of Bengali Muslims into Rakhine over the last century or two, continuing right up to the 2017 crisis. It suggests that many, if not most, of the people claiming to be 'Rohingya' are Bengali migrants, many very recent and often illegal, and that they comprise such numbers (and have such a high birth rate) that they threaten to overwhelm the Rakhine people. They are seen to pose a threat to both Buddhism and national security. This narrative seeks to correct the record, as they see it, by directly combating falsehoods in the 'Origin' narrative, presenting evidence of recent immigration rather than four waves of Muslim migration centuries ago. (Note that, as per the last chapter, in presenting this narrative we allow use of the name 'Bengali' for the Muslims of northern Rakhine State where this reflects the usage of authors of this narrative. This is not as a political statement, but to allow their voice, in their terminology.)

The key authors and most detailed publications include:

- Shwe Zan drafted perhaps the first such document in 1988, entitled 'Study of Muslim Infiltration into Rakhine State'. This was originally only privately circulated, but a revised version was later published in *Influx Viruses: The Illegal Muslims in Arakan* (Shwe Zan & Aye Chan 2005).
- Khin Maung Saw's 1993 conference paper entitled 'The "Rohingyas", Who are they? The Origin of the Name "Rohingya"' (Khin Maung Saw 1994), then a whole series of unpublished documents including 'Islamization of Burma through Chittagonian Bengalis as "Rohingya Refugees"' (2011) and Khin Maung Saw (2005, 2013, 2014). He also wrote two books entitled *Arakan, a Neglected Land and her Voiceless People* (2015) and *Behind the Mask: The Truth Behind the Name 'Rohingya'* (2016).
- Aye Chan, perhaps the most reasoned advocate of this position, wrote 'The Development of a Muslim Enclave in Arakan (Rakhine) State of Burma (Myanmar)' (2005), then a series of papers including

'Rohingya: More a Political Rhetoric than an Ethnic Identity' (2009). See also Aye Chan (2011, 2012), but note that his 2005 paper was republished together with Shwe Zan's paper under the highly provocative title *Influx Viruses: The Illegal Muslims in Arakan* (Shwe Zan & Aye Chan 2005).

- Maung Tha Hla's two books, *The Rakhaing* (2004) and *The Rohingya Hoax* (2009).

- Khaing Myo Saung's *The Bad Colonial Heritage of Arakan and the Expansion of the Bengali Muslims of Chittagong* (in Burmese, 2012; cited in Leider 2015).

One other notable document promoting this narrative is the RNDP (2012) report entitled *Criticizing the Historical Fabrication of Bengali who Assume Themselves as Rohingya and Pretend Themselves to be Taing-yin-thar*, circulated to cabinet ministers and Nay Pyi Taw members of parliament in May 2012 (Thawnghmung 2016). This report was in response to the report a month earlier, entitled *In Respect of the Fact that the Muslim Inhabitants of Rakhine State are Natives by Race and Citizens of the Republic of the Union of Myanmar under Law or by Natural Birth* (NDPD 2012).

The socio-political context of these publications is clear. Shwe Zan's 1988 piece commences with reference to Ba Tha's *A Short History of Rohingya and Kamans of Burma* (Tahir 1998 [1963]), positioning the whole genre as a response to the 'Rohingya' narratives discussed in the last chapter. His revised piece (Shwe Zan 2005) adds mention of the 1991–2 exodus. This paper, together with Khin Maung Saw's 1993 discussion of the origin of the name 'Rohingya', is clearly in many respects a response to the advocacy and international pressure that forced the return of 200,000 Bengali who had fled in 1991–2. The remainder, all written since the mid-2000s, provide a direct counter to the growing voice of Muslim advocates in the West, after significant numbers of Rohingya were resettled in Western countries and are gaining increasing voice.

The 'Infiltration' Narrative

The central message of this narrative is that not only are the Bengalis far too recent migrants to be a *taing-yin-tha*, but that the rapid growth of the population since Independence demonstrates that many are illegal immigrants. They discuss the colonial, civil war, and subsequent history, and argue that the illegal Bengali migrants must not be allowed to gain citizenship by deception. Therefore, they argue, a thorough document verification process is required for the entire Muslim population in Rakhine State, to work out who would be eligible to apply for citizenship and who should be permanently expelled from Myanmar. Bengalis should only be accepted as Myanmar citizens if they strictly meet the requirements of the 1982 Citizenship Law. Many also argue that measures must be undertaken to restrict the Bengalis' excessive population growth and birth rate, which threatens to overwhelm Rakhine cultural and ethnic identity, as well as land and resources.

Most Rakhine historians do accept that some Muslims lived in Arakan during the Mrauk-U Kingdom, but the Muslim population and influence is minimized in their accounts prior to the mass migration during the British era (see ARDHO 2013; Aye Chan 2005; Khin Maung Saw 2005; Shwe Zan & Aye Chan 2005). The RNDP (2012) denies the existence of a long-established Islamic presence in the region, claiming that there is no evidence of any prior to the Mrauk-U period. These Rakhine historians either argue that the pre-1823 Muslims are not the ancestors of the Bengalis, only of other Muslim groups in the country such as the Kaman, or that only a very tiny minority of Bengalis in northern Rakhine are their descendants. Rather, their narrative is that the Bengalis are in Myanmar as the result of British-sponsored immigration, undertaken to enable agricultural expansion during the colonial era—or are refugees from the 1971 Pakistan–Bangladesh civil war, and illegal immigrants from overpopulated Bangladesh. They thus argue that the Rohingya are recent Bengali migrants, who deceptively adopt the history of a small number of pre-colonial Muslims as their own. The previous discussion demonstrates that this is an overstatement, with more Muslims having been in Arakan prior to the British takeover than is admitted here; yet the narrative contains a kernel of truth.

Many Rakhine—and some Burmans—hold a deep fear that they will be overrun by the Bengalis. Surveys conducted in 2012 by the Rakhine Inquiry Commission (UoM 2013) found that 84.7 per cent of Rakhine respondents attributed the violence to alleged Bengali efforts to take over the state. In May 2015, for example, in response to the three Nobel Peace Prize laureates' declaration that the Rohingya face 'nothing less than genocide' (AP 2015), the Rakhine Affairs Minister for Yangon Region said that if genocide was taking place in Rakhine State, then it was against ethnic Rakhine, not the Muslims (Schissler et al. 2015). Such a statement illustrates that local perceptions of victim and violator are diametrically opposed to the image presented in international discourse.

Rakhine histories argue that it is the Rakhine people, not the Bengalis, who are the real victims, robbed of their ancestral homeland, property, and livelihoods by endless Bengali migration. They have been systematically stripped of their rights, property, and identity by the incoming human tide since the colonial period—and particularly via the 1942 massacres. For example, the RNDP (2012) response to Muslim claims that they are a *taing-yin-tha* provides a list of the 140 key villages in Maungdaw Township and notes that 126 of them have Rakhine names, but only 14 have Bengali names, despite the township now being 95 per cent Bengali (Thawnghmung 2016).

These historians thus portray a real sense of existential threat, that they are being progressively displaced from their homeland by a burgeoning Bengali presence. For example, just after winning the April 2017 by-election in the seat of Ann, Dr Aye Maung, Chairman of the Arakan National Party, told *7Day News* that the western part of the country was 'at risk of being conquered' by foreign Muslim intruders. Rakhine State is often referred to as the country's 'Western Gate', the front line in a battle to protect Myanmar from an invasion described as both external, via migration, and internal, via rapid birth rate, interfaith marriage, and forced conversions (Schissler et al. 2015).

Demographic Analysis

It is thus important to determine whether the Muslim population in northern Rakhine State has indeed burgeoned since the British took control, and if it continued to do so until 2017. This is important because, assuming that all those who have fled to Bangladesh eventually do return, the question will resurface as to whether the Muslim population is growing at a rate that threatens to completely overrun the local Rakhine Buddhist population.

A wealth of population data was collected during the colonial era, but much of it varies significantly in rigour and adopts very different classifications around race. Colonial-era data records never used the term 'Rohingya' (Tonkin 2014b), and the ancestors of today's 'Rohingya' appear to be captured under one or more labels such as 'Arakanese Mohammadan', 'Chittagonian', 'Indian', 'Bengali', and so on. The 1931 census, for example, listed 51,615 'Arakan Mohamedans', 252,152 'Chittagonians', and 65,211 'Bengalis'. But there is considerable dispute even by Muslims over which labels refer to 'Rohingya' ancestors, which to seasonal labourers, etc. The definitions for these terms also appear to have changed over time, making it difficult to compare figures directly. This also allows those on both sides to cherry-pick figures.

For example, Charney (1999, p. 264) estimated no more than 20 per cent of Muslims across the state at the end of the seventeenth century. Paton (1826, p. 36), the first British commissioner of Arakan, estimated that 30 per cent of the population was Muslim, based on a quick tour of Arakan immediately after capture. Just a few years later, however, Colonial District Officer Phayre estimated the Indian-descent population of the state at only 15 per cent, not all of whom were Muslim, and added that 'since the conquest of Arakan by the English, a large number of Bengalees have settled' (Phayre 1841, p. 682), suggesting that the 1823 figure was much lower. Thus there is considerable variation even in the first few figures, ranging from something well under 15 per cent up to 30 per cent. The first firm data was the 1872 census, which put the percentage of Muslims in Arakan at 13.28 per cent (Duncan 1875, p. 8), suggesting a figure of no more than 10–13 per cent in 1823.

Fortunately, the colonial authorities did conduct detailed censuses every decade from 1872 until 1941. Smart (1917, pp. 84–6) compiled population and race data from these and the most reliable prior data for Akyab District (approximately central and northern Rakhine State today). His figures for total population are presented in Table 3, to which we have added 1911, 1921, and 1931 census data. What this shows is a rapid increase in the whole population from the commencement of the colonial period; there was an exceptionally high rate during the 1840s. The population doubled in just twenty years, between 1832 and 1852. This is consistent with reports that the region was largely depopulated at the time the British took control, and that many of those displaced by the

Burman occupation returned. It also shows the result of the rapid, massive British agricultural expansion. It is consistent with mass immigration of labourers from elsewhere in British India, as Akyab (Sittwe) quickly became the largest rice exporter in the world during the 1840s. (With the exception of Tenassrim, the rest of Burma was not at that time part of British India.) Population growth in Arakan slowed after the second Anglo-Burmese War, in 1852, after which Rangoon overtook Arakan as the chief rice-exporting hub. Nonetheless, Arakan's population still continued to grow strongly.

Table 3: Overall population estimates for Akyab District, Arakan

Year	Population	Decadal Increase (number)	Increase (per cent)
1832	109,645	—	—
1842	130,034	20,389	18.6%
1852	201,677	71,643	55.1%
1862	227,231	25,554	12.7%
1872	276,671	49,440	21.8%
1881	359,706	83,035	30.0%
1891	416,305	56,599	15.7%
1901	481,666	65,361	15.7%
1911	529,943	48,277	10.0%
1921	576,430	49,487	9.33%
1931	637,580	61,150	10.6%

Source: 1832–62 data from estimates in *British Burma Gazetteer* reports and 1872–1901 from census data, both as reported by Smart (1917, p. 84); 1911–21 data from Grantham's census report (1923, p. 6), and 1931 census data from Bennison (1931, pp. 2–6).

An even clearer picture emerges when we look at Smart's analysis of the race data from the 1872, 1901, and 1911 censuses. His analysis is particularly useful, as it was conducted before the Second World War and the extreme nationalism of the 1920s, and thus before any contemporary narratives began to seriously colour interpretations. His findings are summarized in Table 4.

From the 1921 census, data about religion is more accessible than race data. Table 5 reports 1921 and 1931 census data. The 1941 census was interrupted by the Second World War.

Table 4: Comparison of the 1872, 1901, and 1911 census data for Akyab District, Arakan

Race	1872 Census	1901 Census	1911 Census
Arakanese	171,612 (62.0%)	239,649 (49.8%)	209,432 (39.5%)
Mahomedan	58,225 (21.0%)	154,887 (32.2%)	178,647 (33.7%)
Burmese	4,632 (1.7%)	35,751 (7.4%)	92,185 (17.4%)
Hindu	2,655 (1.0%)	14,455 (3.0%)	14,454 (2.7%)
Other	39,547 (14.3%)	36,924 (7.7%)	35,225 (6.6%)
Total	276,671 (100.0%)	481,666 (100.0%)	529,943 (100.0%)

Source: Smart (1917, p. 86).

Table 5: Comparison of religion data from the 1921 and 1931 census, Akyab District, Arakan

Religion	1921 Census	1931 Census
Buddhist	315,140 (54.5%)	337,661 (53.0%)
Mahomedan	208,961 (36.1%)	242,381 (38.0%)
Animist	36,806 (6.4%)	40,038 (6.3%)
Hindu	14,719 (2.5%)	16,685 (2.6%)
Other	814 (0.1%)	815 (0.1%)
Total	578,361 (100.0%)	637,580 (100.0%)

Sources: (Grantham 1923, pp. 24–5; Bennison 1931, pp. 238–9).

Comparing the Muslim data across Tables 4 and 5 presents a compelling picture. The Muslim population in northern Arakan clearly grew much faster than the Burman–Arakanese Buddhist population. In absolute numbers, Muslims grew more than fourfold between 1872 and 1931, while the Buddhist population grew less than twofold. They shot as a proportion of the population from 21 to 38 per cent. It is thus quite understandable that many Arakanese might have felt that their land was being overrun by Muslims: in a real sense, it was.

The 1931 census found that 92.7 per cent of people in Akyab District were born in Burma (Bennison 1931, p. 28), meaning that by then Chittagonian seasonal labourers were only a very small proportion of the Muslim population in Akyab. Almost all were born in Arakan—even if most families had migrated from India in the earlier part of the colonial period.

This data contradicts the 'Rohingya' narrative claims they are not the descendants of migrants. The colonial administration so heavily promoted Indian migration that during the early 1900s Burma had the world's highest rate of migration, outstripping even New York (Charney 2009; Taylor 2009). By 1921 some 55 per cent of Rangoon was Indian (Charney 2009), and 480,000 new Indian migrants arrived in Burma during the year 1927 alone (Hall 1956, p. 159). It would be most astounding if Arakan did not have similar rapid Indian migration—and, unsurprisingly, the evidence does not support the 'Rohingya' narrative on this point. Instead, it strongly suggests that by the end of the colonial era the vast majority of Muslims in northern Rakhine State were the descendants of colonial-era migrants.

The implications of this high rate of immigration did eventually come to concern to the colonial authorities. In his report on the 1911 census, Webb expressed concern that, due to Bengali immigration, 'if the present tendencies continue, the existence of the Arakan as a separate branch of the Burma racial group will cease in the ordinary course of time' (Webb 1912, pp. 190, 257; see also Leider 2015). Smart, reflecting back on earlier records, commented:

> In 1879 it was recorded that those who were bona fide residents, though recruited [into seasonal agricultural work] by immigrants from Bengal, were, for the most part, descendants of slaves captured by the Arakanese and Burmese in their wars with their neighbours. ... They differ little from the Arakanese except in their religion and in the social customs which their religion directs; in writing they use Burmese, but amongst themselves employ colloquially the language of their ancestors. Since 1879 immigration has taken place on a much larger scale and the descendants of the slaves are resident, for the most part, in the Kyauktaw and Myohaung [Mrauk U] townships. Maungdaw township has been overrun by Chittagonian immigrants. Buthidaung is not far behind and new arrivals will be found in almost every part of the district. (Smart 1917, pp. 89–90)

Financial Secretary James Baxter's *Report on Indian Immigration* expressed concern that the high rate of Muslim migration from Chittagong was problematic and 'contained the seed of future communal troubles' (Baxter 1941). Unfortunately, it seems that these concerns have now come to fruition, compounded by almost a century of state-sponsored discrimination.

So, has the population continued to explode since Independence? Or has it only grown in line with the Buddhist population since then? Burma/Myanmar has only conducted three censuses since Independence: in 1973, 1983, and 2014. The 1973 census (UoB 1973) did not break down religion or race data to the state or district level, so we do not have data. The 1983 census (UoB 1983) gives religion data at the state level, but not ethnicity. Religion data can also be interpolated for the 2014 census, using their estimate of 1,090,000 people not enumerated in northern Rakhine State as representing the size of the Muslim population for the state, plus the Kaman. Table 6 thus provides estimates of the proportion of the Muslim population in the whole of Arakan/Rakhine as well as Akyab District, adding data from the religion tables from the 1921, 1931, 1983, and 2014 censuses and summarizing the data above. The continuing increase in the Muslim proportion of the population is very apparent.

Table 6: Comparison of the proportion of Muslims in Akyab District and the whole of Arakan/Rakhine, 1826–2014

Census	Akyab District (Northern Rakhine)	Whole of Arakan/Rakhine
1826 (estimate)	–	(10–13%)
1872	21.0%	13.3%
1901	32.2%	–
1911	33.7%	–
1921	36.1%	24.0%
1931	38.0%	25.3%
1983	–	28.5%
2014	–	35.1%

Sources: Duncan (1875, p. 8); Smart (1917, p. 86); Grantham (1923, pp. 24–5); Bennison (1931, pp. 238–9), UoB (1983, pp. 1–16); UoM (2016, pp. 2–3).

Origin of the 'Rohingya' Name and Identity

All this data leads us to draw several significant conclusions. First, there is strong evidence of a reasonable population of Muslims in Arakan before the British took possession, mostly descendants of slaves. The Burman–Rakhine are wrong to dismiss the existence and history of this pre-1823 Muslim population. However, the evidence suggests that this population was something around 10–13 per cent of the population of Arakan in 1823. However—and importantly—our second conclusion is that this initial population was swamped by a huge influx of Muslim immigrants from British India during the colonial era, particularly Bengalis and Chittagonians. They migrated mainly during the first five decades or so of colonial rule, settled in Arakan, and became the majority of the Muslim population in northern Rakhine State. The Muslims are wrong to downplay the size of this migration. The logical conclusion, expressed most eloquently by Leider (2015; also 2014, 2017a), is that the history presented by the Rohingya is a 'hybridized history', in which the majority of settlers deny their migrant origins and claim the history of the pre-existing minority community as their own, for political purposes. The migrants have grafted themselves onto the pre-existing community, mostly descendants of slaves forcibly relocated. Concern about this was expressed as early as 1960, when Seit Twe Maung (1960) expressed concern at the extent to which 'Chittagonian settlers' had usurped the identity of 'indigenous Arakanese Muslims'.

The idea that this hybridized community is a distinct ethnic group called 'Rohingya' appears to date from the early twentieth century. Historically, the name 'Rohingya' appears to be derived from the Bengali pronunciation of an old name for 'Rakhine' (see earlier discussion of Buchanan 1799). As an official name for the Muslims of northern Arakan, the term, even the spelling, was debated by Muslim leaders and students during the late 1950s and early 1960s (Leider 2018a; Tonkin 2018). For example, the spelling 'Rwangya' was noted immediately after the war, and Tahir (Ba Tha) used the name 'Roewhengyas' for several years before switching to 'Rohingya' only in the 1963 document discussed in Chapter 3. One of the name's earlier publicly recorded uses was on 10 March 1950, when a group calling themselves the Rohingya Elders of North Arakan gave an official address to Prime Minister U Nu in Maungdaw (Jilani 1999, pp. 462–3). Tonkin (2018) finds not a single reference to the name in any official records or private correspondence during the colonial era. Rather, a political movement appears to have emerged around the name in the 1950s. Leider (2015) notes many examples of major declarations by Muslim leaders from northern Arakan during the 1950s that do not use the term, giving strong evidence that the name was not popularized before the 1960s. Indeed, it is not, evidence would thus suggest, a deeply historical name for a distinct and indigenous ethnic group, but a newer name coined to describe what we would suggest is 'an emerging ethnicity', forged by the socio-political imperatives of the past century.

Many Rakhine writers see a sinister motive in this. For example, Maung Tha Hla expresses his views in *The Rohingya Hoax* that to him the name 'Rohingya' is

> a belied term employed by the alien Muslim separatists, with the object of advancing a legal claim to ethnic grouping of the Union of Burma [*sic*] … synonym of alien Chittagonian separatists or jihadist Mujtahid … an ethnological fraud … devised by the pugnatious [*sic*] Chittagonian Muslims … to win a free Islamic enclave in the Rakhaing [*sic*] State … pretence of a new race … in order to give a legitimate reason for the institutionalization of them as an ethnic group of Burma in support of their demand for the Muslim state. (Maung Tha Hla 2009, pp. 10–11)

This claim, however, is highly problematic. While the 'Rohingya' narrative is based partially on falsehood, any extent to which it is a political ploy is only to gain their legitimate political rights. Any recourse to falsehood or manipulation should never have been necessary. The citizenship laws at Independence granted full citizenship to anyone who had been resident in Burma in the last seven of the ten years prior to either the Second World War or Independence. Citizenship laws since then have all allowed pathways for migrants to become citizens. Under any of these laws, even those Muslim migrant settlers resident in Burma for a generation or more before Independence should already have citizenship, let alone those whose ancestors were in Burma pre-1823. On this basis, only a small number of cases should be under any question. But decades of systemic discrimination, marginalization, and disenfranchisement, particularly under Ne Win's tenure, rather than the migrant past of some of the Muslims, has led to the current political nightmare. Furthermore, granting citizenship should have bestowed equal rights within the political community, rather than being trumped by exclusionary *taing-yin-tha* politics based on dubious mythology. In other words, it is our opinion that the necessity for the Muslims to adopt a hybridized history was driven by the discrimination, marginalization, and ethnic politics perpetrated by the Burman and Rakhine, and was primarily created to try to lay hold of rights they should already have had, by law.

This brings us to the end of our two chapters on historical narratives. The reason we have given such a detailed discussion of history is not because we believe that everything about the conflict can be explained or encapsulated by history, but because most key actors—especially most Muslim advocates—appeal so frequently and continuously to history to express their grievances and claims. Some tend to assume that history alone is enough to understand why conflict rages. That is not our argument. Our argument is that this is how many key actors—especially Muslim advocates—articulate their grievances and claims, so we need to start with their understanding and analysis of their perspectives. Our critiques and recommendations only have relevance when anchored in these articulations, and in our view much more detailed examination of history is one important, largely overlooked, component in moving towards a long-term resolution to this conflict (Leider 2018b). However, history is only one factor, and cannot explain all aspects of the contemporary situation, and is not enough to resolve the conflict. Not everything is path dependent. The next part, therefore, explores a range of other analytical perspectives, to broaden our analysis and understanding.

PART III

CONFLICT ANALYSIS

PHILOSOPHICAL LANDSCAPE
OF CONFLICT ANALYSIS THEORY

The previous part examined in detail the competing historical narratives underlying this conflict, narratives recited ad nauseam by many advocates to express their understanding of the origins and nature of the conflict, and to articulate their grievances and claims. As a long-running, intractable conflict, historical narratives and collective memory are heavily co-opted by each side, to mobilize both internal and external support. Understanding these narratives is necessary, but not sufficient, to a robust understanding of the contemporary conflict.

This section thus moves beyond this critique and deconstruction of historical narratives, to analyse the conflict against a range of theoretical academic models. But what theoretical lens should we adopt? There are many. Scholars have debated ways to understand and analyse conflict for millennia.

Surveying the philosophical landscape of conflict analysis, there are two major dichotomies in the way scholars have attempted to explain conflict and collective violence: one ontological, the other epistemological (Webb 1995). Ontological theories of conflict fall across a spectrum of 'agency' and 'structure'. Agency is generally taken to refer to the capacity of individuals to act independently and make free choices on their own, in ways that influence events. Structure, by contrast, refers to the recurrent patterned socio-political arrangements that appear to influence or limit the choices, actions, and opportunities of individuals. Most modern social theorists take structure and agency as complementary forces (Jary & Jary 1991). For example, Giddens' (1984) 'structuration theory' proposes a 'duality of structure' in which social structure is both the medium and outcome of agency—in other words, structure and agency are interdependent.

Epistemologically, scholars of conflict and violence oscillate between accounts that try to *explain* the social world and accounts that try to *understand* social action. Explanatory theories are premised on the idea that social action can be analysed with reference to a series of causal laws that cut across human space and time, and are thus timeless and ahistorical. By discovering such laws, the presumption is that not only is it possible to investigate and explain social action, but also to predict future action that falls within similar scenarios. On the antipode of causal explanation, there are theories that look at the meaning of social action. Shared values, rules, and ideas shape the context of meaning within which humans act. Social meaning is thus historically and culturally specific, and can be only studied within a certain time and space—that is, within a certain historical and spatial context. Therefore, we need to take into account the perspectives of the social actors and the way they are manifested in certain episodes of social reality.

This section examines a wide range of these conflict analysis approaches, exploring how well they apply to Myanmar's 'Rohingya' conflict, drawing from both agency and structural approaches that attempt to either explain or understand the conflict. Chapter 5 considers the mutual existential fears triggered by a tripartite security dilemma scenario, the role of the state, and the economic aspects of the conflict from greed and political economy perspectives. Chapter 6 then analyses the conflict in terms of ethnicity, identity, and territorial grievances.

5

SECURITY DILEMMA, MINORITY COMPLEX, GREED, AND POLITICAL ECONOMY

This chapter explores the nature of the conflict against the concepts of demographic and ethnic security dilemma, dual minority complex, the role of the state, the 'greed' argument, and a political economy approach. The tripartite security dilemma and minority complex ideas illuminate the deep sense of existential threat experienced by all parties. We then move into a discussion about the role of the state in the conflict, then the economic aspects of the conflict, analysing from 'greed thesis' and political economy perspectives. The next chapter will consider the 'grievance' arguments of identity, ethnicity, and territory.

A Tripartite Security Dilemma

A useful starting point in examining the conflict is to consider the depth and origin of the main actors' perceptions of existential threat, their sense of struggle for group survival in the face of fears for the future. This is nicely encapsulated in the concepts of 'ethnic security dilemma' and 'minority complex'.

The classic articulation of the 'security dilemma' comes from international relations. It suggests that the anarchical nature of the international system, in which all parties have limited knowledge of other countries' intentions, leads states to maximize their military capability to increase their security and ensure their survival (Herz 1951; Butterfield 1951; Jervis 1976, 1978; Waltz 1979; Mearsheimer 2001). Posen (1993) adapts this concept to intra-state conflict, to explain the ethnic violence that led to the disintegration of both Yugoslavia and the Soviet Union after the Cold War. He proposes that the anarchy that occurs in states during transitions (democratization, collapse, revolution, or regime change) is similar to the anarchy prevailing in the international system. Thus, according to Posen, two conditions are present during transitional periods that amplify the security dilemma between ethnic groups. The first is a heightened level of group awareness and solidarity, which offers a ready ability for offensive or defensive mobilization. Ethnic groups uncertain about each other's intentions will judge the other through the lens of history, often the worst examples of past inter-ethnic relations. The second condition, Posen suggests, is social and geographical isolation, which increases the potential for ethno-nationalist extremism. Groups more segregated from one another, and more isolated from their elite, become more vulnerable to rumour, fear, and overreaction. Segregation and isolation lead groups to take measures to protect themselves, which may be seen as threatening by other groups, creating a security dilemma escalation. Since Posen's original publication, the ethnic security dilemma concept has been employed by numerous scholars as an explanatory tool for ethnic conflict in Yugoslavia, the former Soviet republics, Africa, and the Middle East (de Figueiredo & Weingast 1999; Lake & Rothchild 1996, 2001; Fearon 1998; Fearon & Laitin 1996; Walter 1999a; Roe 1999, 2005).

The Muslim and Buddhist communities in Rakhine State have long experienced a significant degree of segregation, which has been acute since 2012. The authoritarian history of the country has likewise created a sense of isolation between the people of Rakhine and the Burman-led institutions of state. Poverty and geography also isolate rural populations from their elite. Thus, during a time of heightened uncertainty due to political transition, the history of past communal and separatist violence has allowed all three main groups to experience very high levels of perceived threat. Rumour and fear have been rampant. The confluence of segregation, isolation, transition, and troubled history have provided the perfect preconditions for an ethnic security dilemma since 2010.

Figure 1: Asymmetries of power and the tripartite nature of the Rakhine State conflict

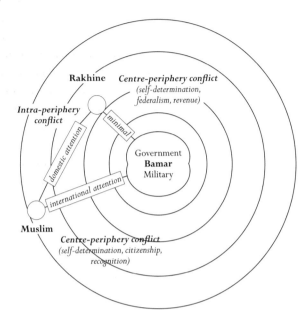

Source: authors' own work.

We have repeatedly described the tripartite nature of the Rakhine State conflict, which exists as three inter-layered but deeply asymmetrical political struggles. This is illustrated in Figure 1. In the following section, we analyse the applicability of an ethnic security dilemma analysis in each of these three axes.

1. Rakhine–Muslim Security Dilemma

The first of these conflict axes is the intra-periphery conflict between the ethnic Rakhine and Muslims. Communal tension between Buddhists and Muslims has a long history, right across Myanmar, since at least the early part of the colonial era (Crouch 2016). We have already noted the massacres and dislocations in Arakan during the Second World War, and the cycles of violence and relative peace every few decades since then. According to the ethnic security dilemma argument, during a time of transition such as post-2010 Myanmar, this history together with high level of segregation predisposes all groups towards a return to violence, when other provocations exist.

The prevailing antipathy between the two groups is about encroachment or disenfranchisement, depending on the perspective. This is complicated by competing territorial claims since Independence. Rakhine and Muslim nationalist insurgencies have already been noted, competing for overlapping territory (Ware 2015). Since before Independence, Rakhine nationalists have fought for control of the whole of Arakan/Rakhine, while Muslim groups have fought for control of northern Rakhine State.

As previously noted, the 2008 constitution makes any *taing-yin-tha* who constitute a majority in two adjacent townships potentially eligible for a 'self-administered zone' (Thawnghmung 2016). The Muslims of northern Rakhine State constitute a third of the state's population, and a majority in the three northern townships of Maungdaw, Buthidaung, and Rathedaung. Were the Muslims granted *taing-yin-tha* status, it would be hard for the government not to also grant them a self-administered zone. This would be in direct violation of the claims made by the Rakhine elite for territorial political control over the whole state. Competing territorial claims and a history of violence therefore stoke existential fears.

This competition has created deep suspicion and distrust, if not outright hostility. Together with debates about citizenship, identities, and now, mass crimes, this distrust has almost obliterated the sharing of information between groups. No group knows whether the other side is intending to, or is even able to, sanction rogue members, an absolutely central requirement to prevent violence spiralling when a few members of one group harm members of the other group (Lake & Rothchild 1996; Fearon & Laitin 1996). This is a key dynamic of the ethnic security dilemma, a loss of confidence and trust resulting in ethnic mobilization against the other at the first sign of threat. The triggering of the 2012 violence captures this perfectly. After the rape and murder of the Rakhine Buddhist woman, and then the reprisal attack on Muslim bus travellers, both groups perceived these incidents as part of orchestrated attacks, and escalated retaliation. Rakhine mobs held the Muslims responsible *in toto*, and Muslim mobs held ethnic

Rakhine responsible *in toto*. Both sides quickly mobilized, with no communication or trust between elites that might facilitate de-escalation. And neither group held any confidence in the Tatmadaw or state institutions to provide justice or security. Similar dynamics contributed to the 2017 crisis.

Asymmetric information also extends vertically within groups, between elites and the masses. Incomplete information has an impact on the mass base of groups. Ethnic entrepreneurs mobilize by propagating narratives that heighten fear and build a perception of insecurity, cultivating notions of victimhood and injustice. This is consistent with Bar-Tal's ideas about the psycho-social factors facilitating mobilization during intractable conflicts. But then, informational gaps create uncertainties about the intentions of their elites, making it highly perilous to assume either peaceful intentions by the other side or elite support. Thus, grassroots (communal) violence becomes a much more likely reaction to any provocation, to protect their own existence (de Figueirdo & Weingast 1999, pp. 271–81).

In Rakhine State, social media further exacerbated this dynamic, helping to spread fear among group members, while the lack of information sharing between groups and vertical information asymmetries with group elites stoked uncertainty. Incomplete pictures of reality in both communities were reinforced by rapid sharing of vivid images, fuelling fears and sharing news of provocations without any indications of how their own elite, security forces, or the other side might act to limit harm or defend them. This, of course, also allowed the promotion of misleading or, in some cases, clearly fictitious, reports, further exacerbating the ethnic security dilemma.

Demographic Security Dilemma

There is one other very relevant version of the security dilemma to explore, what Leuprecht (2010) calls the 'demographic security dilemma'. This is the rising fear between populations based on differential population growth rates. The risk is most acute when one population has reduced its fertility rate, but lives alongside a large minority with a high fertility rate.

Demographic data confirms that the Muslims of northern Rakhine State have much higher fertility and crude birth rates than the Rakhine

Figure 2: Fertility and birth rates across Myanmar

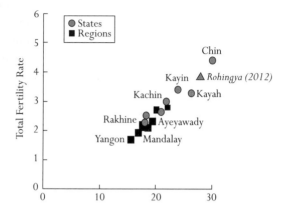

Source: Blomquist & Cincotta (2016). Used with permission.

(Blomquist 2015; Blomquist & Cincotta 2016). Figure 2 shows fertility and birth rates across Myanmar, with data added for the 'Rohingya'. While the Muslim birth rates are no any higher than those of several other minorities from poorly developed parts of Myanmar (e.g. Chin, Kayin, and Kayah), they are considerably higher than that of the Rakhine, making a demographic security dilemma scenario plausible.

A typical response by governments in such situations is to implement stringent population-control policies. However, Leuprecht argues that this is a high-risk strategy, just as likely to stoke violence as to succeed in reducing tensions. In Myanmar, the previous government passed four Race and Religion Protection Laws in 2015, primarily in response to fears over this Muslim demographic security dilemma in Rakhine State. One of these allows local authorities to require children be spaced thirty-six months apart anywhere it is deemed that population growth rates, or rising infant or maternal mortality rates, are negatively impacting regional development (Zaw 2015). There are no penalties enshrined in the legislation, but there are fears that children born outside these rules will be at risk of not being registered by local authorities.

These measures follow other government efforts at demographic engineering in northern Rakhine, dating back to the early 1990s. 'Model villages', often referred to as Na-Ta-La villages, were developed as a way to extend state control into parts of northern Rakhine where its authority was weak (Wade 2017). Land has been progressively taken from Muslim communities, and used for the resettlement of recently released prisoners and homeless Buddhists (both Rakhine and Burman) from other parts of the country. The conditions offered the new settlers have been quite appealing: they have been offered a house, a paddy field, a pair of oxen, and food rations for three years, and only required to reside in northern Rakhine for a minimum three-year period (with the hope they would settle for longer) (Wade 2017). Since about 2008 the government has expanded the Na-Ta-La programme to Buddhists migrating from Bangladesh, mainly those of Rakhine descent. This particular group have been offered enfranchisement after three years' residence; thus the Na-Ta-La villages in northern Rakhine have constituted a quick process for obtaining citizenship (Min Min & Moe Aung 2015). It must be noted, though, that most of the settlers have not possessed the farming knowledge or skills to survive the rural conditions, and often departed the region after the compulsory three-year period (Min Min & Moe Aung 2015).

These measures exemplify the official policy responses aimed at weakening the position of Muslims in northern Rakhine. There is a risk that the demographic security dilemma will escalate already serious tensions in northern Rakhine State, given the demographic age structures of the two main populations, as shown in Figure 3. The largest age group in the Muslim population is the youngest, with every younger age group larger than the next older one. This compares with the Rakhine population, which has brought its birth rate under control in the last decade or so. Thus in the Rakhine community, the number of children now aged four years and below is almost a third less than the number aged between ten and fourteen years. This means that even if population-control policies were successful and brought down the fertility rate (the number of children born per woman) of the Muslims, it will be a couple of decades before the number of Muslim women having children falls. In other words, the age structure shows that the proportion of Muslims will continue to increase for several decades even if the population-control laws are successful. The current four years and below age group will be a bulge of reproductive-age women in a couple of decades. The Rakhine population is likely to stabilize in

Figure 3: Demographic age structure of Rakhine and 'Rohingya' populations

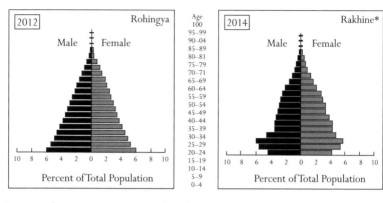

Source: Blomquist (2015). Used with permission, using 2014 census data.

size and then contract in coming decades, while the Muslim population will continue to grow for several more decades first—something which is likely to fuel tensions for decades to come.

The demographic data thus shows that Rakhine fears of a demographic takeover have some merit. Blomquist & Cincotta's (2016) modelling accounts for differential death rates, not just birth rates, and even the best-case scenario posits that the Muslim population will continue to grow in Rakhine State for several more decades (assuming the Muslims all return from Bangladesh). The Rakhine will not be driven out of Rakhine State by this, but the proportions of the population will continue to change. And as the Muslim population growth rate outpaces that of the Rakhine, the perceived threat of absolute and/or cultural extinction is likely to escalate.

As it gets worse, the Rakhine and others in Myanmar must remember that this situation is largely of their own making. Muslim birth rates are in part due to the extremely conservative character of these Muslims, and their perceptions of gender roles. However, the Muslim population growth is also significantly higher due to marginalization by ethnic Rakhine, and to Burman exclusionary politics. By denying the Muslims equal access to education, health care, and the like for decades, they have deprived many Muslims of the usual tools to bring their birth rate down. Indeed, over the past two decades Rakhine birth rates have fallen from levels not much lower than the Muslim rates, while the Muslim rates have not yet begun to decline. In many respects this situation has been created by Rakhine and Burman discrimination. That they feel a threat from a demographic security dilemma is thus largely their own making, and the Muslims must not be further denied equal rights, dignity, and respect because of it.

2. Rakhine–Burman-Led State Security Dilemma

Relations, and conflict, between the Burman-led state and the ethnic Rakhine are characterized by a significant asymmetry of power. At the core of the conflict is the historical political struggle for independence or greater self-determination, and preservation of cultural identity. For the Burman, at stake is national unity, sovereignty, and territorial unity. The Rakhine nationalists' depiction of the past is invested with strong sentiments of injustice, reinforcing distrust of the Burman-led state and its institutions. For example, as Slim (2014) expresses it, Mrauk-U's conquest and humiliation in 1784 is still

> keenly felt as a profound political wrong, permanently symbolized by the destruction of the Royal Palace and the abduction of the Mahmuni [sic] Buddha to Mandalay. Rakhine has felt undervalued ever since its forced inclusion in the Burmese political sphere.

Likewise, U Nu's promise in the run-up to the 1960 elections to discuss also changing Myanmar's constitution from union to a federal system was never delivered, as a result of Ne Win's coup in 1962 (Charney 2009, pp. 100–1). Five decades of military rule and Rakhine struggle have increased the feelings of distrust and insecurity felt by many Rakhine towards the central state—in common with most of Myanmar's minorities.

The key issue in the eyes of most Rakhine today is the need for some form of federalism. Complicating this, though, is not only distrust of the government and military's sincerity, but also a lack of ability to trust that they can make credible, long-term commitments. The ethnic security dilemma revolves around a lack of trust. Lake & Rothchild (1996) and Fearon (1998) both note the problem of governments not being able to provide credible commitment to follow through on agreements, if a change in the balance of power eventuates—a strong possibility especially in transitional environments characterized by volatility and uncertainty. This has long been a major issue in Rakhine State.

The ethnic security dilemma has been further reinforced for many Rakhine during the democratic transition. This can be evidenced by two concurrent developments. First, the Arakan National Party won the majority of seats in northern and central Rakhine at the 2015 election, while most other ethnic nationalities around the country voted NLD. This demonstrates and reinforces the level of Rakhine suspicion and distrust even towards the NLD. Moreover, a strongly ethno-nationalist opposition voice is more likely to increase narratives of suspicion and fear, rather than increase communication and trust. Second, the re-emergence of the Arakan Army as a fighting force in Rakhine State, launching armed offensives against the state, shows that the strategic option of violent confrontation has gained some ground. Such a climate is exacerbated by ethnic nationalist entrepreneurs, who employ memories, myths, and symbols to polarize society, embroiling decisions regarding political action in emotional and psychological factors (as per Lake & Rothchild 1996, pp. 53–5).

For the Burman-dominated state, the ethnic security dilemma relates to the existential threat posed by the separatist aspects of the conflict, as well as issues around the use of resources and economic development. The protection of territorial integrity and state sovereignty has been a long-term strategic mission for the military and the state, embedded as a top priority through the civil wars after independence. It was reinforced by foreign action, such as the shock Kuomintang incursions in the 1950s and consequent fears of intervention by the People's Republic of China (Callahan 2003, p. 146). Thus, the Tatmadaw (at least) has built post-Independence Burman nationalism on a narrative of foreign threat, fear about the survival of the Burmese way of life, and the need for protection from centrifugal ethnic separatism. The army obtained its central role in the state principally by becoming the guarantor of the territorial integrity, sovereignty, and unity of the state. Although recruitment to armed insurgency in Rakhine State has been low, and a major separatist war is highly unlikely, the Rakhine nationalist push for greater autonomy feeds on the sort of separatist sentiment that the Tatmadaw and the state fear. Fear and distrust are only compounded by the fact that similar sentiments are expressed in the separatist struggles in Kachin and Shan States, where tensions are much higher and armed conflict a greater threat. Fear of separatism, therefore, presents as an existential threat to the military, as the guarantor of the unity of the state, as well as to the government.

3. Muslim–Burman-Led State Security Dilemma

Relations between the Burman-led state and the Muslim community in northern Rakhine State are even more asymmetrical. The unstable transition environment at Independence, from British rule to a Burman-led state, increased the insecurity of apprehensive Muslim leaders. The Muslims were looking for some form of political solution that would insulate their community from the perceived threats in Burma and the tectonic geopolitical shifts in the wider region from decolonization. British policy towards the future borders of post-Independence Burma varied significantly after the election of Clement Attlee as British prime minister. The territorial demarcation in Churchill's plan did not include the 'Frontier' areas, whereas when Attlee came to power they were included in plans for independent Burma. These sorts of uncertainties added to Muslim anxieties. Muslim leaders had the impression that the British had promised them some form of self-rule after the end of the Second World War (Yegar 1972, p. 96; Christie 1997, p. 166). Thus, the sense of a security dilemma increased dramatically for them after their call for the creation of a special Muslim region, not separate from Burma but clearly separate from the rest of Buddhist-dominated Rakhine, was rejected in 1947 (Christie 1997, p. 168). The result was such intense Muslim insecurity and fear that some resorted to violence as a defence. Mujahids took up arms before the British departure in January 1948, and lasted until the surrender of the last rebels in 1961.

U Nu's promise of an Arakan federal state in the wake of the 1960 elections, as part of a new Federal Union of Myanmar, raised hopes of an autonomous zone, along with Tatmadaw fears of eventual secession (Yegar 1972, pp. 102–3). The creation of the Mayu Frontier District in May 1961, under military administration, was a welcome compromise, but its abolition by General Ne Win in 1964 was keenly felt by Muslims. Ne Win's logic of denial of rights to the Muslims consolidated this disenfranchisement gradually—first through decree, then the citizenship provisions in the 1974 constitution, then the 1982 Citizenship Law, and so on. Thus, there was a shift away from rivalry between two communal groups that were largely equals, towards greater asymmetry. This was further strengthened by the securitization process during the 1960s, 1970s, and 1980s (Smith 2007), which increasingly presented separatist groups as an existential threat and thus outside the normative and social framework of the political (as per Buzan et al. 1998, pp. 23–4). Securitization against the Karen, the Shan, and then the Kachin stepped up after 1962 (Callahan 2003, p. 224). By the 1970s, after the Bangladesh–Pakistan civil war, the Muslims were also increasingly targeted. However, the significant difference for the Muslims was that other ethnic–separatist groups were always recognized as national races, with rights to full citizenship, and thus deal-making and political settlements (South 2008, p. 34; Charney 2009, p. 125). Muslim insurgents were increasingly pursued as external threats, for which settlement/resolution options were very limited, and the whole Muslim population was implicated by association.

The historical circumstances around the failure to secure self-rule in 1961, as well as the ongoing securitization and externalization of the Muslims over the past fifty years, has intensified their security dilemma. This chronic situation has made the Muslims in northern Rakhine State sceptical of recent democratic reforms and new document-verification processes. Based on their experience and the near-orthodox perception they are potential enemies of the state, many Muslims believe that without the protection of some sort of autonomous zone, even if they regain the vote, a majoritarian system of government will prolong their subjugation through 'democratic' means. Their lack of trust in the democratic transition furthers their sense of ethnic security dilemma, heightening fears. These fears have been augmented by parsimonious reference to the Muslims by Aung San Suu Kyi, the silence in the context of fear making them even more suspicious about her intentions (Murshid 2013).

Limitations of the Model

The concept of an ethnic security dilemma is thus a useful device to make sense of the perplexing tripartite conflict in Rakhine State, but it is not completely free of limitations. The ethnic security dilemma is based on rational choice theory, and assumes that the most rational choice by all sides would be to avoid violence and reach an agreement—it is just the lack of trust that prevents parties from pursuing compromise. However, as we saw in earlier chapters, violence has resulted from openly aggressive intent, not just lack of trust. All instances of violence in Rakhine State, including the October 2016 and August 2017 attacks, involved a process of mobilization against a perceived existential threat. And all sides have had securitizing actors (political leaders, ethnic entrepreneurs, governments, nationalist pressure groups, etc.) who declare a referent object as existentially threatened, legitimizing violent defence of that object as central to survival. The referent object may be some form of collectivity (for example, ethnic Rakhine or Muslims), a set of values and beliefs (for example, historical unity, independence, or infiltration), or symbolically invested material objects (for example, the territorial integrity of Myanmar, independent Arakan, or natural resources) (see Buzan et al. 1998, p. 36).

While information and commitment failures may strengthen the ethnic security dilemma at the communicative level, such failures cannot be seen as the root of the problem. Hostility between the three groups is embedded in opposing narratives that manifest a 'myth–symbol complex' of self-definition and interpretation of history, dynamics which have become as integral to group solidarity as the conflict (Armstrong 1982; Smith 1986, 1999; Kaufman 1996). In this context, the historical narratives enable the politicization of ethnic identities, but also set the boundaries of inclusion and exclusion by direct reference to cultural and historical markers as qualifiers for participation. The probability of conflict and violence is proportional to the degree that the 'myth–symbol complex' embedded in the narratives builds hostility towards adversary groups (Kaufman 1996). The symbols that define the three groups simultaneously reflect values and interests. The narratives portray each party struggling against subhuman evil forces, whilst at the same time it is a struggle for survival and recognition (Kaufman 2001). Thus, even if there were symmetric and full information flow and credible commitment contributing to the amelioration of the conflict, they would not be sufficient to assure groups of their security in Rakhine State.

Another limitation of the ethnic security dilemma model is the assumption that domestic anarchy (as part of political transition broadly conceived) is the cause of insecurity. Such an explanation is persuasive for certain episodes of the long conflict in Rakhine State. For example, the Mujahid rebellion and the 2012 violence occurred in periods of significant transition. Empirically, however, it cannot account for the securitization of Rakhine and Muslims in periods of relative stability. Indeed, given the long-term, direct, and physical oppression the Muslims have faced, it can be argued that they have mostly adopted a remarkable level of non-violence (Vrieze 2013).

Discrimination, disenfranchisement, anti-Muslim sentiment, and the fear of radicalization to militant Islam have not translated into mass mobilization of the Muslim or Rakhine communities. There have long been reports of contact between Muslims in northern Rakhine State and international Islamist extremist groups, reinforcing narratives about the danger of Islamist extremism. This fear leads to the ongoing securitization of Muslims, and intensifies the sentiments of Buddhist nationalists. However, while there have been several instances of individual Muslims, diaspora and other groups advocating a violent response, there have been few Muslims in Rakhine State sharing a common cause with radical Islamist groups, at least until 2017 (Selth 2003, 2004, 2013; Brennan & O'Hara 2015; ICG 2016). The largely non-armed responses by the Muslims must be set against a domestic and regional background of intense minority militarization. From the independence of Bangladesh, to the areas long controlled by the Karen and Kachin, to the military defeat of the Tamil Tigers, the region is marked by cases where the instrumentality of militarization has delivered stories of success. Within Myanmar, at least in the present situation, militarization seems to have secured a seat at the negotiating table for the overwhelming majority of the groups that have mobilized.

The point is simply that internal anarchy is not the only factor that increases the security dilemma in Rakhine State; violence has occurred in periods of relative stability, and in some cases it was initiated by the state. This all highlight the merits, but also the limitations, of the ethnic security dilemma as a means to understand the escalation and mobilization of groups. The complexity of the conflict in Rakhine State, however, leads us to also consider other factors, beyond the 'domestic anarchy' argument.

SECURITY DILEMMA, GREED AND ECONOMY

Double—or Triple—Minority Complex

Another way of examining this conflict is through the lens of a 'double minority complex'. Michael (2007, 2011) coined this term to describe conflicts such as Sri Lanka, Northern Ireland, Israel–Palestine, and Cyprus. Seen from a regional and social–psychological perspective, in each of these conflicts a majority group within a country or region can feel as if they are a threatened minority competing for territorial survival and nationalistic autonomy, faced with a smaller local group closely linked to a populous or powerful neighbour. This, he argues, creates a '*double (in)security* dilemma preoccupying both communities' (emphasis his), or a 'double minority complex'. The point he makes is that accurate mapping of power relations defies simplistic symmetric–asymmetric analysis, and must include cross-border or regional factors (Michael 2011, p. 212). Commenting on the conflict between the Turkish Cypriot minority in Cyprus and the Greek Cypriot minority within the subregional context, he argues that

> heightened insecurity created a defensive mindset that, in the absence of political dialogue, permeated throughout the social fabric of both communities ... [and] led to militarization that, coupled with hardening political rhetoric, contributed to the rise of ethno-nationalism. (Michael 2011, p. 148)

This 'double minority complex' analysis is helpful for the Rakhine State conflict. Without doubt, the Muslim community is a vulnerable and threatened minority. They are poor, lack citizenship, are denied many human rights, and face severe mobility restrictions. This vulnerability has provided socio-political fuel for the adoption of a shared 'Rohingya' identity over recent decades: intense insecurity and extreme threat have forged a nationalistic sense of shared identity out of what even staunch 'Rohingya' advocates agree was originally an ethnically diverse Muslim community.[1]

However, the ethnic Rakhine feel equally vulnerable and insecure, not only as a minority in relation to Burmanization and the Burman-led state, but also in the face of neighbouring Bangladesh, which has one of the world's highest population densities. From a regional perspective, the Muslim demographic threat is not just the birth rate within Rakhine State, but the danger of mass migration from the huge Muslim population just across the border in Bangladesh. Interestingly, and suggesting that the link with Bangladesh may be as much imagined as real, most Muslims in northern Rakhine identified more closely with Pakistan than Bangladesh during the Pakistan–Bangladesh civil war. Nonetheless, many Rakhine have retreated into a 'siege mentality' (Kyaw San Wai 2014), created by fears of ever-increasing religious and territorial encroachment by the human tide of Bangladeshi Muslims, and a political, cultural, historical, economic, demographic, and religious assault by the Burmans. Added to this, many also believe that the international community ignore their concerns in preference for over-sensationalized reports about the plight of Muslims. They see themselves as a very vulnerable and insecure minority.

Taking this analysis one step further, from a regional perspective the Tatmadaw and the Burman-led state, grappling with underdevelopment, a myriad of huge economic and security challenges, plus intense international criticism, also (to some extent) react in ways that belie feelings of vulnerability and insecurity. Bar-Tal & Antebi (1992) note that the state of Israel, for all its military power, lives under a 'siege mentality'. We suggest that many key Burmese actors—especially Tatmadaw leaders, but also the state as a whole—perceive themselves as deeply threatened, and react out of fear more than rational, strategic decision making. As Aung San Suu Kyi put it in comments to the BBC in October 2013: 'Fear is not just on the side of the Muslims, but on the side of the Buddhists as well. There's a perception that Muslim power, global Muslim power, is very great' (Schissler et al. 2015). Such fears can be partly explained by a sense of obligation to protect Buddhism from decline, a legacy that dates back to colonial Burma and the interpretative frameworks adopted by the Burmese to make sense of the British era and respond to colonial influences (Turner 2014). Recent work by these researchers has confirmed widespread discourses across most of the country that portray Muslims as an existential threat, in which Buddhism is vulnerable and needing protection from an intrinsically violent Islam, lest Islam supplant it as the majority religion. Perhaps a 'triple minority complex' helps explain this conflict.

The Role of the State in the Conflict

The state is perceived in a very different light along each of these conflict axes. This highlights the powerful and pervasive influence of government on ethnic identity and relations, both in Myanmar and more generally. Taylor (2009, 2015) has documented the way in which the state has prioritized ethnicity as a defining characteristic of politics in Myanmar, setting up contestation over and between ethnic identities. In the broader literature, the view that the state may shape or reinforce ethnic identities is associated with the historical rise of the modern territorial state, with its principle of membership by proximity (ethnic groups put together in the one state based on proximity rather than kinship or shared history). This has two significant dimensions: first, the territorial state as a mode of political organization became the ultimate end of decolonization and political independence. Second, the territorial imperative of the modern state necessarily includes everyone within its boundaries (Horowitz 2000; Elden 2013). As a result, the state expanded, especially after the Second World War, in terms of both spatial and policy activities. Regimes that traditionally only exercised effective control over the core of their regions have progressively sought to control their peripheries too, through the expansion of bureaucracies and security presence. This development, although initiated outside the colonial context, has also occurred in post-colonial spaces. Decolonized communities have pursued political structures modelled according to the territorial state paradigm.

The expansion of the state has been interpreted in two different ways. For some, the state has been depicted as the non-autonomous agency of a particular social sector, such as a class, elite, or, for our purposes, ethnicity. In such a case, the expansion of the state may be seen as deriving from the attempts of the dominant ethnic group to extend its power and interests across the rest of society (Brass 1984; Brown 1994). In this narrative the state is a non-autonomous actor, concerned not so much with 'nation-building' that would cut across and overcome ethnic particularism as with promoting a specific ethnic agenda (Brown 1994, pp. 23–45; Gurr 2000, p. 64). Most nationalities in Myanmar perceive the state in these terms, and the Rakhine Buddhist and Muslim communities both feel existentially threatened, struggling for survival against a partisan state primarily representing Burman interests and promoting cultural and religious 'Burmanization'.

The second approach in the literature attempting to make sense of state expansion assumes the state to be an independent actor—an institution with its own interests and goals which has the capacity to control and (re)shape society (Coakley 2012; Esman 2004). Thus, the state appears to present itself as a neutral force between opposing ethnic groups, and may seek to act as a neutral facilitator/mediator in conflict, but comes with the aim of integrating opposing views and creating a platform for an overarching identity that would redefine the kernel of the political community around itself. This is clearly the way both the Burman government and the Tatmadaw perceive themselves in the context of Rakhine State.

The state has repeatedly intervened in Rakhine State, to minimize intra-communal violence and prevent foreign infiltration, as it sees things. However, it has only ever managed to stabilize the situation sometimes, and has never resolved grievances, because both Rakhine and Muslim communities have deep grievances against the state and see it as a key actor. In this light, the focus of domestic public opinion on the intra-periphery communal conflict should not be seen as accidental—rather, it reflects the willingness of the dominant ethnic group (the Burmans) to portray the central state/government as a neutral mediator in the conflict, intervening as necessary to maintain security and order for the public good. For example, in a speech by Aung San Suu Kyi on 19 September 2017, regarding Tatmadaw action after the ARSA attacks on security posts, she framed the military response as the neutral actor restoring order in the periphery: "We condemn all human rights violations and unlawful violence. We are committed to the restoration of peace, stability and rule of law throughout the State" (Aung San Suu Kyi 2017, p. 2). As a result of this political posture by the government, the conflict between the Rakhine and the state is often overlooked or downplayed; yet it is vitally important.

The 'neutral' position advocated by the central government has a number of consequences on the conflict dynamics. First, it has furthered the freezing of the conflict, locking the parties into close proximity with no path towards resolution of fundamental grievances available. The denial of options for resolving grievances by both Rakhine nationalists and Muslims has concentrated a vulnerable Muslim population in place, with limited options and no process towards conflict resolution. Second, it has in a perverse sense legitimized the Burmese state's response to the situation, implicitly endorsing the idea that the

Muslims are 'stateless', and at least 'irregular' arrivals—if not 'illegal'. This language actually enhances further the Burmese state's approach to the issue as the neutral mediator, trying to maintain harmony and coexistence via the paradoxical means of partial segregation and mobility suppression. However, this approach only further aggravates both sides and cannot bring about any desirable outcome—certainly not social cohesion, inclusivity, and shared participation in the evolving democratic polity of Myanmar. Third, this neutral posture by the Burman-led government has led to a paralysis in decision making and implementation of policies that might ameliorate the situation.

It is symptomatic of this conflict that even high-level officials in Nay Pyi Taw display extreme fear of talking about the issue, even anonymously, apparently afraid that any comment will provoke negative reactions. Such a response could be read through two different perspectives. It may pinpoint a belief by the state that it is indeed taking a genuinely neutral stance, and has reached a stalemate given the complexity on the ground, unable to proceed without further destabilization. Alternatively, a more sinister interpretation would highlight the instrumentality of its 'neutral' approach—in other words, that many state actors realize they are not neutral, but maintain the posture to secure and promote Burman or state agendas, and remain silent for fear of letting something slip which would confirm the fears of either side, provoking destabilization. If this is indeed the case, while the mobility narrative of 'irregular' arrivals comes at the cost of exporting the issue to the region and beyond, and risks potentially triggering an international response, perhaps it is still regarded as politically and diplomatically affordable compared to the benefit that the ethnic majority enjoys by being isolated from the situation.

As is evident from the analysis, neutrality is a difficult strategy when both the Rakhine and Muslims have grievances against the state. It often forces the state to support the status quo, yet in ways that make distinctions between its populations, and it therefore distributes resources differentially. Neutrality does not deny the possibility of the state being 'captured' by particular ethnic interests for a long period of time. Our fieldwork has confirmed that many Rakhine and Muslims believe that, despite its neutral posturing, communal tensions would diminish if the state prioritized equal economic development and ser-

vice delivery in Rakhine State. Given that most members of both communities lead such marginal existences, competition over scarce
resources is a factor in communal tensions. Any solution must include
stimulating economic development, improving equitable service delivery, and increasing development activity (as opposed to humanitarian
aid). Rakhine politicians and nationalists would prefer to see the funding to flow via their Rakhine State government, ideally directly from
the resources and trade derived from or passing through their state;
either way, greater government engagement in their economic future
and well-being would go part-way to addressing communal tensions.

These observations highlight another role that the state may play,
apart from being partisan or attempting neutral mediation. A better
conception would be to see the state apparatus as a 'competitive arena'
in which communities contend non-violently for relative power and
influence—not to control the state apparatus, as the partisan position
would advocate, but to negotiate relative shares of political power,
distribution of resource wealth, participation in the security sector, and
so on. Such a conception of the state would point towards the need for
a different model of political organization across the country, in the
relations between the centre and peripheries, and embedded processes
for non-violent contestation around relative shares.

Economic Drivers, Resources, and Greed

Resource, revenues, and economic motives are often proposed as a
major cause of violent conflict in Myanmar in general, and in Rakhine
State in particular. Despite having the lowest living standards in the
country, Rakhine has extensive economic potential. As already noted,
Sittwe, the state capital, was once the largest exporter of rice in the
world, but the extensive arable land does not currently produce the
quality and quantity attained in other regions and neighbouring countries. Agricultural land will thus greatly appreciate in value as the ports
and roads are better developed, access to rural finance increases, and
the latest methods are adopted. Fishing also remains underdeveloped
as an industry. Extensive natural gas reserves off the coast are being
developed by international companies in partnership with Burman-led
national companies. Good deposits of minerals such as titanium and

aluminium have been found in the coastal sands (GNLM 2016g), but are not yet being exploited. And the Maungdaw–Rathedaung coastline, with its pristine beaches, is being eyed for potential tourism development—along the lines of Bangladesh's St Martin's Island developments, no more than 10 kilometres off the coast.

In terms of major developments, Myanmar has already set up the Kyaukphyu Special Economic Zone around the second-largest Rakhine city, with its deep-sea port and oil-gas pipelines (GNLM 2017a). It is developing the Kaladan River Multi-Modal Project, to ship goods from the Indian mainland to its isolated north-eastern Mizoram State, via a seaport in Sittwe and then up the Kaladan River by boat to Paletwa (where the AA are most operational), then by road back into India. This will save India on transport costs and generate considerable revenue for Myanmar. The Maungdaw Economic Zone has been set up to expand border trade with Bangladesh, led by a consortium of four companies from Maungdaw and three from Yangon (Myo Pa Pa San 2017). And the government is developing the Ponnagyun Industrial Park just 20 kilometres north-east of Sittwe. Beyond this, the Chinese Belt and Road Initiative includes plans for a Bangladesh–China–India–Myanmar (BCIM) Economic Corridor, which is intended to run from China to Bangladesh and India, right through northern Rakhine State; if this proceeds it could well be the biggest reshaping of regional geo-politics since the colonial era, and the route goes right through this conflict region. All of these factors create potential economic motivations for land and concessions, and thus potentially for conflict.

So the question is whether the Rakhine State conflict, including the treatment of the Muslim population, is primarily about economic motives or whether these are complicating factors in a conflict primarily about something else. There are two main approaches to such analysis in the conflict studies literature: the so-called greed thesis, and a political economy approach. The following sections will consider each in turn.

The 'Greed Thesis'

The 'greed thesis' is a much-discussed concept in conflict studies. Essentially, it argues that competing vested economic interests related to the control of energy, resources, or trade are at the core of conflict (e.g. Benson 2015; Wolf 2015; Felbab-Brown 2017; Forino et al. 2017). 'Greed' motives are usually placed in contrast to 'grievance' motives, traditionally explained as revolving around things like ethnic or racial identity, religion or ideas of homeland (discussed in the next chapter). It echoes arguments that ethnicity and/or religion are co-opted into conflict, rather than being primary drivers, and so shifts the focus to 'greed' motives such as competition over resources (Homer-Dixon 1994) and contestation of the control of economic opportunity (Collier et al. 2003), epitomized, for example, by the 'resource curse' (Le Billon 2001). Our key question is: to what extent is this the case in Rakhine State?

Most readers will not be familiar with the detail of this argument; thus we present the greed thesis from the literature in some detail below, before considering how valid it is in explaining this particular conflict. We give an extended discussion of the applicability of this theory, because it has been so appealing to major donors for many years, and the conclusions of this section are therefore of great relevance to international finance institution policy towards Rakhine.

There has been a marked resurgence in and intensification of ethnic violence since the end of the Cold War, something brought to world attention in the wake of the Rwandan genocide. At about the same time as this was noted, the World Bank and the International Monetary Fund came to realize that the economic policy reforms they demanded of developing countries under their 'structural adjustment programmes' had significant adverse effects on the poor, provoking significant domestic backlash (World Bank 1990). This resulted in a new theoretical interpretation of conflict. Led particularly by those connected to the World Bank, this interpretation came to view local civil wars through the lens of disruption to macro-economic growth and development.

The greed thesis builds on the rational-actor model. Starting with an assumption that vested economic interests are the main motive for civil war, it suggests that ethnic conflict occurs where the economic incentives for the use of violence is calculated as outweighing the cost (Collier & Hoeffler 1998; Fearon & Laitin 2000). It contends that the main objective of rebellion is effective territorial control, in order to control economic resources. This might be realized through capturing the existing state, creating a new independent state through secession, or controlling a liberated zone. Mobilization is conditional on the prospect of a victorious outcome, and thus on the potential for the insurgents to reap the economic benefits of their involvement. Accordingly, this argument postulates that in low-income countries, ethnic violence and civil war occurs primarily around natural-resource sites (Collier & Hoeffler 1998). The risk is higher in countries with larger populations and ethno-linguistic diversity, in that ethnic tension can be used to facilitate rebel mobilization and cohesion, and obstruct efforts by the government to penetrate rebel ranks. Mobilization based on ethnic grievance narratives therefore does not mean that the underlying motive is not 'greed'.

Collier & Hoeffler (1998, 2002, 2004) identify three broad aspects of the conflict mobilization process, and consider associated groups of opportunities for mobilization and rebellion. The first group of opportunities for conflict have to do with financing rebellions. Opportunities exist where there are natural resources to be exploited once territory is controlled, substantial diaspora support, or support from other states sympathetic to the rebels' cause. The second group of opportunities for civil war relate to unusually low costs. Rebellion is said to be particularly likely in countries that rely mainly on primary commodity exports, because of low conflict cost. Low income per capita reduces the cost of foregone income, and low levels of secondary education reduce any prospect of people gaining a high earnings career. A low economic growth rate likewise impairs the prospects for high-income opportunities. Any or all of these mean that there is a low cost of violence compared to perceived reward. A final group of opportunities arise where the military is weak, or in a remote and inaccessible terrain that can be used by rebels as safe havens, plus when there is easy access to weapons, military training, and know-how. Such conclusions favour economic opportunity and utility as an explanation of civil war, which in turn promotes 'greed' over 'grievance' as the motive behind mobilization and violence.

However, two of Collier and Hoeffler's consequent observations also equally inform the 'grievance' discourse: the first is that the risk of conflict and violence doubles where one ethnicity dominates, meaning when the largest ethnic group constitutes between 45 and 90 per cent of the population. This increases the chances of ethnic polarization, and facilitates rebel coordination and recruitment. The second observation is that, on average, there is a 50 per cent recurrence of violence in the first five years, but that this risk fades gradually with time: 'time heals' (Collier & Hoeffler 2004, p. 589). Where these conditions exist, it might imply that grievances are significant, and not just greed.

The policy implications most commonly drawn from the greed thesis are the need for poverty reduction through economic development, and effective governance through the promotion of democratic institutions. The greed theory can be thus said to offer a defence of the liberal orthodoxy in development and peace building, postulating that economic reforms based on a free market, and good (equitable) governance through institutional state building, are the primary means to peace. It also conveniently shifts the blame for conflict to the 'local' (rebel leaders, etc.) and turns away from challenging discussions about promotion of inequalities in liberal capitalism, and the role of the state in conflict and local grievances (Demmers 2017, pp. 107–8). The greed thesis is supported largely by quantitative analysis of a large number of cases. However, the typology of this data does not separate ethnic and non-ethnic civil wars, and amalgamation of results thus favours non-ethnic explanations of civil war. Since ethnic conflict is not treated as a separate category, its significance diminishes in the overall analytical map of civil war (Ballentine & Sherman 2003; Pugh & Cooper 2004).

Applying the greed thesis to the case of Rakhine, we note that significant resources do exist, and that there are very low incomes and education levels. Control of agricultural land and fisheries is paramount for local livelihoods, and local competition does spark communal tensions. Access to and exploitation of natural resources, and control of trade and transport routes, offer potentially significant reward to elite actors, and raise significant concerns for all communities, particularly with regard to the distribution of revenue. Economic motivations thus most clearly do play a role in this conflict.

However, completely disregarding historical grievances, fears, and racial attitudes is difficult in the case of Rakhine, if we seek to explain violent behaviour at both individual and collective levels. Both the AA and ARSA are characterized by quite low levels of material support, and have quite thin recruitment bases, despite widespread popular support for the AA at least. This makes it difficult to primarily attribute the conflict to 'evil greedy local' actors. Thus, while economic factors obviously do matter, it is not clear that rational cost calculations by any rebel elite about their potential gains enter into strategic decisions to engage in conflict violence. Economic factors and resource issues appear more as the product of long-standing grievances about under-development, domination, and exploitation. Similarly, it is equally uncertain how economic factors prolong the conflict in Rakhine State. Is it a conflict mainly about enrichment of certain actors (as an end of itself) at the expense of the wider population, or a struggle for the betterment of the socio-economic situation of the wider Rakhine or Muslim population?

The economic aspects of the Rakhine State conflict revolve around two intersecting spheres: large-scale projects, and primary production (agricultural and fishing). The development of large-scale projects in Rakhine State is based largely on foreign investment, including the Kyaukphyu Special Economic Zone, the Kaladan River Multi-Modal Project, the Ponnagyun Industrial Park, the Maungdaw Economic Zone, and the Belt and Road Initiative. These projects are all politically and legally managed by the central Myanmar government, which presents them as key to lifting the people out of poverty and minimizing ethnic tensions. For example, the Kyaukphyu Special Economic Zone is touted to eventually provide 300,000 jobs (GNLM 2017a), and in the words of the Rakhine State Minister for Finance, Revenue, Economics, and Planning, U Kyaw Aye Thein, when completed, the zone 'will create jobs and result in more development. It can reduce conflict' (Myanmar Times 2017). This view is also seconded by the Maungdaw Border Trade Association chair, U Aung Myint Thein, a Burman, who claimed: 'When the economy has improved, no one will make trouble. That is human nature. Therefore, we will have to push the implementation of the economic zone project at the earliest opportunity' (Myanmar Times 2017).

The second economic sphere, the one most important to the local populations in the short term, is agriculture and fishing—and thus access to arable land and fisheries. A majority of both the Rakhine and Muslim populations depend on these for their survival, and both have tradition-ally been abundant. Even cultivating a small plot can provide basic food security. Thus, any action that restricts access to or affects the distribution of land or fisheries, through implementation of mega-projects, or the reshuffling of demographics and populations, can have a tremendous impact on the already tense relations between communities.

Both economic spheres are significant, but neither approximates to the conditions of the greed thesis. Greed theory views violent conflict as if it were a market, in which individuals invest in conflict and vio-lence to reap private returns (Demmers 2017). There are some aspects of the major projects that could be read in terms of a predatory state, and some cases of land grabbing, particularly in the last year or two, but there is none of the accumulation of benefit by elite local rebel leaders as proposed by the greed thesis, and as perhaps seen, for exam-ple, in the Kachin conflict. There is no capitalization of low costs either, and so far there has been little private exploitation of local resources by ethnic or Yangon–Nay Pyi Taw elites.

International finance institution policy towards Rakhine, therefore, should note that even if the greed thesis sounds appealing, it is hardly applicable. The economic and resource factors in the conflict are far more a product of long-standing grievances about underdevelopment and domination, or even about a predatory state, than about local elite enrichment. The greed approach's explanation of ethnic violence employs a brand of economic theory that builds a link between poverty and violence, and suggests that violence is more probable on the part of the poor because opportunity costs are low. It assumes that in a less developed economy with minimal investment in people, the cost of being killed in war is low. The option to use violence is thus seen to be more probable, because life is cheap (Cramer 2006). But this does not fit the Rakhine context, which did not see mass mobilization until 2017, and, even now, the masses have fled after brief chaos rather than embraced sustained violence.

A wealth of other scholarly attention has pointed out the complexity of the relationship between poverty and conflict, beyond a causal determinism. Poverty can only have a catalytic impact on conflict and violence if there is state repression of non-violent resistance, leading to a build-up of political mobilization. It is thus noted that, globally, most often insurgents do not belong to the poorest or the least educated (Cramer 2009, p. 15; Goodhand 2003; Wolf 1969). Perhaps the involvement of large numbers of people in the 2012 and 2017 violence in Rakhine State might suggest a turning point towards mass mobiliza-tion, due, in part, to poverty, but in over seven decades of conflict since Independence this analysis has not fitted the case of Rakhine. Although Rakhine is the second-poorest state in Myanmar after Chin State, nei-ther has been a hotspot of mass mobilization for organized violent insurgency. There have been many insurgent groups in Rakhine State, yet the mobilization to armed violence has always been relatively low compared to other parts of Myanmar—such as Karen, Shan, or Kachin, where the level of poverty has not been quite as extreme. This does not imply a lack of support for the insurgent goals in Rakhine State, where nationalism on all sides has been very high—just that the greed thesis's presupposition that poverty reduces the cost of violence, and therefore leads more readily to mass mobilization, does not explain the conflict in Rakhine State well.

This observation points to the need for a broader understanding of politics and politicization in conditions of poverty. Populations who live in poverty are not automatically a critical mass for mobilization, and are not a collective that can be automatically manipulated by exter-nal agents (Breman 1993). The processes of social identity formation and change are more complex than this, especially when social dichot-omies such as religion or ethnicity have been imposed either by institu-tions or social relations that serve the interests of individuals or groups (Tilly 1998).

In conclusion, then, in making sense of the conflict in Rakhine State it is more important to focus on social, political, and institutional pro-cesses that create and sustain spheres of inclusion and exclusion, and the interaction of such processes with economic factors within the emerging capitalist system, than on the idea of a low cost of violence because the people are poor.

A Political Economy Approach

Although the greed thesis discussed above does not provide a satisfac-tory analysis of the Rakhine situation, it does provoke thinking about how the interplay of socio-political and economic factors informs the conflict. The major flaw in applying the greed thesis is that it assumes that the conflict is initiated by greedy locals, and does not consider the possibility of predatory states or the economic interests of non-local elites connected to the ethnic majority. A political economy approach explores these ideas better.

Sassen (2017a, 2017b) links the conflict in Rakhine State to land grabs, suggesting that the deepest cause of conflict relates to economic and military interests rather than religious and ethnic issues. The expulsion of the Muslim population has conveniently freed land that has become important to the economic agenda of the military and national elites: cross-border trade, the potential for hotels and tourism along the Maungdaw coast, mineral extraction, etc. This view is also echoed by other analysts (e.g. Forino et al. 2017), who suggest that racial and religious differences have become proxies for a conflict which is predominantly about claiming advantage in the emerging economy in Rakhine State.

Sassen places her analysis within broader patterns of regional and global economic structural change over the past twenty years. Systemic pressures, including stagnation in developed economies, has driven global capital to seek new opportunities, leading to a push into new spaces. This drive for land, assets, and infrastructure unavoidably leads to what Harvey (2006) calls a permanent 'accumulation of dispossession'. There definitely is a new phase of land grabs for, among other things, resource extraction, exclusive economic zones, and building development. Violence, destruction, and appropriation are typical elements of capitalism across all historical phases, but Sassen (2008, 2013, 2014) argues that the current phase of 'advanced capitalism' is underpinned by a financial logic that is inherently extractive, because it places little or no dependence on increasing household income and consumer power for economic sustainability. She thus sees it as less interested than ever in local populations. The displacement of the Muslim population, she suggests, is the product of this new phase of capitalism that, in search for land and primitive accumulation, does not recoil from creating landless and stateless populations, continually excluding, marginalizing, and moving people (Sassen 2016).

Certainly, land grabs and business interest are increasing, and such displacement is closely linked to conflict dynamics in some other parts of the country. Incentives, including concessions for the exploitation of natural resources by rebel groups, the Tatmadaw, and international business consortia, have been integral to the history of ceasefire agreements in Myanmar, as succinctly captured in the concept of 'ceasefire capitalism' (e.g. Woods 2011). The kernel of this argument, in comparison to the greed thesis, is that economic self-interest through the sharing of natural wealth can eliminate violence by armed ethnic groups (Sherman 2003; Snyder 2006; Smith 1999, p. 441). In addition, through the formation of state/military–private partnerships, this process has allowed the government to 'solidify *de jure* sovereignty into *de facto* territorial control' (Woods 2011, p. 749). However, the model of turning the conflict into a mutually beneficial economic agreement between dominant elites has failed, as is evident in the collapse of the ceasefire in Kachin, showing that such 'ceasefire capitalism' can backfire and lead to new rounds of violence (Brenner 2015).

In relation to Rakhine, the contentions of Sassen, and of Forino et al. (2017), are highly questionable. It is difficult to establish any geographical proximity between the major development projects in Rakhine State (especially those in Kyaukphyu, Ponnagyun, and Sittwe) and the location of most past security crackdowns (Maungdaw, Buthidaung, and Rathedaung Townships). Jones (2017) strongly argues that this disconnection between the locus of land grabbing and conflict to date is significant. The only exceptions to this are the emerging economic zone in Maungdaw which, as Jones suggests, has gone largely unnoticed (Mratt Kyaw Thu 2017), and the latent potential of Maungdaw tourism and mineral extraction.

Thus, replacing contestation over race and identity as key drivers with land grabs and 'business interests' does not capture the reality of the situation on the ground. They are a contributing factor, but not explanatory in their own right. Mere economic self-interest does not explain the silence of the progressive forces in Myanmar—groups and activists who have fought long and hard to bring democracy and equality elsewhere in the country—vis-à-vis the violence against the Muslims. It is noteworthy that during our fieldwork, with few exceptions, civil society leaders from other parts of the country showed indifference for the situation of the Muslims, even those from ethnic nationalities that have experienced state oppression and discrimination themselves.

For these reasons, relying on an ideal-typified conception of capitalism, in which market imperatives auto-generate certain class agency, leads to a mono-dimensional and economistic analysis of the conflict that does not fit Rakhine. Such 'market-dependency' arguments ascribe social and political action in ethnic and religious conflict to structural and systemic pressures, grounded on some kind of capitalist internal logic. The totalizing of this transnationalization of capitalism entraps and downplays history as a mere second-order manifestation of the capitalist imperative, regardless of human action (Knafo & Teschke 2017). Such an explanation suppresses agency under wider structural tectonic shifts, eschewing any possibility of considering capital accumulation in Rakhine State as part of a series of diverse processes both historical and contemporary, that benefit capital indirectly rather than directly (Soe Lin Aung 2017). Capitalism has historically played a role in ethnic conflicts, especially with regard to the appropriation of capital by ruling elites, but as Soe Lin Aung (2017) succinctly points out, that appropriation has often indirectly hardened rather than caused conflict, by deepening the existing inequalities and adding layers of disparity between ethnic groups, driving grievances. This, we suggest, is the case in Rakhine State.

These reflections lead to the conclusion that, while socio-political conflict in Rakhine State does not stand in an economic vacuum, economic drivers are insufficient to explain the violence. There is a need to depart from an understanding of social action based on pre-ordained logic. Agents are not passive rule-followers, constrained by macro-forces. Rather, they (re)act in the face of structural pressures, making difference as they progress, and often innovating while in this process. Thus, we need an analysis of agency within particular contexts in order to make sense of the innovative action by individuals and institutions, in the wider framework of the multiple trajectories of capitalism. Concretely, the question in this context is to analyse capitalism as a historically open praxis rather than a theoretically closed category (Teschke 2016). History is not conceived as the nomological manifestation of capitalism, but rather as a genuine terrain of inquiry as people make their own history (Teschke 2016).

The conflict in Rakhine State has strong racial grievance dimensions, amplified by cultural and religious difference. Such a conflict is not an epiphenomenon of primitive accumulation, but it intersects with economic interests in a mutually constitutive way (Chen 2013). Examples include the creation of a new economic zone in Maungdaw and pursuing its development even now, in the absence of most Muslims. They include the settlement of non-Muslims in northern Rakhine State, in a deliberate effort to change the demographics (Wade 2015). Likewise, the decision by the Minister for Social Welfare, Relief, and Resettlement that land that was burnt in Maungdaw, vacant after the August 2017 violence, will be managed and re-developed as state land (GNLM 2017b). And they include the Chinese government's praise for Tatmadaw operations in northern Rakhine State in 2017, given they have such a large share of the mega-projects under way in Rakhine State. While these might all be seen as episodes of primitive accumulation, as important as they are, such economic factors only compound a pre-existing nexus of conflict and violence based on identity difference (racial, cultural, and religious), and competing claims to territory as a 'homeland'.

6

IDENTITY AND TERRITORY GRIEVANCES
IN RAKHINE STATE

The opening to Part III highlighted the structure–agency debate around the drivers and characteristics of conflict. These explored the conflict around security dilemma, double minority, and economic ideas, both structural and rational-actor, as well as the roles of the state as an agent of power, imposition, and change. In concluding the last chapter, we argued that the Rakhine State conflict cannot be fully explained by any of these approaches, but that they all contribute towards a better and fuller understanding of the different dynamics of the conflict. We now turn our attention to the two most common non-material 'grievance' perspectives in the literature, with the aim of highlighting how their interplay shapes and reshapes the trajectories of the conflict: grievance based around identity (or ethnicity) and territory, which have been the kernel of the narrative building we analysed in earlier chapters.

Identity, Ethnicity, and Conflict

Identity and Identity Conflict

Identity is such a widely used term that its meaning is not always clear. Most commonly, the term is used to distinguish between the self and the 'Other', on either the personal or group level. In the field of conflict analysis, identity has gradually replaced social class as the main means in analysing conflict. Analysing conflict around identity became quite prominent in the literature after the end of the Cold War, in light of Rwanda and other civil wars that led to genocide and crimes against humanity (Kaldor 1999). Identity is linked to the existential question of who or what I am, and is usually framed to contrast with who or what I am not. Conceptually, identity is a self-definition question, generating diverse answers, which in turn begs further clarification on a number of sub-questions related to the search for self-meaning. These sub-questions include things such as the extent of freedom of choice vis-à-vis structural and normative restraints, and the impact of narratives, discourses, and symbols.

Broadly speaking, two dimensions of identity are widely discussed in the social science literature, one emphasizing the level of the individual, the other the level of society (Demmers 2017). Individual identity is usually described in terms of the total set of cognitions one has and employs in order to define who and what one is. Social identity is described as that part of an individual's identity that derives from membership in a social group or groups, and the emotional significance apportioned to that membership by the individual (Tajfel 1981, p. 63). However, social identity also transcends individual self-definition, to be anchored in the relationship between the individual and the social context. If social identity relied solely on individual self-definition, that would imply that the moment any individual had a change in their self-understanding, their social identity would also automatically change; this is not the case. Accordingly, social identities are relational, and are predicated on differentiation as much as inclusion: in many ways, 'we are what we are *not*' (Demmers 2017, p. 23; emphasis in the original).

This helps explain the resistance to the name 'Rohingya' within Myanmar. Some of the Muslims in northern Rakhine State are descendants of Muslims who were living in Arakan prior to 1823, mostly of slave origins from the Mrauk-U kingdom period. Most, however, are descendants of colonial-era migrants, or are of mixed ancestry. A majority from both origins now self-identify as 'Rohingya'. In Chapter 3 we identified this as a hybridized history, but in effect the migrant

Muslims have adopted the culture, values, and history of the pre-existing Muslim community in Rakhine State, leaving their past and assimilating the culture of the host (Muslim) population as their own. In any other context, this is exactly what we would expect good migrants to do. The now-intermingled Muslim population claim 'Rohingya' as their cultural—even ethnic—name. We analyse this as a new ethnicity emerging over the last century. Ethnicity always evolves in response to distinct socio-political pressures, so this should not be overly surprising. But the point is that while their self-understanding and self-identity has evolved, their social context has not. From a social point of view, particularly due to the legacy of the exclusionary politics of Ne Win, the Muslims of northern Rakhine State are still categorized and treated by others as if as if no change has occurred (Verkuyten 2005, p. 62)—as if they are a recently arrived migrant community. They are tolerated as guests in the country, at best, and the rest of Myanmar vehemently denies that they are even a coherent ethnic group, let alone a *taing-yin-tha* (indigenous national race).

This is how identity conflict arises: when self-understanding of one's identity and the external social identity ascribed by others in the same socio-political space are incompatible. In other words, identity conflict arises when groups think one way about themselves, but are perceived in incompatible ways by others, and thus feel a need to fight to validate who they see themselves to be.

Part II highlighted how Ne Win and the Tatmadaw, particularly after the 1962 coup, sought to ascribe an external social identity to both the Rakhine and the Muslim population in northern Rakhine State. Ne Win's logic of denial, winding back U Nu's promises and abolishing the Mayu Frontier District, for example, consolidated Muslim disenfranchisement, first through decree, then through codification of the status of *taing-yin-tha* in the 1974 constitution, then the 1982 Citizenship Law, then the 2008 constitution. The military, which to the Muslims represented the Burmese state, has attempted to appropriate the historical space, dominate the narratives about them, and monopolize the means of ascription of social identity. It is important to note the vast asymmetry of power in controlling the ascription of social identity. And the military/state have attempted to control Rakhine identity too, while the frequent Rakhine reference back to their lost kingdom and struggle to restore their lost fortunes is a key part of their attempt to resist this state-led ascription of social identity.

Every society has normative frameworks that outline acceptable and unacceptable modes of behaviour, based on the set of values and ideas that characterize particular groups. Some rules that encapsulate these normative frameworks may be written, institutionalized, and hard to change; others may be more flexible, unwritten, and amenable to change. Social identities can be formed, reshaped, denied, or promoted within societies, but in each case, power and agency determine who is promoted and who is denied, who is accepted and who is rejected. Historically, the modern state has been a significant agent of social identity formation. It monopolizes both physical and symbolic power in order to classify people in relation to citizenship, ethnicity, and culture, among other things—using an array of material and symbolic resources which range from persecution and forceful suppression, to the education curriculum and appropriation of language and history (Brubaker & Cooper 2000; Ferguson & Gupta 2002).

One of the great challenges of decolonization, in much of the world, has been that of unifying clans, tribes, and ethnicities which often shared little affinity before colonization. The notion of 'nation building' was widely adopted around attempts to forge an overarching sense of national social identity, although, as in Myanmar, this has often been more a case of projecting the culture of the largest ethnicity and expecting minorities to assimilate rather than developing a truly overarching shared identity.

The Reification of Ethnic Political Identities

We have already traced how the politics of ethnicity was gradually institutionalized in post-Independence Myanmar, through the evolution of the importance ascribed to the notion of *taing-yin-tha*, and the incremental demarcation of ethnic boundaries of inclusion and exclusion. Interestingly though, neither the original 1947 constitution, nor either of the subsequent 1974 and 2008 constitutions, include a list of *taing-yin-tha*. Cheesman (2017, pp. 468ff.) describes the taxonomic adventures of the military regime in iterating the 135 *taing-yin-tha* since Independence.

Colonial rule (1826–1948) significantly influenced Burma's ethnopolitical map. Prior to British colonization, ethnicity had a different, more social, role than as one of the key determinants of demographic mapping. Pre-colonial Burma's formations of social identity were defined far more along lines of loyalty and tribute than bloodlines and purity (Lieberman 1978). The idea of social categorization on the basis of *lu-myo* (race) was already familiar in both the Rakhine and Burmese kingdoms. Cultural, social, and racial differences were therefore not unknown. However, the pre-colonial conception of *lu-myo* appears to have been more fluid and porous than the model of ethnicity and race imported from Europe. Wars, loyalties, and royal leadership in precolonial Burma had less to do with identity and more to do with allegiance (Charney 2009), and we note the ability of identity groups to cross boundaries, being able to subscribe to different religious, cultural, and normative practices without reference to ethnic demarcation.

For example, the status of minorities was largely determined by access to political power or the lack thereof, rather than race per se. Marginal upland people were deemed backward, but their estrangement from political power was not so much dependent on religious, racial, or ethno-linguistic categorization by others as on their social and geographical habitat away from states and cities (Leach 1970 [1954]; Renard 1988). Scott (2009), for example, argues very convincingly that this was largely deliberate on their part, attempting to live in locations and ways that rendered them ungovernable by the dominant kingdoms. At the same time, in pre-colonial times members of *lu-myo* identity groups appear to have had the curious ability to change *lu-myo* (race). Both Leach (1970 [1954]) and Sadan (2013) note the ability of Kachin to 'become Shan', and provide examples of families simultaneously claiming both Kachin and Shan identity, based on a change of residence, name, religion, and other cultural practice. We have already noted that the Burman chronicles present *lu-myo* in social terms, able to accommodate the assimilation of conquered peoples without loss of original identity. While this was used to justify Burman hegemony and expansionism, it demonstrates very different ideas about race and ethnicity to those imported from Europe. And importantly, we note some not dissimilar dynamics in Rakhine State. For several centuries, for example, many Mrauk-U rulers simultaneously adopted both Buddhist and Muslim titles, most surviving court literature is in Persian rather than Arakanese or Pali, and the royal courts apparently promoted Muslims to the very highest positions in the kingdom—apparently without significant concern about racial, cultural, or religious difference (Karim 2014; d'Hubert 2014). Thus, in pre-colonial practice across Burma, there appears to have been a degree of mobility and flexibility built into the concept of *lu-myo* that does not fit traditional European understandings of race or ethnicity. Unfortunately, this has largely been lost.

The idea of minorities conceived primarily along ethnic, racial, and religious lines was thus a concept largely imported by the British, who were almost obsessed about defining people according to racial, ethnic, and linguistic identity (Taylor 1982). Their use of the terms nationality and race, and their obsession with collecting not only revenue data in things like decadal censuses, but enumerating and reporting race, ethnicity, language, and religion data, introduced a new narrative. For the British, these were scientific typologies of the colonial space based on anthropological observations, and justified white Europeans at the top of a hierarchy of races that included diverse, categorized, local populations. These British ideas, derived from romantic nationalism as found in Lord Byron's lines and the writings of nineteenth-century Europeans such as Mill, Mazzini, and Herder, were supplemented by improved cartography that offered great accuracy in defining the territory and territorial control attributed to each race (the material point of reference of a 'nation's' cradle (Elden 2013).

Such categorization was fundamental in the colonial context, where such divisions would facilitate the efficiency of colonial administration. Ethnicity became a powerful tool for population control and effective administration of the colony. The implementation of laws and policies on the basis of identity markers allowed the British to divide the population systematically under categories and sub-categories (Taylor 2007). For example, by the time of the 1885 Anglo-Burman War, in which the British captured Upper Burma, they came to the conclusion that the ethnic minorities needed protection from the Burmans (Thant Myint-U 2001; Taylor 2015). Thus, on taking control, they immediately divided Burma into 'Ministerial Burma' (Burman-dominated lowlands, including Arakan) and the 'Frontier

Areas' (mountainous, ethnic nationalities). The categorization of 'martial races' then allowed them to justify exclusion of the Burmans from military service, while allowing recruitment from minority groups. Gradually British rule became perceived by the local population as a colonial enterprise protected by foreigners, assisted by foreign ethnicities (Smith 1999). The British brought foreign minorities along with them, to run their Burmese colony, including Muslims from the Subcontinent (many employed in the security and administration of Rakhine). With the British distinction between autochthonous and non-autochthonous groups, the colonizers introduced new cleavages that were anchored to the emerging, European-conceived, notions of race, border, and territoriality. Thus, putative identities that were once fluid, porous, and flexible were turned into something brittle, static, and absolute. During the colonial era in Arakan, and in Burma at large, there was therefore the initiation of a process, which Ne Win in particular continued after de-colonization, that involved the apprehension of ethnic identity, a product of human social interaction, then its presentation as an unalterable fact, predetermined by nature (Berger & Luckman 1967).

It also provides the basis to understand the current ethnic puzzle in Rakhine State and its territorial delineations. Distribution of power, as well as material and non-material public resources, follows the asymmetric relationships between the Burman-dominated central government and the two major communities in Rakhine State, the Rakhine and the Muslims.

This politicization of ethnicity was, of course, also part of wider processes around decolonization and independence (Taylor 1982, 2007). A reification of ethnic identities was part of a global shift in post-1945 world politics, focused around anti-colonial struggles. The language of nationalism and self-determination became the ideological vehicle for all colonized peoples entering the national liberation struggle. Following the example of national self-determination movements in Europe, they pursued independence along the same grounds. In order to do that, they adopted the language of ethnicity and claimed the ideology of nationalism, arguing that as distinctive human groupings, as their own nations, they should be entitled to self-rule (Laoutides 2015).

In Myanmar, growing anti-colonial sentiment led to the rise of nationalism, first as an attempt to reclaim lost identity pride and subsequently as a means to mobilize resistance against the British. Although ethnicity and race entered Myanmar's politics most directly during the struggle for independence, in the 1920s and 1930s (Taylor 2015), it emerged through a much longer social process. Turner (2014) shows how ordinary Buddhists in Burma progressively responded to colonial policies, eventually channelling the minds of many young, anti-colonial Burmese towards nationalism. The Burmese understood British rule through the interpretative framework of *sasana* (religious) decline. Progressively a new imaginary—the moral Buddhist lay community—was developed, and assumed the task of protecting the religion from further erosion. Early Buddhist lay organizations during British rule thus first sought to preserve Buddhism, by minimizing the colonial influences that sought to reshape and control Buddhism and Buddhists. By the 1920s Buddhism had changed from the object of political organizing into an instrument of organizing for political ends (Turner 2014, p. 139). Accordingly the evolving nationalist agenda employed the pre-existing model of Buddhist social organization, then imbued it with instrumental political value after Independence.

Importantly, the struggle for independence in Burma originated within the Young Men's Buddhist Association, and drew heavily on racial and religious loyalties, fanning nationalism along racial (and religious) lines, rather than instilling confidence in an emerging overarching Burma-wide identity. The creation of the General Council of Burmese Associations as well as the Dobama Asiayone attest to the fact that the evolution of the nationalist agenda was a multi-layered and perplexed process, easily perceived as based on race and religion (Nemoto 2000). This was exacerbated in Arakan, in the events of the Second World War, during which the Muslims found themselves on the opposite side to the Burman and Rakhine. This further cemented the characterization of the Muslims as on the wrong side of nationalism.

The reification of ethnic identities under the British thus became the foundation for the nationalist struggle, the subsequent politics of ethnicity in Myanmar (Taylor 2015), and Ne Win's elevation of the politics of indigeneity (*taing-yin-tha*) as a means of projecting control—through domination over most minorities and exclusion of others (Cheesman 2017).

Building Ethnic Hegemony

To understand the ethnic identity conundrum better, we need to explore theories of the process of identity building and ethnic conflict a little further. As discussed above, identity involves the creation of images about oneself and others. Volkan (1988) introduces the idea of the 'externalization of identity', through which a shared sense of identity is built and passed on through culture (familiar objects/discourse of one's environment) and the process of socialization. Thus various symbols, such as national anthems, particular foods, religious figures, flags, and so on are used as channels of identity externalization. Reference to other groups can also be instrumental in this, whether with positive or negative connotations (Ross 1993). However, group identity is strengthened and in-group cohesion greatest when there are clear enemies (those who are outside the group), myths of a glorious past (narratives of superiority or the grandeur of a golden age to which they desire to return), myths of collective traumas (invasions, massacres, losses, always covered with a strong sense of injustice), and clearly demarcated territory which can define the zones of inclusion and exclusion.

For Ross (2007), identity issues are at the heart of any ethnic conflict. Individuals feel connected through a shared identity, built on a perception of common past experiences and expectations of shared future ones. This connection strengthens the social categories that determine group and individual behaviour. Social action and innovation take place within the framework of culture, the system of beliefs and meaning that individuals and groups use to interpret reality. If minorities are significantly different, they are less likely to assimilate, and thus can become targets for the externalization of the majority's negative feelings and self-images, attracting suspicion and antipathy because of their 'different' characteristics (Volkan 1988).

Different cultural practices and behavioural expressions can become conflict factors because they evoke meanings, images, and metaphors rooted in collective memories. Thus, cultural interpretations or narratives become central to one group's interpretation of another. Culture provides a group with essential accounts of the world, with group narratives giving an account of their origin, history, and conflicts with outsiders. Ethnic hatred may become more intense if the targeted minority is linked to narratives of past deep trauma upon the majority, such as a defeat in war, past dominance of the minority over the majority, and so on. In that case, according to Ross, after the balance of power changes in favour of the majority, the minority may become a target of ethnic cleansing, massacre, and genocide.

Burmanizing Burma, Demonizing Rakhine and Muslims

Ross and Volkan's analysis resonates in Rakhine State on multiple levels. The Rakhine lost their glorious kingdom to the invading Burmese army in 1784, and a significant contributing factor in the decline and eventual fall of Mrauk-U was the massacre of Shah Shuja and his Muslim followers a century earlier. For the Burman, Rakhine State represents one of their first significant losses of territory to British colonialism, and the Muslims are perceived as closely linked to the colonial administration, security, and money-lending practices, all of which alienated many Burmese.

The nationalist struggle for independence in the 1920s, with its mantra of 'Do-Bama' (we Burman), grew into a push for the re-indigenization of Burma in the 1930s. Re-indigenization was implemented post-Independence, but its conception dates to the last phase of the colonial period after the separation of Burma from British India in 1937 (Nemoto 2000; Egreteau 2011). The nature of this Burman-centric nationalism, and ethnic clashes during the Second World War, created an escalation of centrifugal ethnic forces; a plethora of largely ethnic-based groups rebelled at Independence in 1948.

Post-colonial nation building was led by Prime Minister U Nu and a Burman-dominated elite, while General Ne Win led the military to victory in the intense civil war. In Rakhine State, ethnic Rakhine separatist ambition was an important aspect of most insurgent rebellions, while the Mujahid rebellion raged for well over a decade in the north of the state. In the end, U Nu's willingness to negotiate significant levels of autonomy for the Muslims, even after the Mujahids had been defeated, became one of the key justifications for Ne Win's coup in 1962.

The Burmese government's major instrument for the re-establishment of control was the armed forces, which underwent a systematic process of Burmanization by expelling and excluding ethnic minorities from its ranks, transforming it into a powerful ethnic Burman apparatus (Callahan 2003). This process of Burmanization was mirrored in other state institutions, through policy programmes on several aspects of economic, political, and cultural life (education, land reform, promotion of Buddhism as the official religion, etc.). Although the political rhetoric was encapsulated by the idea of 'unity in diversity', the process of Burmanization created a preferential system in government and society that promoted ethnic Burmans. This was exacerbated after Ne Win took power in 1962, with significant ramifications for Muslims and those of Indian origin—including the Muslims of northern Rakhine State. The Ne Win government's idea of stability and nation-building was through the imposition of the culture, history, and dominant self-narrative of the Burman majority onto all minority groups, and the exclusion of non-indigenous elements who entered Burma during the period of British control. This left the Rakhine as a suppressed, marginalized minority, to be either assimilated or alienated. And it cast the Muslims as non-indigenous, foreign, excluded, and dangerous.

The situation of the Muslims in northern Rakhine State therefore deteriorated significantly after 1962, enhanced by the Ne Win regime's elevation of the ideology of *taing-yin-tha* as the definitive indigenous national races. This became the means to assign autochthony to the population. Progressively, *taing-yin-tha* became the test for full citizenship rights (Cheesman 2017). Thus in Rakhine State the Burman leadership, particularly Ne Win and the Tatmadaw, adopted identity politics in an exclusive fashion as a means to subjugate (if not assimilate) ethnic Rakhine, and to marginalize and exclude the Muslims. For the Muslims, non-autochthony placed them at the very outer zone of the population groups in Myanmar, progressively eroding their right to participate in the political community.

Following the enunciation of ethnicity as the main characteristic of the political order, old identities were re-fashioned, new identities have been articulated, and historical memory has been re-imagined by ethnic entrepreneurs for various purposes. Questions of identity and ethnicity have been prominent in the existential threat felt by each group. Although the type of threat may vary, it is perceived as real in all cases, with serious consequences. For the Muslims, the feeling of existential threat stems from the violence they have experienced over the past seventy-five years, at the hands of either the Rakhine (1942 and 2012) or the military (1978, 1991–2, 2016–17). Their collective memory of persecution is further strengthened by a narrative of indirect or structural violence, constituted by collective discrimination in the form of restrictions on movement, denial of citizenship, forced segregation, and internal displacement.

These traumatic experiences reflect the hegemonic macro-discourses, and have influenced the language of fear and threat employed by the Muslims. It results in a siege mentality, the self-image of a homeless and helpless population suffering ongoing gross injustice (Anderson 1983). This has forged a sense of shared identity out of what was originally an ethnically diverse community of Muslims in Arakan. The emergence of a common identity has been constituted dialectically, in contrast to 'the Other', the common oppressor. The Muslim narrative thus draws on forms of defensive nationalism, creating a shared identity out of common oppression (Anderson 1983). This, however, suggests that both the object and the agency of identification are not static, but constituted through a process of displacement or projection (Bhabha 1994, p. 162). This observation recognizes the complexity, relative contingency, and openness of the processes by which identities are constructed in everyday practices, thus transcending the single macro-narratives of identity formation (Rattansi 1999).

The demonization of the Muslim population based on a process of alienation from the national body politic can thus offer some insights into violence and conflict in Rakhine, as can the systemic pressure to subjugate or assimilate the ethnic Rakhine. Identity politics, and the building of a negative image of the Other as a means of enhancing in-group cohesion, elevation, and survival, can explain the accumulation of negative narratives leading to episodic low-intensity intra-communal Rakhine–Muslim conflict—and some of the military crackdowns. However, is all violence in Rakhine State related to questions of identity?

We suggest that many accounts of violence that in the first instance appear, or are presented as, ethnic conflict are actually underpinned by motives other than identity. This, we suggest, is particularly true of many of the everyday stories of conflict we have heard during interviews. We suggest that there is a major disconnect between what elite actors and the organizations that claim to represent local communities promote as their cause, and the dynamics of everyday lives, interactions, and aspirations.

Ethnic Conflict, Complexity, Fluidity, and Micro-Level Violence

Ethnic Conflict and the Danger of Collectivization

There has been a long academic debate about the causes and characteristics of conflict. 'Ethnic' conflict, as the conflict in Rakhine State has long been framed, is almost always understood as a form of 'grievance' (perceived or real), such as recognition in the distribution of political power (Geertz 1973; Horowitz 2000), incompatible cultural values (Huntington 1996), or a loss of identity (Sen 2006).

The 'ethnic' assumption about conflict in Myanmar does not constitute an intellectually isolated anomaly, being in tune with established analytical frameworks for the study of internal conflict and civil wars along identity lines. Recent scholarship highlights the oversimplifications involved in simply identifying conflict as 'ethnic'. Such portrayals almost universally fail to recognize the diversity of actors and identities, and have a strong tendency to encompass all members of different 'ethnic' groups into the conflict in distinct, binary, and enduring social categories (Cordell & Wolff 2010; Esman 2004; Gurr & Harff 1994; Wolff 2006). This line of inquiry presupposes that 'ethnic identities' exist as distinct and concrete social categories, and that tensions caused by differences in identities constitute the primary source of collective violence and conflict. Analysis thus attempts to unveil the exact types and nature of ethnic identities present, and the structure and patterns that lead to inequality and conflict. This simplification leads to an essentialist understanding of what is, in fact, highly dynamic, leading to an extreme reification of the variable 'ethnicity'. Hard and collective notions portray 'ethnic groups' as almost exclusively normative groups, and as singular agents with clearly defined wills that act comprehensively as individuals.

Ethnic identities do not exist in a vacuum, but emerge in response to particular, dynamic socio-political contexts. Lived ethnic identity and socio-cultural tradition is inherently fluid, diverse, and riven by division. The danger is, however, that the polarizing narratives used to mobilize nationalism means that use of the notion of ethnic identity in relation to conflict almost inevitably implies an inelasticity of internally homogenous and externally bounded groups, that does not reflect the realities of the social world (Malesevic 2004). It is interesting to note how much this is a distortion of traditional pre-colonial ideas and practice about the fluidity and dynamism of *lu-myo* (race or ethnicity). Conflation of conflict into an 'ethnic' label also tends to engage all members of collectivities as part of the conflict, when in reality it may only be a specific segment of such a collectivity, and may interpolate elements into a unified whole, erasing or ignoring distinctions and difference (Gilley 2004; Murer 2012). Thawnghmung (2012) has powerfully and quite personally demonstrated this problem in relation to the Karen conflict, documenting the alternate, non-violent views and struggle for equality of 'other' Karen, particularly in Yangon and the Delta, as opposed to those in Karen State. Her narrative highlights how the views of more moderate segments are easily overlooked in the face of dominant nationalist discourses driven by the government, military, or ethnic armed groups. The same dynamics, we suggest, apply to each of the major actors in the Rakhine conflict.

A range of Myanmar researchers who label the conflict as 'ethnic', such as Kramer (2010), Smith (1991, 1999, 2007), and South (2008), do offer nuanced and detailed analysis and are not overly drawn into this collectivization. While seeing conflict through an 'ethnic lens', the complexity in their treatment illustrates the point that 'ethnicities' should not be seen in terms of static, binary social categories, but as complex social realities. Ethnic cohesion varies from very loose and socially insignificant ascriptions to highly intense forms of interaction and organization. Thus, ethnicity must be seen as a discussion not about coherent social groups, but about dynamic social relationships and sets of historically framed processes, and we could probably examine the relations between groups better if we separated them from the ascribed social categories (Brubaker 1998, 2004).

In this light, consolidation of a sense of belonging among a group takes place during the course of a conflict. High levels of group cohesion may be the result, rather than the cause, of the conflict (Demmers 2017). We would thus argue that it is more useful to think about 'ethnicity without groups', or about nation-ness as set of contingencies, discursive frames, political projects, or organizational routines, than as discrete groups of people. An explicit distinction between groups (Rakhine and Muslim) and organizations (ARSA or AA) reduces the reification process, but also overcomes the oppressing tendency to cage individuals into involuntary associations, and groups into unmalleable identities (Malesevic 2004). It is important to treat 'ethnicities' as categories of social practice, not discrete and static entities with clearly defined membership, and recognize that in violent conflict more often it is organizations and not 'ethnic' groups that engage in violent actions. The relationship between organizations and groups is quite ambiguous, but the two cannot be equated. Thus, while Burmans, Rakhine, and Muslims are broadly in conflict, it is predominantly the Tatmadaw, the Arakan Army (AA), local militias, and the Arakan Rohingya Salvation Army (ARSA) who engage in violence.

This discussion is very relevant for Rakhine. If the level of recruitment for violence can be seen as a measure of the degree of cohesion between organizations and ethnic communities, then an interesting story unfolds. On the one hand we have the AA, and the nationalist armed groups before it, who claim to be fighting on behalf of the Rakhine. None ever enjoyed massive recruitment success, and the AA formed, trained, and operated exclusively in the Kachin region for years to build strength before returning to Rakhine. This observation indicates that despite the very strong sense of Rakhine nationalism and the significant role played by the Arakan National Party in national politics, there remains a lack of legitimacy for the AA's use of violence. Dynamics in the Rakhine–Burman conflict are still far below the threshold that would trigger any mass recruitment for organized violence, which in turn would increase the AA's legitimacy as a representative of the Rakhine. There is some limited support from Rakhine villagers and elite in terms of finance and intelligence, but this does not yet reflect any major change in the AA's narrow support base. Further, it is also noteworthy that the AA does not use any rhetoric against the Muslims. Rather, its website has a statement claiming that it strives for self-determination by an open, religiously diverse Rakhine, in which basic human rights are guaranteed for all (AA 2014). This statement, in response to an accusation in *Foreign Policy Magazine* that it has an anti-Muslim agenda, clearly implies an invitation for Muslims to join the AA and fight their common enemy together, namely domination by the military and the Burman-led state.

Similarly, at least until 2017, recruitment to mass violent resistance by Muslim ethnic entrepreneurs has had relatively low success. It has been widely noted by scholars that the Muslims of northern Rakhine State have never previously been a particularly radicalized population, even taking into account the Mujahid rebellion (Selth 2003, 2004, 2013; Yegar 1972, 2002; Horsey 2016). Recruitment to the Rohingya Solidarity Organization and the Rohingya Independence Front was never high. The exception appears to be ARSA's recruitment in the lead-up to the recent 25 August 2017 attacks, which Tatmadaw Commander-in-Chief Min Aung Hlaing (2017a, 2017b) estimates involved up to 4,000 ARSA combatants and 10,000 ARSA recruits. Certainly, there has long been a fear that discrimination against the Muslim population would lead to further recruitment to violence, and ARSA's strategy appears to have specifically sought to induce a popular uprising by Muslims against the state apparatus, to liberate a region from military and state control. If these numbers are accurate, this is approaching the degree of popular support for the Kachin Independence Army or the Karen National Union. However, the speed with which these people and the wider community fled to Bangladesh supports stories that many of these '4,000 ARSA combatants' were coerced or quickly recoiled from violence. Interestingly, and in line with the AA rhetoric, ARSA made explicit statements that the enemy they are fighting is not non-Muslim communities in Rakhine State, but the security forces (although that clearly later broke down in the massive reaction to the 25 August attacks). Our point is simply that there is a real distinction between the organization and the ethnic group—whether ARSA and the Muslims, the AA and the Rakhine, or the Tatmadaw and the Burman population—and yet that distinction can be ambiguous or hard to identify.

No less ambiguous is the relation between individual micro-level violence and inter-communal violence, such as in 2012. Whilst communal violence took place in 2012, it was not the rule up to this point in this conflict. The trigger, the rape and murder of the Buddhist woman by Muslim men, was certainly a heinous crime. Yet somehow, a violent crime by individuals became reframed as shared guilt or risk by the whole collective. The crime was not inter-communal violence, yet the response became read as inter-communal in nature, framed that way by ethnic entrepreneurs seeking to anchor their narratives in particular events. One of the problems in Rakhine State is that every crime, every action of micro-violence by individuals from any side, is now framed and read through the lens of communal violence or state persecution, whatever the initial motive.

The segregation of communities, as has taken place since 2012, only increases the probability of future violence. This includes the indefinite housing of Muslims in IDP camps with no ability to return to previous homes or livelihoods, and the loss of common space for interaction. In our repeat visits to Rakhine, we have observed changes in the local economy and society; life continues, and perhaps the well-being of most Rakhine improves, albeit at a very slow pace. But change does not include the Muslim community which, being isolated in IDP camps or village-tracts away from the developments, just witnesses these changes without any opportunity to partake. This disequilibrium increases temporally, with the difficulty of reintegration growing the longer communities are kept separate. The same will apply to those who have fled to Bangladesh—the longer they remain out of the country, the harder their reintegration will be. Prolonged segregation and marginalization therefore increase the possibility of recruitment to organized violence, motivating more members of the 'ethnic group' to respond in a manner closer to the limited number who previously seriously proposed violence as a solution.

The above analysis problematizes the links between organizations and communities in Rakhine State and brings to the fore some of the cleavages among the communities with regard to the ethnic conflict. Ethnic groups are not coherent blocs that clash with one other. Violence is not necessarily a product of unified action, but rather of an informal negotiation between diverse supra-local and local actors, with complicated sets of interests. Although the setting may look catastrophic, diverse local actors still pursue their own aims by operating and employing the overarching ethnic macro-cleavage. Facilitated by the wider conflict, people set out to pursue and settle their personal agendas, which may be personal rivalries over land, business interests, family feuds, etc. (Kalyvas 2007; Keen 2008). For example, while the State Councillor's office has reported that '163 informants' were killed by ARSA to protect the secrecy of the August 2017 attacks (UoM 2017b), our interviews confirm at least one instance in which the crime was the result of a personal vendetta that had nothing to do with the conflict. The point is that, because the conflict as read is an 'ethnic' one, unjust personal, economic, or other actions become subsumed under that heading, which is both a dangerously narrow reading of the conflict and allows individual crimes to be perpetrated with impunity.

This appropriation of ethnic conflict cleavages is not limited to physical violence, but expands to other sectors of human interaction, including the economy. The macro-cleavages distort interpretations of everyday incidents in rural areas, which become read through the lenses of ethnic conflict. The decisions of local businesses or farmers to not hire labour from a different group is often interpreted not as economic (price, skill, time efficiency, etc.), but rather as because of ethnic cleavages, becoming another reason for 'grievances'. Similarly, we have heard so many local accounts of buffalo going missing that this may be an urban myth, but the blame for animals having gone missing from Rakhine villages is always apportioned to neighbouring Muslims, without further investigation. The narrative is directly informed by the wider ethnic cleavages, turning a local, minor, and possibly easy to resolve issue into a major point of collective friction that reinforces the macro-cleavage.

Framing Conflict and Violence

It is important to note that the conflict in Rakhine State, in all its three axes, is socially and discursively constructed. The chapters elaborating the competing historical narratives demonstrate the interpretative clash for control of the 'facts' about the origins, causes, and actors driving the conflict. The interactive construction of meaning, involving both elites and masses (in different ways and modes), has been described as 'collective framing' (Tarrow 1994, 1998). Violent episodes in history become coded and described against the frame of a macro-conflict narrative. Collective framing redefines social conditions through a condensed and selective simplification process, which associates certain objects, situations, or experiences with a population's cultural predispositions. Such a process constructs larger frames of meaning invested with notions of grievance (Snow & Benford 1992). This redefinition of reality aims at mobilization, by amplifying perceptions of injustice and subconscious emotional appeals for remedial action. The interactive nature of meaning construction is evident, in that the 'meaning builders' are themselves also consumers of the cultural and traditional meanings they seek to re-appropriate. The aim of these 'entrepreneurs' is to imbue narratives with their own values and tailor the direction of social action toward their political goals (Tarrow 1994). As we saw in previous chapters, each group competes for the dominance of its interpretation, using its historical narrative as a means of reappropriating contemporary meaning and action.

Thus if social entrepreneurs encode ethnic difference as integral to a particular violent incident, such as the triggering of the 2012 intercommunal violence, the incident is quickly attributed to the wider frame of ethnic conflict (Horowitz 2001, p. 131). This applies to both contemporary and historical events. Since 2012 we have witnessed how the contesting frames of violence have created what Horowitz (2001) describes as a conflict about the nature of the conflict, leading to new rounds of violence. Gradually the framing of each violent episode, and the meanings attached to it, expand the dynamics of violent conflict. The original causes of the conflict become progressively less important in understanding why violence recurs (Brass 1996). Increasingly, the role of the internet and social media as a 'framing space' has become an important parameter in the way meaning is constructed and reappropriated. Cyberspace is employed for fast flows of information, but its speed and brevity predispose the propagation of simplified, inaccurate, and even deliberately fabricated misinformation, which can build a false sense of reality that can influence social action and instigate further mobilization.

Frame analysis must not be confined to conflict actors in Rakhine State, but should be expanded to consider the way other agents—such as the diaspora, journalists, INGOs, policy makers, diplomats, and analysts—make sense of the conflict. It has been noted earlier how many key informants ritualistically begin any interview with a long presentation recounting historical narratives as the canvas for analysing contemporary episodes of the conflict. Similarly, members of the international community (broadly defined) widely frame their analysis of every event around particular aspects of the conflict, remaining blind to or silent about other aspects. We can see this in the way the tripartite nature of this conflict is often flattened to be simply about state persecution of 'the Rohingya ethnic minority'. International attention is largely fixated on the centre–periphery conflict between the state and the Muslim community. Amplified through the voices of many diaspora advocates, this re-framing transforms the conflict from a traditional ethno-cultural agenda into one that adopts a humanitarian-based and internationally appealing moral complexion, free of any need to recognize the fears and needs of the Rakhine, and reconcile with them as the basis of future peaceful coexistence (Leider 2015). Domestic attention focuses on the intra-periphery conflict between the ethnic Rakhine and the Muslims—now framed around ARSA attacking local civilians—constructing this in ways that do not acknowledge the role of the state in causing conflict. Likewise, the conflict between the state and the ethnic Rakhine receives minimal attention.

This change in the dynamic and focus of the conflict, underpinned by the 2012 inter-communal violence, coincided with the beginning of the transitional political period: transitions towards greater democracy and mass political participation in Myanmar. The rapid introduction of modern forms of mass politics into an authoritarian society created the space for ethnic entrepreneurs to exploit group antipathies and pursue group action that could lead to forms of political violence (Walter 1999b). This development lends support to a wider argument in the literature on the relation between political violence, the level of openness, and the electoral structure of a political system (Muller & Weede 1994; Horowitz 2000; Mann 2005). The political and economic transition of Myanmar opened up the space for local actors to operate in a fashion inconceivable under the pre-2011 military rule. The continued emphasis on the ethnic composition of Myanmar in the public discourse, enhanced by the emergence of ethnic parties, has elevated the prospect of political violence being seen instrumentally as the means for party unity and electoral success (Burke 2016). Certainly, the military-backed USDP party courted the Muslim vote in the 2010 elections in a manner that aggravated ethnic Rakhine fears, and Rakhine nationalist parties have not been slow to articulate positions opposed to Muslim interests. Thus, framing is a process of appropriating meaning, and it always occurs within the parameters of ideologies, cultural dispositions, and perceptions, from within and without (King 2004). The Rakhine State conflict is no exception.

Territory

One final key theoretical area in the conflict studies literature remains to be considered, namely the relationship between territory and ethnicity. This is important to analyse because, in international politics, control of territory has become a *sine qua non* condition for international recognition of a political community (Toft 2006). Territorial coherence also shapes perceptual judgements of ethnic affinity. Control of territory thus creates conditions that emerging ethnic groups could meet, opportunities that could be exploited. However, linking territory to recognition and international support elevates the value of possession, making territory increasingly indivisible and territorial conflicts more highly intractable.

There are two possible explanations for this. First, ethnicity is often employed as the main narrative for survival in international politics, thus it is reappropriated with an existential moral value that makes claims to territory by ethnic groups (and states) legitimate, and hard to negotiate. Second, the post-Second World War world order places emphasis on territorial sovereignty and the stability of nation-states, as crystallized in the UN Charter's protection of the territorial integrity of member states. This core norm of the international system offers an advantage against any challenge to the boundaries of existing states (Crawford 2006), although conversely, significant loss of control over territory undermines claims to national sovereignty. Again, this raises the stakes in territorial conflict.

The modern understanding of the sovereignty and indivisibility of territorial states evolved in Europe, through the transformation of the notion of political community and its relation to territory (Hall 1999; Krasner 1993, 1995–6; Teschke 2003). Hard and fixed borders gradually replaced more fluid distinctions between political communities (Elden 2013). The emerging national collectives problematize diverse notions of minority identity, leading numerous groups of people to be incorporated (sometimes violently) into the 'national' mainstream body politic, within clear territorial demarcations (Hall 1999, pp. 132–71; Tilly 1993). In Europe, statism contributed to the gradual establishment of common language groups and cultures, and there emerged a sense of identity increasingly defined as 'nation' (Mann 1993, pp. 571–90). Progressively, there was a confluence between the people as a political community and the demarcated territory that they claimed as the locus of realizing—institutionally, economically, and politically—their distinctiveness as a collectivity. Nation and territory have thus become intrinsically linked in European-history-derived ideas.

People organize and categorize themselves politically within a spectrum of options ranging from voluntary membership to territorial proximity and birth membership. These alternatives to political organization are not exclusive to each other; occasionally they collide, and ethnic conflict often can be explained and understood with reference to such collisions. The individualistic assumptions of Western thought have, however, had a major impact on formal institutions far beyond the West. Part of this legacy is the modern nation-state, which in a very short period of three hundred years has become the default model of political organization globally. Based on territorial sovereignty, it encompasses everyone within its boundaries under a unified administration. But even in this context, ethnicity continued to be an organizing principle of community within the state, providing perceptively firmer ground for political association than egalitarian individualism.

Under colonial rule in Burma, this boundary-drawing process took ethnic intersects into account and consolidated ethnicity as an unalterable dimension of politics, depicted territorially. Any large-scale territorial demarcation would have been arbitrary in Burma. The pre-colonial Burman Kingdom, including Rakhine, was operating administratively in zones starting from the highly centralized core in Mandalay, going outwards within decreasing spheres of influence based on socio-political distance from the centre. The region around the capital was directly administered, most of lowland Burma was governed by royally appointed nobles, and many other areas, such as most of Shan, were ruled through hereditary clan chiefs. Yet other areas, like most of Karen and Kachin, were occasionally required to pay tribute, but were not administratively ruled in an ongoing sense. Thus the British decided to divide Burma in somewhat arbitrary fashion into two major zones after 1886: Ministerial and the Frontier areas. Arakan's inclusion in Ministerial Burma by the British legitimized the conquest of Arakan by the Burmans a few decades earlier, and justified Burma proper and Arakan being seen as a unified space—an idea that was not attuned to the Arakanese national narrative. Perhaps this largely explains why Rakhine State was created as late as 1971, one of the last to be created within the Union of Myanmar.

What the British did, which was more important for ethnicity, was to change the scale of the polity by several degrees. The colonial borders were artificial, not because the new demarcation was indifferent to their ethnic composition, but because they were, on average, many times larger than the political systems they displaced (Horowitz 2000). With migration, trade, and a central bureaucratic structure, among other things, it became necessary to establish social relations far beyond the village or locality (Smith 1999). The massive volume of transactions overwhelmed and exceeded the reach of pre-existing sentiments of community. There was thus a need for a new set of social arrangements able to handle the transformation on the ground; however, the evolution of citizenship as the means to transcend particularistic identification, minimize uncertainty, and facilitate relations among strangers was out of the question. Colonials were not citizens, but subjects (Horowitz 2000). Whereas in Western Europe the ideological developments that led to a full-blown conception of citizenship evolved over centuries without external interference, in Burma these changes took place over decades, and ethnicity proved a powerful and fairly prompt way to organize the body politic in preparation for political independence.

After the end of the Second World War the right to self-determination was incorporated in the UN Charter and became part of the international legal arsenal of decolonization (Crawford 2006). But in former colonies, usually demarcated according to administrative convenience under the principle of *uti possidetis* rather than local forms of group identity, peoples who had once had little to do with each other found themselves members of the same state. Or, in some instances such as Rakhine, people who had recent traumatic experiences, like the clashes between Muslim and Rakhine in 1942, were left grouped together in the same state. Thus, the narrow interpretation of self-determination as a legal norm by the UN deprived many groups of a chance to pursue peaceful claims for autonomy within the boundaries of international law. This laid the grounds for ethnic and separatist conflicts (Tomuschat 2006), with control of territory sometimes proving successful for secession or establishing realms of autonomy under international law.

Territory and ethnicity provide two different principles for political organization. However, in the context of Rakhine, they collide to produce a perplexing puzzle of relations and claims between Muslim, Rakhine, and Burman/state actors—claims which in turn lead to a set of paradoxes, but also explain the current conflict in Rakhine State. Myanmar is a post-colonial state, with boundaries unaltered from those it had as a colony since 1937, when British Burma became a separate colony from British India. Thus, from the international community perspective, all inhabitants of this space are recognized as members of the political community of Myanmar. However, the internal organization of the political community quickly became based on ethnicity rather than territory, allowing elevation of the idea of a political community made up of ethnicities rather than individual citizens. This created the space for Ne Win and the Tatmadaw elite to prioritize the idea of *taing-yin-tha* (indigenous national race), as already explored. The locus of membership in the political community in Myanmar has thus moved from territory (those who inhabit the land are by definition citizens of the body politic) to race (those who belong to a list of *taing-yin-tha* are by definition full citizens).

The dialectical relationship between territoriality and ethnicity in Rakhine State persists in an environment of difficult coexistence. Placing heterogeneous groups under the same territorial organization is complicated and challenging. Whilst territorial proximity appears as inclusive—all within the territory are to be treated equally—ethnic determination of the political body has become exclusive. This process did not originate from honest and friendly intentions, but builds upon a reappropriation of meaning and context, with the aim of imposing a particular understanding of history and social relations which is—at the very least—not mutually agreed upon. It has thus unleashed a struggle for domination of the territorial space by competing groups with different agendas.

Burma descended into ethnic and separatist chaos at Independence in 1948, as already discussed. We have also already explored the competing claims by ethnic Rakhine and Muslim groups since Independence, with Rakhine groups seeking autonomy or secession for the whole of Rakhine, by violent or political means, and the Muslims repeatedly seeking some form of autonomy or secession for the north of the state. But because the Muslims have to some extent always been considered external to the Burmese polity, and increasingly so under Ne Win's *taing-yin-tha* truth regime, their claims to autonomy have been seen to most directly challenge the notion of national sovereignty under UN principles. This, in part, helps to explain the military obsession—over decades—with crushing Muslim secessionism far more ruthlessly than other secessionist conflicts across the country.

Perhaps the international prioritization of territorial control as a precondition for international recognition also helps explain the emergence of ARSA. It is highly unlikely that northern Rakhine State could ever gain independence as a nation-state, and this does not appear to be the strategy of ARSA. Perhaps it primarily aims to destabilize Myanmar, or to achieve a de facto state arrangement where it controls 'liberated' territory for a time. But perhaps the more recent evolution in international thinking about state sovereignty is also a factor. Particularly since the emergence of the Responsibility to Protect through the UN in the 2000s, state sovereignty has come to be seen as less absolute, and more conditional upon fulfilling responsibilities towards the people of the country. One could imagine ARSA believing—or at least imagining—that international support and pressure on the Myanmar state to grant them autonomy would be strengthened by gaining de facto control of territory, given their powerful historical narrative of injustices and the well-documented contemporary oppression of the Muslims.

The source of government legitimacy over Rakhine is not an outcome of the long presence of Burmans in Rakhine, but rather of historical developments (colonization, decolonization, *utis possidetis*, protection of territorial integrity under international law), further invested by the mythology of a shared history of related peoples with a common ancestry. The claims of Rakhine nationalists to legitimacy stem from their long history in the land. Muslim advocates say that some of their ancestors coexisted with the Rakhine for centuries. Along with colonial-era migration and increased mobility, the two populations have now co-inhabited the region for a long period, certainly long enough to legitimize their presence along the lines of the territorial principle.

Thus, in conclusion, much in this conflict involves questions of identity and territory. However, to the extent that this conflict is about identity, commonly conceived of in terms of ethnicity, it also resonates strongly with all the concerns about such a label. Analysis of conflicts framed as 'ethnic' commonly collectivize groups as if they were inelastic and static, internally homogenous and externally bounded blocs, and this has happened in the Rakhine State conflict. They are not. Likewise, analysis cannot overlook the multitude of micro-cleavages, or the reinterpretation of criminal activities, micro-violence, and political or economic interest in favour of a flattened narrative about the conflict. The racial groups remain distinct from the social entrepreneurs and organizations mobilizing for conflict, and their constructions of meaning. In the same manner, the importance of territory cannot be overlooked. For the military, territorial integrity is linked with the exercise of sovereignty, and secessionist action by a group considered to be external, such as the Muslims, is a particularly significant threat. But for the Muslims, gain of territorial control potentially strengthens international recognition of and support for their cause as standing against unjust oppression. However, at its core this is not an identity or ethnic conflict revolving primarily around difference, or a territorial dispute, as much as a conflict about political inclusion, recognition, and equality.

No solution is simple, but any resolution must embrace these realities while charting an alternative to political organization along ethnic lines. And somehow, a territorial definition of citizenship must emerge, with genesis of an inclusive *demos* in the new democratic, post-transition Myanmar. We will explore some of these ideas in the next chapter.

7

THE INTERNATIONAL COMMUNITY

RECOMMENDATIONS AND CONCLUSIONS

So, where to from here?

The previous chapters have described and analysed the conflict from as many angles as possible, including the perspectives of each major actor and against a diverse range of theoretical approaches found in the literature. The key question now is: given the current crisis and the mass dislocation of over a million Rohingya Muslims, who might potentially never return, is there any way back? Is there any path from here that could lead to conflict resolution and a future non-violent coexistence in Myanmar, one that deals with grievances and injustices, de-escalates perceived threat on all sides, and leads to greater equality and rights? Or has the current situation spiralled into an irreversible situation resulting in the ethnic cleansing of more than half the Muslim population (whether by deliberate intent or a more unintended outcome of long-term discriminatory policy)? And what of the remaining 600,000 Rohingya Muslims still living in Rakhine State? Is there possibility of resolution, non-violence, rights, and a bright future for those people?

This chapter will summarize the most important findings from our analysis, and explore them in the context of the recommendations made by the Kofi Annan-led Advisory Commission on Rakhine State

(Annan et al. 2017b). These recommendation are widely recognized as the best proposals to date towards resolution of the underlying issues and long-term drivers of the conflict, although they were handed down just before the latest violence and so do not deal with the latest injustices and human flight. This chapter will therefore explore the Commission's recommendations, how these would affect the underlying conflict drivers and grievances, and consider any further factors or actions required for any peaceful resolution. It discusses the need for a complete reframing of the underlying issues away from race and indigeneity, pointing to the pathway for this, and highlighting the opportunity it poses for the wider peace process. It considers the actions and advocacy of the international community, and some of the impacts this is having, and could have, on the conflict. And it concludes with a grave warning of the moral hazard posed by international community action or advocacy, signalling the need for far more informed and strategic international responses.

Key Findings from our Analysis

Key themes running throughout this book, presented with extensive evidence and discussion, are the deep historicity of the conflict, the complexity of actors and mutual existential fears, and the fact that this conflict is not about the denial of citizenship, statelessness, economic interests, identity, ethnicity or territory per se. Rather, it is primarily about the possibility and extent of inclusion, on equal terms, of the Rohingya and (to a lesser extent) the Rakhine in the political community that constitutes the Union of Myanmar.

This is a deeply historical conflict. Burman–Rakhine rivalry and conflict date back centuries. Rakhine–Muslim tensions go back at least two hundred years. There have been repeated mass dislocations since at least the Second World War, several on a scale similar to the present one. In one sense, what has happened over the past couple of years is not new or unique, but it does present significant new dangers. We have documented at least four previous mass displacements and refugee crises from northern Rakhine, prompting and prompted by very significant historical grievances. And we have highlighted the extent to which all protagonists draw extensively on those historical narratives to articulate present grievances, legitimize contemporary political claims, mobilize their populations, and promote their protracted victimhood to gain external support. The fact that a majority of those displaced in 1978 and 1991–2 did eventually return offers hope that the same may be achievable today. But even in the worst-case scenario where this group doesn't return, the longer-term grievances and drivers must still be dealt with, for the sake of the remaining Muslims, the ethnic Rakhine, the other minorities caught in the midst of this—and for the future of the whole Myanmar state.

This led us to discuss the three major axes of the conflict in some detail, illustrated by detailed examination of: a) recent communal violence between Muslims and Rakhine; b) the armed conflict and non-violent political struggle between Rakhine nationalists and the Burman-led state; and c) the extensive violence between Muslims and the security forces of the Burman-led state.

We then examined the situation as an 'intractable conflict', focusing on it particularly as a stalemate of historical narratives. Chapters 3 and 4 thus explored the four key historical narratives used by ethnic entrepreneurs to frame the conflict, for psycho-social mobilization and to convey their protracted victimhood and historical injustices. For want of names, we called these the Rohingya 'Origin' narrative; the Rakhine 'Independence' narrative; the Burman 'Unity' narrative; and the Rakhine–Burman 'Infiltration' narrative. These were presented largely in their own terms, then analysed and critiqued. We concluded that there is strong evidence for a Muslim community in northern Rakhine well before the Burman conquest in 1784, in addition to the Kaman Muslim population, which thus should be considered indigenous (*taing-yin-tha*) under Myanmar definitions. However, this community intermarried with and was in many ways swamped by a massive wave of migration during the colonial period, resulting in a very mixed-ancestry community today, almost impossible to separate into 'indigenous' and 'non-indigenous' groups, as the state seeks to do. Importantly, the migrants largely assimilated with the pre-existing Muslim population, adopting their history as their own, which is usually regarded as a positive attribute of migrants.

While the Rohingya community is wrong to downplay the impact of colonial-era migration, which was very large, so too are the Burman

and Rakhine wrong to exclude the Muslim population from the definition of 'indigenous'. There was rapid population growth due to migration, but there is also a genuinely indigenous aspect to the Muslim
community of northern Rakhine State. The Rohingya have a genuine
claim to a hybridized or mixed–indigenous ancestry. Some ancestors
of most of those who call themselves Rohingya almost certainly do
pre-date the arrival of the British, and the 1823 watershed presupposes
rigid, fixed racial identities not reflected by the fluidity of intermarriage and social mixing across contemporary Myanmar. This assimilation of migrants into an indigenous people should be seen in positive
terms, particularly in the light of the high rate of mixed-blood ancestry
across the rest of Myanmar today.

The *taing-yin-tha* definition of indigeneity, and the politics that drives
it, are not inherent in history or the context. Rather, they are weapons
of exclusionary politics, largely perpetrated by General Ne Win and the
military regime after the 1962 coup, and should be consigned to history
along with the xenophobic and autarkic authoritarianism of that period.
The *taing-yin-tha* dogma at the heart of this conflict is built on a Burman
mythology of common ancestry and history, which is a key driver of the
multiple conflicts across the country. Its centralizing, Burman-
hegemonic, and exclusionary dimensions undermine national unity, and
for reform to proceed in contemporary Myanmar the nation must move
beyond such things. Without leaving this poisonous politics of ethnicity
behind, and reframing the debate entirely away from race and ethnicity,
it is hard to see how a sustainable long-term peaceful solution could
ever be achieved—in Rakhine State or nationally.

Based on this historical analysis, Chapter 5 then considered the manner in which existential fears are triggered and sustained by all parties.
We looked at the tripartite ethnic security dilemma posed by the oblit-
eration of trust and communication in a time of political transition and
uncertainty, and found this to be a significant factor. The fact that the
reduced Rakhine birth rate makes the Muslim birth rate appear particularly high also sparks demographic security dilemma concerns,
which are likely to continue to destabilize for decades to come. This
must be planned for in any resolution. Further, in seeking to understand the complex web of existential fears, analysis must include cross-
border and regional dynamics. Power relations in the Rakhine State

conflict defy simplistic symmetric–asymmetric analysis—meaning that from a regional and social–psychological perspective, it is not only Muslims but also a large number of Rakhine (and even many Burmans) who feel extremely vulnerable. All parties thus react like existentially threatened minorities; this is a 'double-' or 'triple-minority complex'. Indeed, with so many Rohingya now in Bangladesh, and the growing rift between Muslim and Buddhist countries in the region, there is the worrying possibility that the notion of a 'Muslim' Bangladesh threatening 'Buddhist' Rakhine, or 'Muslim' South/Southeast Asia threatening 'Buddhist' Myanmar, may come to drive fear responses by the ethnic Rakhine, or the whole Myanmar state, even more strongly. Conflict resolution must address these fears, real or perceived.

We also observed that the Myanmar state is far from neutral in this conflict, and thus cannot mediate or bring stability as an impartial outside arbiter or actor. Until the state recognizes its complicity in creating and driving the conflict, and approaches negotiation humbly as an actor rather than a mediator, lasting resolution is unlikely.

Our analysis then turned to economic considerations. We explored the conflict from the perspective of the 'greed thesis', a very popular lens through which to read civil war, especially among major international donors, and a political economy approach, finding that the traditional understanding of the 'greed thesis' does not apply in this instance. There is no evidence that the conflict follows lines of rational calculation of material reward and opportunity cost, especially not by local ethnic leaders. There is, however, evidence that the significant new investment and economic development plans for the state mean that the vested interests of military, Burman, and Rakhine elites have become a complicating factor. This political economy is neither instigator nor primary driver of the conflict, but it has become a very real factor adding to the complexity of the situation and posing significant new dangers. It is particularly problematic that most of the Muslim population of Maungdaw are refugees in Bangladesh at precisely the same time as their land has suddenly been identified as having greater economic value than ever—for cross-border trade, hotel and coastal tourism, mineral extraction, etc. The danger of a long-term ethnic cleansing outcome for economic gain is now very real, whether pre-planned or otherwise. If the Myanmar authorities are at all sincere in seeking to resolve this situation, they must take decisive steps, *immediately*, to protect the economic interests of the vulnerable Muslim community that has fled recent violence, and ensure their repatriation with full security and restitution.

Chapter 6 then analysed the conflict in terms of ethnicity, identity, and territorial grievances, finding that it closely fits the model of an identity conflict, as described in the conflict studies literature. The reification of ethnic political identities in Myanmar since Independence, a concept largely imported by the British, has been exploited by Ne Win and the Tatmadaw for six decades, to exclude colonial-era migrants and pursue an assimilative 'Burmanization' agenda. The end result has been decades of ethnic conflict across the country, and in Rakhine State the demonization of both the ethnic Rakhine (to some extent) and the Muslims (primarily). This combination of Burman chauvinism and anti-Indian/anti-Muslim sentiment is one of the most fundamental drivers of this conflict, along with contestation for control of territory. However, as is often the case, labelling this conflict 'ethnic' has led to a dangerous sense of collectivization, in which all members of each group are falsely assumed to have identical interests and support all the same causes. Care and nuance must be maintained. The role of ethnic entrepreneurs, and the inflammatory temptation to reframe every crime or micro-level violent incident as 'ethnic conflict', regardless of circumstances, needs to be recognized and addressed.

Finally, territorial control (or the disruption of state control over territory) is a key factor in this conflict. Territory is of great importance to the Burman-led military, because it echoes core international norms, embedded in the United Nations Charter, about respect for territorial integrity and state sovereignty, which are perceived as guaranteeing the principle of non-interference in the domestic affairs of another state. However, as the *sine qua non* condition for international recognition of a political community, control of territory has also become an important tool in the pursuit of claims for autonomy by both Rakhine and Muslim groups. This driver, as a tool of leverage and international recognition/support, can explain the recent violent attacks by both the Arakan Army and, particularly, the Arakan Rohingya Salvation Army. This analysis highlights the fact that the issues of governance—meaning at least equitable representation for both Rakhine and

Muslims, in a system guaranteeing recognition, rights, physical security, and cultural survival—is central to any long-term, sustainable conflict resolution. Indeed, the long-term protection and recognition of the rights of a returned Muslim community when granted citizenship may, ultimately, require some form of limited autonomous region for the Rohingya.

The Kofi Annan-Led Advisory Commission Recommendations

The international community is clamouring for solutions, desperately seeking both proposals for policies that might turn the situation around and ways to gain leverage to force the Myanmar government to accept them. The most comprehensive and practical recommendations to date are those that were presented to the government on 24 August 2017, by the Kofi Annan-led Advisory Commission on Rakhine State (Annan et al. 2017b). These recommendations, of course, preceded the 2017 violence and mass exodus from northern Rakhine, but remain the best starting point for conflict resolution.

Aung San Suu Kyi's office and the Kofi Annan Foundation established the Commission in September 2016, with a mandate to identify the factors that had resulted in violence, displacement, and underdevelopment in Rakhine State, and to develop recommendations to address these. The nine-member committee comprised three internationals (led by Kofi Annan), and six nationals: two Burmans, two Rakhine, and two Muslims (although none were Rohingya). The Commission conducted extensive meetings over the course of a year, with national political and military leaders, Rakhine government officials, and representatives from a diverse range of political parties, religious institutions, civil society, village leaders, residents of various villages and IDP camps including ethnic minorities, plus the private sector, international agencies, regional governments, and so on. The Commission delivered its final recommendations just hours before the August 2017 ARSA attacks, so the situation on the ground has changed dramatically since then. However, Aung San Suu Kyi and the NLD government have continued to commit themselves to implementing *all* of these recommendations, as quickly as the conditions on the ground allow, giving them significant domestic and international purchase. And they are, as already stated, the most well-researched, comprehensive, and practical recommendations towards a long-term solution made to date.

Of the eighty-eight recommendations made in the Commission's final report (Annan et al. 2017b), quite a few are challenging to the government's position, yet they are very important if peace is to be achieved. All recommendations, without exception, deserve implementation. There is not space here to review all aspects of the report's findings, which include recommendations around essential areas such as economic and social development, education and health service provision, control of the drug trade, etc., as well as political participation, inter-communal cohesion, security-sector reform, access to justice, Bangladesh and regional relations, etc. Most significantly, the report highlighted our point that this conflict has multiple axes, and that, for example, the conflict relationship between the ethnic Rakhine and the state cannot be ignored in seeking a long-term solution.

It is difficult to single out any recommendations as more important than others, but in the light of the preceding analysis and recent events, a number stand out as being of particular priority—as well as particular difficulty. These include:

1. *Allow an impartial and independent investigation of the serious human rights allegations.* This was recommended in the interim report in March 2017 (Annan et al. 2017a), and reiterated in August, but the government and military have consistently obstructed all efforts to set up any investigation involving external actors. For example, they have continually blocked the UN Human Rights Council's fact-finding mission, named in May 2017. The government, and Tatmadaw, continue to present themselves as neutral actors mediating a communal conflict, and ARSA as a separate issue of state security, despite being heavily involved as a conflict actor. It is hard to see any resolution until the government and military admit their complicity, and allow impartial and independent investigation. This must be a high priority, but would involve a difficult political capitulation by Aung San Suu Kyi, the NLD, and the Tatmadaw.

2. *Expedite a simpler citizenship-verification process (not just a document-verification process), and ensure that those who are verified as citizens enjoy all benefits, rights, and freedoms associated with citizenship.* The report goes on to recommend that the process must be transparent, effi-

cient, and based in legislation, well discussed and communicated across Rakhine State, with a clear timeline for various stages, and allow greater flexibility around documentation. This would be a massive reversal of policy, and would face significant internal opposition from Rakhine and Buddhist nationalists. It will be all the more difficult in the current climate, and with more than half the Muslim population displaced to Bangladesh, most fleeing with few documents or possessions.

3. *Abolish distinctions between different types of citizenship, guarantee that individuals will not lose their citizenship or have it revoked where this will leave them stateless, and enable those who have lost their citizenship or had it revoked to reacquire it if failing to do so would leave them stateless.* Further, the report recommends finding provision for all individuals who reside permanently in Myanmar to acquire citizenship by naturalization, particularly if they are stateless. As the Annan report succinctly points out, the 1982 Citizenship Law creates different types of citizenship with different rights, both in terms of acquiring and passing on citizenship and of political involvement and possibility of governance. This is a key reason why most Muslims in northern Rakhine State have resisted the current document-verification processes. Not only do they not trust the system, based on prior experience, but they have decided that it is worth fighting on for citizenship with full rights, rather than accept the type of more limited citizenship the 1982 law ostensibly offers them on paper.

4. *Re-examine the current linkages between citizenship and ethnicity.* In our analysis, this is key to the conflict, as above. Burman Privilege and the obsession with *taing-yin-tha* (indigenous races) categorization is a key driver of conflict across the country, and especially in Rakhine State. It is centralizing, Burman-hegemonic, and exclusionary. Any long-term resolution to the conflict in Rakhine will require the de-politicization of ethnicity and race in Myanmar, with a recognition of genuinely equal citizenship rights for all individuals. We discuss this further below. However, such a fundamental change in the political structure of Myanmar, and challenging entrenched Burman privilege, will be an extremely difficult change to sell, both to the Tatmadaw, who have the numbers in parliament to block constitutional change, and to the wider population. This is key, but

we fear this is almost impossible for a government with so little real power and so little moral courage.

5. *Ensure freedom of movement for all, de-linked from citizenship verification.* This would mean that all individuals in Rakhine State should be able to move freely around the country irrespective of whether they hold verification, registration, or citizenship documentation. Such freedoms would go a very long way towards reassuring Muslims nervous about returning from Bangladesh, but would be exceptionally hard to implement without significant backlash from nationalist groups and the Tatmadaw. Very careful communication, clear leadership, and reliable law enforcement will be needed, attributes the government currently lacks.

6. *Close the IDP camps.* As above, this is essential for conflict resolution and rights, and for reassuring Muslim refugees in Bangladesh that it is safe to return, but it would be extremely difficult for a government with so little real power and so little traction with nationalist groups to implement without stoking racial tensions and risking communal violence. The stalemate over this for more than five years since the 2012 violence highlights the extreme sensitivity of this issue, and the lack of progress demonstrates the inability of parties to talk and negotiate. The fear is that any refugees returning now from Bangladesh will end up in something akin to new, additional IDP camps, rather than being able to return to village life. Significant leadership and social entrepreneurship would be required to implement this peacefully, yet it is essential if resolution is to be achieved.

7. *Allow unfettered humanitarian and media access.* Again, this would involve a difficult political capitulation by Aung San Suu Kyi, the NLD, and the Tatmadaw, but it would go a long way towards signalling change to a sceptical international community and Muslim refugee population in Bangladesh. It would also lay a foundation for an impartial and independent investigation.

8. *Provide equal and expanded access to health and education.* These recommendations are essential on several levels. Not only are healthcare and education essential in their own right, but, together with improving economic opportunities, they are the most sure way to bring down birth rates, helping defuse the demographic security

dilemma over the longer term. Education can also be one of the most effective institutions to foster social inclusion and cohesion, as well as notions of non-violence.

9. *Increase monitoring of security forces, including CCTV surveillance of checkpoints, and provide language training for security forces working in Muslim areas.* This would be of huge benefit, and a significant confidence-building measure towards the Muslim community, but there is a genuine fear that the NLD has no real power to implement such measures over the military. This reform must be agreed and instituted by the Tatmadaw.

10. *Combat hate speech.* Much of the propagation of narratives and mobilization for recent violence has occurred via social media. As noted in the discussion about the ethnic security dilemma as well as the framing of conflict and violence, groups more segregated from one another, and more isolated from their elites, are more vulnerable to rumour, fear, and overreaction. Successfully combating hate speech will thus not only require effective counter-messaging by peace-oriented groups, but also efforts to mitigate the social segregation between Burman, Rakhine, and Muslim, both online and physically. It will also require engagement by elites from each group, communicating assurance that they are working to investigate rumours, and that there are non-violent mechanisms they will use to deal with reported injustice without requiring mass mobilization. Such action would limit the ability of various entrepreneurs to frame episodes of—probably criminal—violence that are irrelevant to the conflict as parts of a mobilizing process related to the conflict. Thus, not only is government messaging essential, but so also is finding and empowering elites able to act as social entrepreneurs of peace and stability.

11. *Facilitate engagement between the communities, and joint activities at the township and village level, including sporting and cultural events.* Our analysis suggests that a key contribution to the communal violence so rampant in 2012 and 2017 has been the framing of the conflict, as well as the ethnic security dilemma. The latter is caused in large part by a loss of trust and the severing of the channels of communication that might de-escalate issues while they are still minor infringements. Trust building and processes to restore channels of

communication, at local and elite levels, are essential. But in the current climate, activities such as this could only be implemented safely in limited sites further from the most recent violence; in regions like Mrauk-U and Kyauktaw Townships perhaps, rather than Maungdaw or Buthidaung.

12. *Equal participation, representation, and access to justice.* This is absolutely essential if a long-term solution is to be found, but extremely difficult to move forward without the above steps being taken.

Necessary but Insufficient: What Else?

The recommendations of the Advisory Commission on Rakhine State report are thus essential, and many strike at the core of issue in the Rakhine conflict. This is the best set of recommendations and framework to date. However, our analysis highlights other gaps, which must also be addressed if an enduring resolution is to be found. Further, the change in circumstances caused by the 25 August ARSA attacks, the massive military response, and the mass flight of refugees to Bangladesh has changed the situation on the ground, requiring additional recommendations. Based on our detailed analysis in the preceding chapters, we reiterate three of the above recommendations as even more important than ever:

1. *Move on citizenship quickly, openly, and transparently, with the social policy to support it.* Perhaps the only pathway that might actually see the majority of refugees return from Bangladesh, and achieve long-term resolution, is to link the document-verification process for return to Myanmar with a full, transparent citizenship-verification process. Doing so quickly might be sufficient to convince a frightened refugee population to return. Conversely, it is highly unlikely that most of the Muslim refugees will return now without some form of citizenship guarantee. And unless they return quickly, vested interests are likely to grab land and economic opportunities in ways that further undermine security and create new, exaggerated grievances, laying a foundation for future violence and instability in the region. Quick and significant progress by the government on citizenship verification is essential if any resolution and return is

going to occur. Citizenship alone, however, is not sufficient. Even if all Rohingya were offered citizenship with immediate effect, this would not change the situation on the ground without wider policy reform (for example, inclusive economic development, education and healthcare delivery, freedom of movement, and programmes to communicate social change). The way many Kaman Muslims, full citizens and a recognized *taing-yin-tha*, were caught up in the 2012 violence demonstrates this point. A citizenship process with clear guarantees, timeline, social policy, and effective messaging, together hold the only real possibility of refugee return.

2. *Open an international inquiry, and ensure mechanisms to hold the perpetrators of mass atrocities fully to account, on all sides.* This will be resisted by the Tatmadaw and other powerful groups, but justice issues must be dealt with. This is a highly sensitive issue and one that cannot necessarily be addressed by forms of retributive justice. In post-conflict transitional environments, the concept of justice transcends the traditional framework of punishment or retribution. In such a context, transitional justice constitutes a judgement that would enable the state itself to act as a moral agent (Borneman 1997). It is the symbolism of the criminal trial that enables the community to become a unified moral community (Koskenniemi 2002). Such an effort needs to consider on the one hand the most effective way to overcome collective traumatic experiences and on the other the long-term impact on the future relations between the communities. Thus, forms of truth commission or similar may be more effective than sending perpetrators to the International Criminal Court, but the populations cannot move past historical grievances without some sort of justice being seen to be done.

3. *Remove the link between citizenship and ethnicity.* This means making the political community the community of citizens, not *taing-yin-tha*. This would be a momentous change, possibly unattainable in practice, but the question of political participation in the Union of Myanmar stands at the heart of both this conflict and the political transition in the country. A national opportunity exists here, for the whole peace process and democratic transition. For decades the idea of ethnicity as the ultimate qualifier for inclusion promoted an ultra-communitarian ideal of citizenship, based on selective ascrip-

tive criteria underscored by the old regime. The conflict in Rakhine is the starkest example of the failure of this approach, in an ethnically diverse country and in a world characterized by high levels of human mobility and interconnectedness. Such an approach fails to capture the dynamic character of ethnicity, which changes over time in response to socio-political context. Imposing a static interpretation of ethnicity, so situated in the historical past, attempts to freeze identity development, and thus to create a picture of a political community that is neither flexible nor representative of the situation on the ground.

This is not only a key issue in Rakhine, but at the heart of democratic reform in Myanmar. To move into the future so desired across the country, an unfreezing of identity and a re-evaluation of relationships between people and groups is essential. It is time to move beyond the Ne Win-era *taing-yin-tha* framework. Ethnicity as a cultural practice and social representation of identity is of immense value. But to deal with conflict nationally, especially in Rakhine, and to facilitate democratic reform, the political community needs to be recognized as the community of citizens—the genesis of an inclusive *demos* in the new democratic, post-transition Myanmar, in which cultural diversity between equals is celebrated in non-hierarchical and non-exclusionary terms.

Beyond these, our analysis in preceding chapters identifies a number of additional factors that must also be addressed—particularly given subsequent events. These include:

1. *Measures must be undertaken to protect land, assets and economic interests until the refugees return, before vested interests claim land and economic opportunities, and it must be assumed that the refugees will return.* This could go a long way towards proving that genuine security is possible, and re-building the trust required to repatriate the Muslims. There are already significant concerns about land grabbing, including, for example, plans to build a new Border Guard Police base in Buthidaung on 600 acres of land belonging to Muslim farmers (Moe Myint 2018a).

2. *The government must show real solidarity with all victims and vulnerable people in Rakhine State, on all sides, and provide tangible support for the*

human rights of all, without implicating all members of a group in the violence perpetrated by a minority.

3. *Some party or parties are clearly trying to prevent implementation of the Annan report findings; an investigation is needed to determine any involvement by Tatmadaw, security forces, and local non-Muslims.* It cannot be assumed that the sole perpetrator is ARSA. Real action to counter such opposition to the implementation of the report's recommendations is required.

4. *The Tatmadaw must be opened to scrutiny and shown to be accountable, somehow.* It must be noted again, though, that Aung San Suu Kyi and the NLD government have no formal power over the military.

5. *The state, including the government, must acknowledge that it is as an actor in conflict, not a neutral mediator, and approach negotiations on that basis.*

6. *Mechanisms to facilitate person-to-person links between elite actors on all sides are required, to establish lines of communication, build trust, and create processes by which more minor incidents and grievances might be defused quickly and non-violently.* This relates directly to point 10 above, requiring careful identification of the right elite social entrepreneurs. This could, and should, be a first step towards wider negotiations. The single biggest obstacle here is that the government has labelled ARSA as 'terrorists', making any negotiation almost impossible. But in the interests of de-escalation and first steps towards resolution, channels around this and identification of elite Muslim peace entrepreneurs who are recognized and respected within their communities will be essential, and these people really need to be connected with the ARSA leadership somehow. This must be a priority.

7. *A pathway towards dialogue and negotiations is necessary, and this conflict must be linked into the national political dialogue frameworks, despite some unique features.* Again, the 'terrorist' label is immensely counterproductive on this score. Security issues must be dealt with, and any international Islamist extremist linkages severed, but there must be a mechanism for the negotiation to deal with the legitimate fears and concerns of the Muslim and Rakhine populations. Negotiations should involve the government, military, ANP, religious nationalists, AA, and Muslim representatives.

8. *The demographic security dilemma must be planned for.* Assuming for a moment that all of the Muslim refugees in Bangladesh do return to

Rakhine State, the Muslim proportion of the population will continue to grow for several more decades. This is in part due to decades of discrimination, in which restricted mobility, livelihood options, and education/health-care service delivery has prevented the environment that most commonly lowers birth rates. Communicating this in a manner addressing ethnic Rakhine fears while respecting rights and aspirations is essential. Lifting all mobility restrictions on the Muslim population would go a very long way towards addressing this, allowing the burden from the growing Muslim population to be spread nationally rather than concentrated in one small corner of Myanmar.

9. *History must be dealt with*. The stalemate of historical narratives cannot be ignored, neither is the Burman-led state in a position to impose a 'correct' historical narrative. The Annan report urges looking beyond the past to a renewed vision for a dynamic future—but this cannot be at the expense of re-thinking the past. Almost all grievances underlying this conflict are rehearsed through historical narrative. These narratives are presented in exclusive and irreconcilable terms, ignoring the fears, grievances, and collective memory of the other community. But, in addition to conflict, these communities have shared and achieved many great things together, and historically Arakan modelled success as a cosmopolitan centre at the crossroads of civilizations; it still could do so once again! Means must be found for exploring and documenting a more evidence-based understanding of Arakan/Rakhine history. This would be one acknowledging a Muslim presence pre-1823, the historical grandeur of Arakan, the assimilative expansionism of central Burma, extensive colonial migration, and the social destruction during the Second World War, all in a way that could ultimately bring communities together.

10. *The issue of the name 'Rohingya' must be addressed openly and rationally*. The Muslims of northern Rakhine claim this name as a self-identity. Continuing to call them 'the Muslims of northern Rakhine' is clumsy, and inaccurately makes their primary marker of identity 'Muslim'. The people themselves want to move away from an identification primarily as 'Muslim', and their narrative history accounts suggest that they primarily want to be accepted as equals

in society. By de-politicizing ethnicity and de-linking it from membership in the political community, it should be possible for Myanmar to accept 'Rohingya' as a cultural expression within the country, a social phenomenon—even an emerging 'ethnicity'. Either way, attempts to deny or avoid the name cannot continue forever, and ultimately, so long as it does not rob or harm others, people surely have a moral right to name themselves and forge their own sense of personal and communal identity.

Moral Hazard: A Final Warning

As a final warning, based on the recommendations above, we consider how the international narrative about the plight of the Rohingya may provide the wrong signalling to local actors and lead unintentionally to further cycles of violence—with the highest price to be paid by the most vulnerable. This is not a concluding remark, but a warning we wish to sound of a scenario that might unfold if the path of the recommendations discussed above is not followed. This is not an intellectual exercise, but a grounded warning based on well-documented experiences from other geographical contexts in recent history.

The attacks against military posts hours after the release of the Annan report raise questions about the strategic aims of such an operation, and pose a final, very significant, warning to the international community. Why did ARSA orchestrate and execute violent attacks, given that the content of the interim report was known, and favoured concessions to the Muslim population? Why undermine the Muslim civilian position by causing a disproportionate crackdown by the military, which led to over 670,000 people fleeing to Bangladesh? Why proceed with a rather suicidal act of rebellion, which did not stand a chance of success and put Muslims into harm's way en masse?

One explanation of ARSA's decision to risk massive retaliation is related to the role of the international community and its involvement in internal conflicts over the past twenty-five years. There has been an emphasis on the promotion and protection of human rights, strongly manifested through narratives of victimhood, and the possibility of military intervention to prevent mass atrocities, which has been extensively documented under the rubrics of humanitarian intervention and post-conflict peace building. The emergence of what Leider (2017a) calls a 'New Wave Rohingya' movement post-2012, employed by the Rohingya diaspora, has accentuated this, by internationalizing their plight globally and increasing their visibility, attracting civil advocacy by transnational agencies. This has been in tune with a process of global victimhood developed after the Second World War, underpinned by the evolution of the human rights discourse and an emerging global civil advocacy of the vulnerable that generated normative and political pressure for remedial justice (Bonacker 2013). Simultaneously, the internationalization of the Rohingya's plight has appealed to a keen audience in Islamic countries, where the discussion was not so much about the violation of human rights as the persecution of peaceful and defenceless Muslims (without embracing human rights language).

In this context, intervention is defined broadly as involvement that ranges from non-consensual military deployment to political, diplomatic, and economic support to the minority—either officially by patron states or unofficially by non-state actors or agencies. The crucial element here is that the primary—but not necessarily the only— incentive for intervention is an intention to protect civilians from genocidal violence. This humanitarian concern may be founded on the discourse of human rights and the responsibility to protect, which is employed by a wide range of Western state and non-state actors as well as non-Western countries and international organizations (including the Organization of Islamic Cooperation).

Equally, humanitarian concerns in Islamic societies may be founded on the sense of experienced, shared victimhood of religious kindred, without a strong foundation on human rights. What is important here is that humanitarian intervention conveys strategic benefits to the minority that is identified as needing protection.

Kuperman (2005, 2008) demonstrated, in relation to Bosnia Herzegovina and Kosovo, how the promise of international intervention on behalf of a minority might increase the risk of ethnic conflict, by offering an otherwise inferior conflict party a credible prospect of victory (see also Janus 2009). He argued that the emerging norm of international humanitarian intervention 'may exacerbate some violent conflicts and thereby cause precisely the human tragedies it is intended to avert' (Kuperman 2008, p. 50). Humanitarian intervention has been seen as a means to prevent massive violation of human rights, such as genocide, ethnic cleansing, and crimes against humanity. However, even the possibility of humanitarian intervention to protect a minority has the potential to encourage risk-taking by minority groups that expect international involvement, whether in the form of military intervention, or in other ways that would boost their legitimacy as an interlocutor.

In the case of Rakhine, international involvement can be broken down into several different parts. First, a vocal diaspora has been very active since 2012 in Western and non-Western countries, championing the idea that genocide and ethnic cleansing are occurring, advocating to parliaments, co-opting key international figures, and running high-profile events. While this is understandable, it has raised the hopes of Muslims in Rakhine of international support for their cause. Second, a large humanitarian response to 2012 was widely perceived, by Muslims, Rakhine, and the state, to favour the Muslims, given that they were disproportionately affected by the violence. Third, a range of international voices, mostly Western human rights agencies, have called for recognition of human rights violations in Rakhine. And fourth, Islamic countries and networks have shown strong solidarity with the cause of the Rohingya. The 2012 violence attracted significant international attention and galvanized transnational advocacy, which has amplified their voice and increased dramatically the pressure on other governments to act on behalf of the Muslims.

This international environment of increasing publicity in support of the Muslims in northern Rakhine was the background against which ARSA launched its first military operation in October 2016. Tactically the chances of major success were always minimal, and the attacks triggered a harsh, five-month security crackdown. During that time, international messages of support only increased. It is quite possible that this could have been interpreted by ARSA as an increased opportunity for some sort of real international support, whether the mobilization of foreign fighters and financing, or the leverage of greater humanitarian engagement forcing the NLD government and Tatmadaw to stand down. It is quite possible, and very concerning, to think that expectations of increased international support may have encouraged the August 2017 attacks, with hopes of drawing attention and triggering a far greater international outcry against the military and forcing the government into a political solution. To the extent that this has occurred, ARSA gravely miscalculated the military response, but it is highly likely to have encouraged both the leadership and recruits.

The Annan Commission interim report called for civil and political rights, but it was well short of recommending the collective rights and autonomy that ARSA has made central to its political manifesto. There are very real moral hazard concerns that—and this this is just a scenario, yet quite a plausible one—ARSA launched the attacks and put Muslim civilians into harm's way to achieve three strategic aims. First, through the tragedy of the massive refugee flows, to increase public outcry and pressure on the Myanmar government. Second, disproportionate military retaliation against civilians would attract more sympathizers among Muslims both locally and internationally, and thus enlarge the pool of potential recruits for future operations. Third, the attacks would block any implementation of Annan's recommendations that fall short of ARSA's political aims. Rather, their calculation may have been that the attacks and the military crackdown would confirm to the international community and, through them, the Myanmar government, that the most just and safe option for political accommodation would be some form of autonomous rule in northern Rakhine, which has been ARSA's primary goal since 2016.

In other words, it may be plausible that the motivation for the August 2017 attacks was not a miscalculation by ARSA as much as a tactical response to the increased international outcry about in the situation in northern Rakhine. If this is the case, then we have a serious moral hazard situation, making responses by the international community even more problematic, and which suggests that ARSA may consider high-risk action against the Tatmadaw again, to put other civilians into harm's way. Intentionally engaging in a losing war to attract international intervention in order to win is a high-risk strategy that, as we have seen in other theatres, has an unjustifiably high premium in loss of civilian life.

The very possibility of such a scenario should scare all of us in the international community, and lead us to a very sober re-evaluation of our engagement. To us, the only way forward is a form of principled engagement that works hard to bring the parties together, around a negotiated solution. The sort of high-profile, confrontational international public shaming that we have seen to date is unlikely to help resolve the situation, risks moral hazard, entrenches belligerent responses, and tends to sideline moderate voices that may seek an alternative path in a less politicized environment. But this takes deeper understanding, and more long-term and costly engagement, and it does not engender the international recognition of taking the high moral ground, publicly and loudly. But we strongly believe that the analysis of this book demonstrates that the only possible path to resolution of the Rakhine conflict remains highly principled but committed engagement.

NOTES

THE VEXED QUESTION OF NAMES

1. Note that in Burmese the name *Yakhine* was recognized for the state from the time of the 1974 constitution, so the trend in name change in many ways dates from 1974, although Arakan remained the official English-language version of the name until 1989. It has to be remembered, too, that—despite the history and demands of the Arakan peoples—Arakan/Rakhine was not demarcated as a state under the 1947 constitution, or any period prior to 1974.

1. COMPLEXITIES, MISCONCEPTIONS, AND CONTEXT

1. The dates for the war vary from text to text. The British formally declared war on Burma on 5 March 1824, and began an invasion of Arakan in January 1825, occupying Mrauk-U by the end of March. Arakan became British territory as a result of the Treaty of Yandabo, signed on 24 February 1826. Thus listing the war as 1824–6 is most correct.

2. RECENT VIOLENCE AND SIGNIFICANCE

1. The eleven videos were uploaded to the YouTube channel Hwgiagodhahdiwm VshwogaGAkq (https://www.youtube.com/channel/UCsE3K0tQdXoa1HLuLLYNCEA) on 11 October 2016, although it is not clear whether this was the first upload site.
2. Likewise, on 16 August ARSA also uploaded a video featuring Abu Ammar 'Junooni', also known as Hafiz Tohar, its alleged leader. Surrounded by a group of masked men armed with assault rifles, he explained that ARSA has existed for three years without targeting civil-

ians—Rakhine or Muslim—and called on the government not to oppress the Muslim minority in Rakhine State.

3. However, these findings should be treated very cautiously, given the problematic nature of survey-based research in a country such as Myanmar. In addition, there are some concerns that some of the questions and methodology adopted for this Asia Barometer survey (Welsh & Huang 2016) were overly leading, adopting translations of categories and wording not well tailored to the Burmese context.

3. THE ROHINGYA 'ORIGIN' NARRATIVE

1. Ne Win's coup took place before statehood could be granted to Arakan, which did not then achieve statehood until 1973. However, the decision to make Arakan a state in the Union of Myanmar was made in 1961, and publicly announced.

2. Min Saw Mun (the name used in Karim 2000 and others) is spelled in a variety of ways in different texts, e.g. Mengh-tsan-newun in Phayre (1844), Min Sowa Mun in Siddiquee (2014), Mong Saw Mwun in Maung Tha Hla (2004), and Mañḥ Co Mvan in Leider & Kyaw Minn Htin (2015). Some historiographical texts call him Narameikhla (or Nara Mit Lha) when he first became king and Min Saw Mun only when he reconquered his throne. His Persian/Muslim name was Solaiman Shah.

4. RAKHINE–BURMAN NARRATIVES: 'INDEPENDENCE', 'UNITY', 'INFILTRATION'

1. Manuscripts listed by Zaw Lynn Aung (2009, 2010, 2013) as being held in the Myanmar National Library are Sithu Gamani Thingyan's 1887 *Rakhine Razawin* [Palm-leaf manuscript number 2297], *Rakhine Razawan Kho Min Razagri Sadam* (called *Min Razagri Sadam*) (no date), and *Rakhine Razawin* (no date) [Palm-leaf manuscript number 1483]. At the Yangon University central library, he lists *Rakhine Razawin Akauk Shyauk Htoon* (1848) [Palm-leaf manuscript number 96336], *Rakhine Ayepon* (1849) [Palm-leaf manuscript number 49887], *Razawingyi* (1851) [Palm-leaf manuscript number 9837] and *Dannyawady Arei: To Pon Hnin Maha Razawan* (no date), [Palm-leaf manuscript number 5302]. He also notes one in the possession of U Htun Yi (Researcher on Myanmar Literature): *Rakhine Razawan,Rakhapura* (1870).

2. Three palm-leaf manuscripts are listed by Zaw Lynn Aung (2009, 2010, 2013), as being held in the Oriental and India Office Collection of the British Library in London: Nga Mi's 1842 *Rakhine Razawin* from the

collection of Phayre complete, with his personal notes in the margin, an 1884 *Rakhine Razapon*, and the *Rakhine Razawin Nge*.

5. SECURITY DILEMMA, MINORITY COMPLEX, GREED, AND POLITICAL ECONOMY

1. Rohingya nationalists claim that their ethnic origins trace back to the Arabs, Moors, Pathans, Moghuls, Bengalis, and Indo-Mongoloid people (e.g. ARNO 2013a; CBRO 2014; Islam 2011; Siddiqui 2014). They attempt to trace their history in Arakan to much earlier than other authorities accept, and argue that this sense of becoming a single community occurred at a much earlier date than we postulate here.

BIBLIOGRAPHY

AA. 2014. 'Condemnation Letter'. *www.thearakanarmy.com*, post-dated 5 August 2014 by the Arakan Army Commander-in-Chief, available at http://archive.is/J5oYn 18.

AFP. 2012a. 'Myanmar Declares Emergency in Unrest-Hit State'. Agence France-Presse, 10 June.

———— 2012b. 'Myanmar Imposes Curfews after Riots'. Agence France-Presse, 10 June.

———— 2012c. 'Suu Kyi Tries to Defuse Myanmar Sectarian Strife'. AsiaOne News, 6 June.

Ager, S. 2017. 'Rohingya (Ruáingga)'. *Omniglot*, available at www.omniglot.com/writing/rohingya.htm.

Alam, M. A. 1998. 'Publisher's Notes', in *A Short History of Rohingya and Kamans of Burma*. Chittagong: Institute of Arakan Studies, p. 1.

———— 2000. *The Rohingyas: A Short Account of their History and Culture*. Dakha: Arakan Historical Society.

———— 2014. 'A Short History of Arakan and Rohingyas', in M. M. Siddiquee (ed.), *The Rohingyas of Arakan: History and Heritage*. Chittagong: Ali Publishing House, pp. 37–89.

Ali, S. M. 1967. 'Arakan Rule in Chittagong (1550–1666 AD)'. *Journal of Asiatic Society of Pakistan* 12 (3): 333–51.

Amnesty International. 1992. *Union of Myanmar (Burma) Human Rights Violations against Muslims in the Rakhine (Arakan) State*. London: Amnesty International.

———— 2017a. '"My World is Finished": Rohingya Targeted in Crimes Against Humanity in Myanmar', 18 October, available at https://www.amnesty.org/en/documents/asa16/7288/2017/en/.

———— 2017b. 'Myanmar—"We are at Breaking Point": Rohingya: Persecuted in Myanmar, Neglected in Bangladesh', 19 December 2016, available at https://www.amnesty.org/en/documents/asa16/5362/2016/en/.

———— 2017c. '"Caged without a Roof": Apartheid in Myanmar's Rakhine State', 21 November, available at https://www.amnesty.org/en/documents/asa16/7484/2017/en/.

Anderson, B. 1983. *Imagined Communities: Reflections on the Origin and Spread of Nationalism*, rev. edn, London: Verso.

Anin, A. 2002. 'Towards Understanding Arakan History: A Study on the Issue of Ethnicity in Arakan, Myanmar'. Unpublished manuscript, Yangon.

Annan, K., Win Mra, Aye Lwin, Tha Hla Shwe, Mya Thida, Saw Khin Tint, Khin Maung Lay, G. Salamé, & L. van den Assum. 2017a. *Interim Report and Recommendations*. March. Yangon: Advisory Commission on Rakhine State.

———— 2017b. *Towards a Peaceful, Fair and Prosperous Future for the People of Rakhine: Final Report of the Advisory Commission on Rakhine State*. August. Yangon: Advisory Commission on Rakhine State.

AP. 2015. 'Nobel Laureates Appeal for End to Persecution of Rohingya'. Associated Press, 28 May, available at www.cnsnews.com/news/article/nobel-laureates-appeal-end-persecution-rohingya.

ARDHO. 2013. *Conflict and Violence in Arakan (Rakhine) State, Myanmar (Burma): What is Happening, Why and What to Do*. Mae Sot: Arakan Human Rights and Development Organisation.

Armstrong, J. A. 1982. *Nations before Nationalism*. Chapel Hill: University of North Carolina Press.

ARNO. 2007. 'Facts about Arakan Rohingya National Organisation'. Press release, 4 October, available at http://www.rohingya.org/portal/index.php/arno/arno-press-release/159-press-release—facts-about-arakan-rohingya-national-organisation.html.

———— 2013. 'Facts about the Rohingya Muslims of Arakan'. Arakan Rohingya National Organisation, available at http://www.rohingya.org/portal/index.php/learn-about-rohingya.html.

Aron, G., & D. Gilmore. 2017. 'Navigating Change: Crisis and Crossroads in the Rakhine State Context'. CDA Collaborative Learning Projects, available at http://cdacollaborative.org/publication/navigating-change-crisis-crossroads-rakhine-state-context/.

ARSA. 2017a. 'ARSA Commander Addresses Int'l Community & Messages to Various Ethnic groups including Rakhine', available at https://www.youtube.com/watch?v=xMSgxAc0LtE.

———— 2017b. 'Statement 2: Current Unrest Triggered by Burmese Military to Derail @KofiAnnan Commission Report on Arakan State', 24 August [Twitter], ARSA_The Army @ARSA_Official, available at https://twitter.com/ARSA_Official.

———— 2017c. 'STATEMENT #ARSA On Humanitarian Pause—

Categorically Denies Allegations of Links with Transnational Terror Groups', 14 September [Twitter], ARSA_The Army @ARSA_Official, available at https://twitter.com/ARSA_Official.

———— 2017d. 'Urgent Statement: #Arakan State Situation We are Defending against the #Burmese Colonizing Forces', 24 August [Twitter], ARSA_The Army @ARSA_Official, available at https://twitter.com/ARSA_Official.

———— 2017e. 'URGENT: Rakhine Political Groups & Intl Govts MUST Immediately Put Pressure on Burmese Army to Stop Using Rakhine Civilians as Human Shields', 27 August [Twitter], ARSA_The Army @ARSA_Official, available at https://twitter.com/ARSA_Official.

———— 2017f. 'ARSA Commander Addresses Rohingya Diaspora & the World; Warns Myanmar Military'. YouTube, 16 August, available at http://bit.ly/2AhDSHX.

Asia Watch. 1992. *Burma: Rape, Forced Labour and Religious Persecution in Northern Arakan*. New York: Human Rights Watch/Asia 4 (13): 28.

Aung San Suu Kyi. 2017. 'Speech Delivered by Her Excellency Daw Aung San Suu Kyi, State Counsellor of the Republic of the Union of Myanmar on Government's Efforts with Regard to National Reconciliation and Peace'. Official transcript, Naypyitaw, 19 September, available at www.mofa.gov.mm/wp-content/uploads/2017/09/SC-speech-transcription-Final-_19–9–2017_.pdf.

Aye Chan. 2005. 'The Development of a Muslim Enclave in Arakan (Rakhine) State of Burma (Myanmar)'. *SOAS Bulletin of Burma Research* 3 (2): 396–420.

———— 2009. 'Rohingya: More a Political Rhetoric than an Ethnic Identity'. Unpublished paper read at School of Oriental and African Studies, London University, 9 August.

———— 2011. 'Burma's Western Border as Reported by the Diplomatic Correspondence (1947–1975)'. *International Social Research Bulletin* 2: 1–14.

———— 2012. 'The Kingdom of Arakan in the Indian Ocean Commerce (AD 1430–1666)'. *Suwannabumi* 4 (1) (Pusan University of Foreign Studies Southeast Asian Area): 1–26.

Aziz, A. 2018. 'BGB Recovers Yaba Worth Tk33.6 Crore in Teknaf'. *Dhaka Tribune*, 22 February.

Bahar, A. 2010. *Burma's Missing Dots: The Emerging Face of Genocide*. Bloomington: Xlibris.

Ballentine, K., & J. Sherman (eds). 2003. *The Political Economy of Armed Conflict: Beyond Greed and Grievance*. Boulder: Lynne Rienner.

Bar-Tal, D. 1998. 'Societal Beliefs in Times of Intractable Conflict: The Israeli Case'. *International Journal of Conflict Management* 9: 22–50.

BIBLIOGRAPHY

———— 2001. 'Why Does Fear Override Hope in Societies Engulfed by Intractable Conflict?' *Political Psychology* 22: 601–27.

———— 2003. 'Collective Memory of Physical Violence: Its Contribution to the Culture of Violence', in E. Cairns & M. D. Roe (eds.), *The Role of Memory in Ethnic Conflict*. Basingstoke: Palgrave Macmillan, pp. 77–93.

———— 2007. 'Sociopsychological Foundations of Intractable Conflicts'. *American Behavioral Scientist* 50: 1430–53.

———— 2013. *Intractable Conflicts: Socio-Psychological Foundations and Dynamics*. Cambridge: Cambridge University Press.

———— 2014. 'Collective Memory as Social Representations'. *Papers on Social Representations* 23: 5.1–5.26.

Bar-Tal, D., & D. Antebi, 1992. 'Siege Mentality in Israel'. *International Journal of Intercultural Relations* 16: 251–75.

Baram, H., & Y. Klar. 2016. 'In Defence of the In-Group Historical Narrative in an Intractable Intergroup Conflict: An Individual-Difference'. *Political Psychology* 37 (1): 36–53.

Baxter, J. 1941. *Report on Indian Immigration*. Rangoon: Superintendent, Government Printing & Stationery.

BBC. 2012. 'Burma Police Clash with Muslim Protesters in Maung Daw'. BBC News, 8 June, available at from www.bbc.com/news/world-asia-18368556.

Bennison, J. J. 1931. *Census of India, 1931—Part II: Tables*, vol. XI. Rangoon: Government Printing & Stationery.

Benson, J. 2015. 'Blood Teak: How Myanmar's Natural Resources Fuel Ethnic Conflicts'. *The Diplomat*, April 30.

Berger, P., & T. Luckman. 1967. *The Social Construction of Reality: A Treatise in the Sociology of Knowledge*. London: Penguin.

Bhabha, H. 1994. *The Location of Culture*. London: Routledge.

Bhattacharya, B. 1927. 'Bengali Influence in Arakan'. *Bengal, Past and Present* 33: 139–44.

Blomquist, R. 2015. 'Ethno-Demographic Dynamics of the Rohingya–Buddhist Conflict'. *Georgetown Journal of Asian Affairs* 3 (2): 94–117.

Blomquist, R., & R. Cincotta. 2016. 'Myanmar's Democratic Deficit: Demography and the Rohingya Dilemma'. New Security Beat (Wilson Centre), 12 April, available at https://www.newsecuritybeat.org/2016/04/myanmars-democratic-deficit-demography-rohingya-dilemma/.

BNI. 2017. *Deciphering Myanmar's Peace Process: A Reference Guide 2016*. Chiang Mai: Burma News International.

Bonacker, T. 2013. 'Global Victimhood: On the Charisma of the Victim in Transitional Justice Processes'. *World Political Science* 9 (1): 97–129.

Borneman, J. 1997. *Settling Accounts: Violence, Justice and Accountability in Postsocialist Europe*. Princeton: Princeton University Press.

BIBLIOGRAPHY

Brass, P. 1984. 'Ethnic Groups and the State', in P. Brass (ed.), *Ethnic Groups and the State*. London: Croom Helm, pp. 1–58.

———— 1996. *Riots and Pogroms*, New York: New York University Press.

Breman, J. 1993. 'The Anti-Muslim Pogrom in Surat'. *Economic and Political Weekly* 28 (16): 737–41.

Brennan, E., & C. O'Hara. 2015. 'The Rohingya and Islamic Extremism: A Convenient Myth'. *The Diplomat*, June 29.

Brenner, D. 2015. 'Ashes of Co-optation: From Armed Group Fragmentation to the Rebuilding of Popular Insurgency in Myanmar'. *Conflict, Security and Development* 14 (5): 337–58.

Brescó, I. 2016. 'Conflict, Memory, and Positioning: Studying the Dialogical and Multivoiced Dimension of the Basque Conflict'. *Peace & Conflict: Journal of Peace Psychology* 22 (1): 36–43.

Brown, D. 1994. *The State and Ethnic Politics in South East Asia*. London: Routledge.

Brubaker, R. 1998. 'Myths and Misconceptions in the Study of Nationalism', in J. A. Hall (ed.), *The State of the Nation*, Cambridge: Cambridge University Press, pp. 272–306.

———— 2004. *Ethnicity Without Groups*. Cambridge, MA: Harvard University Press.

Brubaker, R. & F. Cooper. 2000. 'Beyond Identity'. *Theory and Society* 29 (1): 1–47.

BSPP. 1967. *Taingyintha Yingyehmu Yoyadaledônzan-mya: Kayin* [National race cultures and customs: Karen]. Rangoon: Burma Socialist Programme Party.

———— 1971. *Taingyintha Lumyomya-e Nègyèzangyinye Thamaing* [History of the national races' anti-imperialism]. Rangoon: Burma Socialist Programme Party.

Buchanan, F. 1799. 'A comparative vocabulary of some of the languages spoken in the Burma Empire'. *Asiatick Researches or Transactions of the Society instituted in Bengal for inquiring into the History and Antiquities the Arts, Sciences and Literature of Asia*, Asiatic Society of Bengal 5: 219–40.

Burke, A. 2016. 'New Political Space, Old Tensions: History, Identity and Violence in Rakhine State, Myanmar'. *Contemporary South East Asia: A Journal of International and Strategic Affairs* 38 (2): 258–83.

Burma Times. 2016. 'Two (AA) Rebels Captured in Kyawktaw Township'. *Burma Times*, National News, 12 January.

Butterfield, H. 1951. *History and Human Relations*. London: Collins.

Buzan, B., O. Wæver, & J. de Wilde. 1998. *Security: A New Framework for Analysis*. Boulder and London: Lynne Rienner.

Callahan, M. 2003. *Making Enemies: War and State-Building in Burma*. Ithaca: Cornell University Press.

CBRO. 2014. 'Facts about the Rohingya Muslims of Arakan'. Canadian

BIBLIOGRAPHY

Burmese Rohingya Organization, available at http://rohingya.webs.com/arakanhistory.htm.

CDNH. 2017. *Building Resilience to Communal Violence: Lessons from Rakhine State.* Yangon: Center for Diversity and National Harmony.

Chan, F. 2017. 'ISIS, al-Qaeda Drawn to Crisis in Rakhine State'. *Straits Times,* 20 September.

Charney, M. 1993. 'Arakan, Min Zawagyi and the Portuguese: The Relationship between the Growth of Arakanese Imperial Power and Portuguese Mercenaries on the Fringe of Mainland Southeast Asia 1517–1617'. MA thesis, Ohio University, published in *SOAS Bulletin of Burma Research* 3 (2) (Autumn 2005) 974–1145.

———— 1998a. 'Crisis and Reformation in a Maritime Kingdom of Southeast Asia: Forces of Instability and Political Disintegration in Western Burma (Arakan), 1603–1701'. *Journal of the Economic and Social History of the Orient* 4 (2): 185–219.

———— 1998b. 'Rise of a Mainland Trading State: Rakhine under the Early Mrauk-U Kings, c. 1430–1603'. *Journal of Burma Studies* 3 (1): 1–35.

———— 1999. 'Where Jambudipa and Islamdom Converged: Religious Change and the Emergence of Buddhist Communalism in Early Modern Arakan (Fifteenth to Nineteenth Centuries)'. Ph.D. thesis, University of Michigan.

———— 2000. 'A Reinvestigation of Konbaung-Era Burman Historiography on the Beginnings of the Relationship between Arakan and Ava (Upper Burma)'. *Journal of Asian History* 34 (1): 53–68.

———— 2002. 'Centralizing Historical Tradition in Precolonial Burma: The Abhiraja/Dhajaraja Myth in Early Kòn-baung Historical Texts'. *South East Asia Research* 10 (2): 185–215.

———— 2004. 'From Exclusion to Assimilation: Late Precolonial Burmese Literati and "Burman-ness"'. SOAS, available at https://eprints.soas.ac.uk/10327/.

———— 2009. *A History of Modern Burma.* Cambridge: Cambridge University Press.

Chaudhuri, K. N. 1985. *Trade and Civilization in the Indian Ocean: An Economic History from the Rise of Islam to 1750.* Cambridge: Cambridge University Press.

Cheesman, N. 2015. *Opposing the Rule of Law: How Myanmar's Courts Make Law and Order.* Cambridge: Cambridge University Press.

———— 2017. 'How in Myanmar "National Races" Came to Surpass Citizenship and Exclude Rohingya'. *Journal of Contemporary Asia* 47 (3): 461–83.

Chen, C. 2013. 'The Limit Point of Capitalist Equality Notes toward an Abolitionist Antiracism'. *EndNotes,* No. 3, September, available at https://

endnotes.org.uk/issues/3/en/chris-chen-the-limit-point-of-capitalist-equality.

Christie, C. J. 1997. *A Modern History of South East Asia: Decolonization, Nationalism and Separatism*. London: I. B. Tauris.

CNA. 2016. 'Rohingya Crisis Sparks Muslim Protests in Asian Capitals'. Channel NewsAsia, 26 November.

Coakley, J. 2012. *Nationalism, Ethnicity and the State: Making and Breaking Nations*. London: Sage.

Collier, P., V. Elliott, H. Hegre, A. Hoeffler, M. Reynal-Querol, & N. Sambanis. 2003. *Breaking the Conflict Trap*. Washington, DC: World Bank.

Collier, P., & A. Hoeffler. 1998. 'On Economic Causes of Civil War'. *Oxford Economic Papers* 50: 563–73.

——— 2002. 'On the Incidence of Civil War in Africa'. *Journal of Conflict Resolution* 46 (1): 13–28.

——— 2004. 'Greed and Grievance in Civil War'. *Oxford Economic Papers* 56: 563–95.

Collis, M. C. 1925. 'Arakan's Place in the Civilization of the Bay: A Study of Coinage and Foreign Relations'. *Journal of the Burma Research Society* 15 (1): 34–52.

Cordell, K., & S. Wolff. 2010. *Ethnic Conflict: Causes, Consequences, Responses*. Cambridge: Polity Press.

Cramer, C. 2006. *Civil War is not a Stupid Thing: Accounting for Violence in Developing Countries*. London: Hurst.

——— 2009. 'Violent Conflict and the Very Poorest,' Chronic Poverty Research Centre, Working Paper No. 129, pp. 1–26.

Crawford, J. 2006. *The Creation of States in International Law*. Oxford: Oxford University Press.

Crotty, M. 1998. *The Foundations of Social Research: Meaning and Perspectives in the Reseach Process*. St Leonards: Allen & Unwin.

Crouch, M. (ed.). 2016. *Islam and the State in Myanmar: Muslim–Buddhist Relations and the Politics of Belonging*. New Delhi: Oxford University Press.

d'Hubert, T. 2014. 'Pirates, Poets and Merchants: Bengali Language and Literature in Seventeenth Century Mrauk-U, Capital of Arakan (Myanmar)', in T. de Bruijn & A. Busch (eds.), *Culture and Circulation: Literature in Motion in Early Modern India*. Leiden: Brill, pp. 47–74.

——— 2015a. 'The Lord of the Elephant: Interpreting the Islamicate Epigraphic, Numismatic, and Literary Material from the Mrauk U Period of Arakan (ca. 1430–1784)'. *Journal of Burma Studies* 19 (2): 341–69.

——— 2015b. 'Patterns of Composition in the Seventeenth-Century Bengali Literature of Arakan', in F. Orsini & K. B. Schofield (eds.), *Tellings and Texts: Music, Literature and Performance in North India*. Cambridge: Open Book, pp. 423–44.

d'Hubert, T., & J. Leider. 2008. 'Traders and Poets in Mrauk-U: On Commerce and Cultural Links in Seventeen Century Arakan', in R. Mukherjee (ed.), *Pelagic Passageways: Dynamic Flows in the Northern Bay of Bengal World before the Appearance of Nation States*. New Delhi: Ratna Sagar, pp. 345–79.

de Figueiredo, R. J. P., & B. R. Weingast. 1999. 'The Rationality of Fear: Political Opportunism and Ethnic Conflict', in B. Walter & J. Snyder (eds.), *Civil Wars, Insecurity and Intervention*. New York: Columbia University Press, pp. 261–302.

Demmers, J. 2017. *Theories of Violent Conflict: An Introduction*. London: Routledge.

Denzin, N. K., & Y. S. Lincoln (eds.). 2005. *Handbook of Qualitative Research*, 3rd edn. Los Angeles: Sage.

Duncan, H. T. 1875. 'Appendices, Arakan Division', in *Report on the Census of British Burma taken in August 1872*. Rangoon: Government Printing.

DVB. 2012a. 'Riots Erupt in Arakan State'. Democratic Voice of Burma, 8 June.

———— 2012b. 'State Media Issues Correction after Publishing Racial Slur'. Democratic Voice of Burma, 6 June.

———— 2018. 'Arakan Army Suspected of Involvement in Bo Bo Min Thaik's Murder'. Democratic Voice of Burma, 6 February.

Egreteau, R. 2011. 'Birmanie: "Birmanisation"', in J. Medeiros (ed.), *Le Mondial des Nations*. Paris: Éditions Choiseul, pp. 260–82.

———— 2015. 'Burmese Indians in Contemporary Burma: Heritage, Influence, and Perceptions since 1988'. *Asian Ethnicity* 12 (1): 33–54.

Ei Ei Toe Lwin. 2012. 'Team Appointed to Probe Killings'. *Myanmar Times*, 11 June.

———— 2013. 'Meiktila Violence Work of "Well-Trained Terrorists"'. *Myanmar Times*, 1 April.

Elden, S. 2013. *The Birth of Territory*. Chicago: University of Chicago Press.

Esman, M. 2004. *An Introduction to Ethnic Conflict*. Cambridge: Polity Press.

Fearon, J. D. 1998. 'Commitment Problems and the Spread of Ethnic Conflict', in D. A. Lake and D. Rothchild (eds.), *The International Spread of Ethnic Conflict*. Princeton: Princeton University Press, pp. 107–26.

Fearon, J. D., & D. Laitin. 1996. 'Explaining Interethnic Cooperation'. *American Political Science Review* 90 (4): 715–35.

———— 2000. 'Violence and the Social Construction of Ethnic Identity'. *International Organization* 54 (4): 845–77.

Felbab-Brown, V. 2017. 'Myanmar Manoeuvres: How to Break Political–Criminal Alliances in Contexts of Transition'. Crime-Conflict Nexus Series, No. 9, United Nations University Centre for Policy Research.

Ferguson, J., & A. Gupta. 2002. 'Spatializing States: Toward an Ethnography of Neoliberal Governmentality'. *American Ethnologist* 29 (4): 981–1002.

BIBLIOGRAPHY

Forino, G., J. von Meding, & T. Johnson. 2017. 'Religion is Not the Only Reason Rohingyas are being Forced out of Myanmar'. *The Conversation*, September 12.

Fortify Rights. 2016. 'Supporting Human Rights in Myanmar: Why the US Should Maintain Existing Sanctions Authority', 2 May, available at http://www.fortifyrights.org/downloads/Fortify_Rights_and_UEG_Supporting_Human_Rights_in_Myanmar_May%202016.pdf.

Galtung, J. 1969. 'Violence, Peace, and Peace Research'. *Journal of Peace Research* 6 (3): 167–91.

Gerin, T. 2016. 'Myanmar Army Vows to Eliminate Armed Ethnic Rebels in Rakhine State'. Radio Free Asia, 8 January.

Geertz, C. 1973. *The Interpretation of Cultures*. New York: Basic Books.

Giddens, A. 1984. *The Constitution of Society: Outline of the Theory of Structuration*. Cambridge: Polity Press.

Gilley, B. 2004. 'Against the Concept of Ethnic Conflict'. *Third World Quarterly* 25 (6): 1155–66.

GNLM. 2016a. 'AA Insurgents Ambush Tatmadaw Columns'. *Global New Light of Myanmar*, 6 March, pp. 1, 3.

———— 2016b. 'A Dilemma of Peace: Miliatary MPs Justify Continued Conflict with AA'. *Global New Light of Myanmar*, 5 May, p. 1.

———— 2016c. 'Press Release Regarding the Attacks on the Border Guard Police Posts in Maungtaw Township—14th October 2016'. *Global New Light of Myanmar*, 14 October, pp. 1, 3.

———— 2016d. 'Security Tightened: Nine Policemen Killed, Five Injured, One Missing in Border Attacks'. *Global New Light of Myanmar*, 10 October, pp. 1, 3.

———— 2016e. 'State Counsellor Offers New Year Message'. *Global New Light of Myanmar*, 18 April, pp. 1, 3.

———— 2016f. 'Tatmadaw Aims to Remove AA Insurgents from Rakhine State'. *Global New Light of Myanmar*, 8 January, pp. 1, 3.

———— 2016g. 'Rakhine Seabed Tested for Mineral Deposits'. *Global New Light of Myanmar*, 11 February, p. 9.

———— 2017a. 'Economic Opportunities in Rakhine State'. *Global New Light of Myanmar*, 20 May, pp. 5–7.

———— 2017b. 'Redevelopment of Maungdaw Region as per Disaster Management Law—Dr Win Myat Aye'. *Global New Light of Myanmar*, 27 September, p. 9.

Goodhand, J. 2003. 'Enduring Disorder and Persistent Poverty: A Review of the Linkages between War and Chronic Poverty'. *World Development* 31 (3): 629–46.

Gommans, J. 1995. 'Trade and Civilization around the Bay of Bengal, c. 1650–1800'. *Itinerario* 19 (3): 82–108.

BIBLIOGRAPHY

Gottman, J. (ed.). 1980. *Centre and Periphery: Spatial Variation in Politics*. Beverly Hills: Sage.

Grantham, S. G. 1923. *Census of India, 1921—Part II: Tables*, vol. X. Rangoon: Office of the Superintendent, Government Printing, available at www.networkmyanmar.org/images/stories/PDF17/1921-Census-Extract.pdf.

Gray, D. E. 2009. *Doing Research in the Real World*. Los Angeles: Sage.

Green, P. 2013. 'Islamophobia: Burma's Racist Fault-Line'. *Race & Class* 55 (2): 93–8.

Green, P., T. MacManus, & A. de la Cour Venning. 2015. *Countdown to Annihilation: Genocide in Myanmar*. London: International State Crime Initiative of Queen Mary University of London.

Griffiths, A. 2015. 'Three More Sanskrit Inscriptions of Arakan: New Perspectives on its Name, Dynastic History, and Buddhist Culture in the First Millennium'. *Journal of Burma Studies* 19 (2): 281–340.

Gurr, T. R. 2000. 'Ethnic Warfare on the Wane'. *Foreign Affairs* 79 (3) (May/June): 52–64.

Gurr, T. R., & B. Harff. 1994. *Ethnic Conflict in World Politics*. Boulder: Westview Press.

Gutman, P. 1976. 'Ancient Arakan: With Special Reference to its Cultural History between the 5th and 11th Centuries'. Ph.D. thesis, Australian National University.

Habibullah, A. B. M. 1945. 'Arakan in the Pre-Mughal History of Bengal'. *Journal of the Asiatic Society of Bengal* 11 (1): 33–8.

Halbwachs, M. 1992. *On Collective Memory*. Lewis A. Coser (trans). Chicago: University of Chicago Press.

Hall, D. G. E. 1956. *Burma*, 2nd edn. London: Hutchinson's University Library.

——— 1968. *A History of South-East Asia*. New York: St Martin's Press.

Hall, R. B. 1999. *National Collective Identity: Social Constructs and International Systems*. New York: Columbia University Press.

Hammack, P. L. 2010. 'Identity as Burden or Benefit? Youth, Historical Narrative, and the Legacy of Political Conflict'. *Human Development* 53: 173–201.

Hancock, L. E. 1998. 'The Patterns of Ethnic Conflict'. *Ethnos-Nation* 6 (1–2): 9–28.

——— 2014. 'Narratives of Identity in the Northern Irish Troubles'. *Peace & Change* 39 (4): 443–67.

Handel, Z. 2008. 'What is Sino-Tibetan? Snapshot of a Field and a Language Family in Flux'. *Language and Linguistics Compass* 3: 422–41.

Harper, K. 2017. 'Will the World be Silent in Face of the Rohingya Calamity? The Time has Come for a UN Commission of Inquiry'. *Just Security*, 27 February.

BIBLIOGRAPHY

Harvey, D. 2006. *Spaces of Global Capitalism: Towards a Theory of Uneven Geographical Development*. London: Verso.

Harvey, G. E. 1925. *History of Burma from the Earliest Times to 10 March 1824, the Beginning of the English Conquest*. London: Longmans, Green & Co.

———— 1946. *British Rule in Burma 1824–1942*. London: Faber & Faber.

———— 1947. *Outline of Burmese History*. London: Longmans, Green.

Herz, J. 1951. *Political Realism and Political Idealism: A Study in Theories and Realities*. Chicago: University of Chicago Press.

Hill, C. 2013. *Myanmar: Sectarian Violence in Rakhine: Issues, Humanitarian Consequences, and Regional Responses*. Canberra: Australian Parliamentary Library, Department of Parliamentary Services.

Hla Pe, U. 1985. *Burma: Literature, Historiography, Scholarship, Language, Life, and Buddhism*. Singapore: Institute of Southeast Asian Studies.

Ho, E. L., & L. J. Chua. 2016. 'Law and "Race" in the Citizenship Spaces of Myanmar: Spatial Strategies and the Political Subjectivity of the Burmese Chinese'. *Ethnic and Racial Studies* 39 (5): 896–916.

Hobsbawm, E. 1990. *Nations and Nationalism since 1780: Programme, Myth, Reality*. Cambridge: Cambridge University Press.

Hobsbawm, E., & T. Ranger (eds.). 1983. *The Invention of Tradition*. Cambridge: Cambridge University Press.

Homer-Dixon, T. F. 1994. 'Environmental Scarcities and Violent Conflict'. *International Security* 19 (1): 5–40.

Horowitz, D. 2000. *Ethnic Groups in Conflict*. Berkeley: University of California Press.

———— 2001. *The Deadly Ethnic Riot*. Berkeley: University of California Press.

Horsey, R. 2016. 'Myanmar Border Attacks Fuel Tensions with Rohingya Muslim Minority'. *Commentary Asia*, International Crisis Group, 12 October.

Houtman, G. 1999. *Mental Culture in Burmese Crisis Politics: Aung San Suu Kyi and the National League for Democracy*. Tokyo: Tokyo University of Foreign Studies.

Htet Kaung Linn. 2016. '"The Army Insists we Give Up our Weapons, It's a Major Obstacle"'. *Myanmar Now*, 8 July.

Htet Naing Zaw. 2018. 'Generals Prep $15M of New Fencing For Border With Bangladesh'. *The Irrawaddy*, 23 February.

Human Rights Watch. 2000. 'Burmese Refugees in Bangladesh: Still No Durable Solution', 1 May, available at https://www.hrw.org/report/2000/05/01/burmese-refugees-bangladesh/still-no-durable-solution.

———— 2013. '"All You Can Do is Pray": Crimes against Humanity and Ethnic Cleansing of Rohingya Muslims in Burma's Arakan State', 22 April, available at https://www.hrw.org/report/2013/04/22/all-you-can-do-pray/crimes-against-humanity-and-ethnic-cleansing-rohingya-muslims.

———— 2017a. 'Burma: New Satellite Images Confirm Mass Destruction: 288 Villages, Tens of Thousands of Structures Torched'. 17 October, available at https://www.hrw.org/news/2017/10/17/burma-new-satellite-images-confirm-mass-destruction.

———— 2017b. 'Burma: 40 Rohingya Villages Burned Since October'. 17 December, available at https://www.hrw.org/news/2017/12/17/burma-40-rohingya-villages-burned-october.

———— 2017c. 'Massacre by the River: Burmese Army Crimes against Humanity in Tula Toli'. 19 December, available at https://www.hrw.org/report/2017/12/19/massacre-river/burmese-army-crimes-against-humanity-tula-toli.

Huntington, S. 1996. *The Clash of Civilizations and the Remaking of World Order*. New York: Simon & Schuster.

Hutt, D. 2017. 'The Cowardice of Aung San Suu Kyi: Is The Lady Still a Champion of Rights and Democracy?'. *The Diplomat*, 1 March, available at http://thediplomat.com/2017/03/the-cowardice-of-aung-san-suu-kyi/.

Ibrahim, A. 2016. *The Rohingyas: Inside Myanmar's Hidden Genocide*. London: Hurst.

ICG. 2012. 'Myanmar Conflict Alert: Preventing Communal Bloodshed and Building Better Relations'. Alert Asia, 12 June 2012. Brussels: International Crisis Group.

———— 2013. 'The Dark Side of Transition: Violence against Muslims in Myanmar'. Asia Report No. 251. Brussels: International Crisis Group.

———— 2014. 'Myanmar: The Politics of Rakhine State'. Asia Report No. 261. Brussels: International Crisis Group.

———— 2016. 'Myanmar: A New Muslim Insurgency in Rakhine State'. Asia Report No. 283. Brussels: International Crisis Group.

———— 2017. 'Myanmar's Rohingya Crisis Enters a Dangerous New Phase'. Asia Report No. 292. Brussels: International Crisis Group.

IOM. 2018. 'ISCG Situation Update: Rohingya Refugee Crisis, Cox's Bazar, 25 February'. International Organization for Migration, Inter Sector Coordination Group.

Irrawaddy. 2017. 'In Troubled Rakhine State, Focus Turns to Mountains'. *The Irrawaddy*, 27 June.

Irwin, A. 1946. *Burmese Outpost*. London: Collins.

Islam, N. 2011. 'Muslim Influence in the Kingdom of Arakan'. Kaladan Press Network, 15 November, available at http://www.kaladanpress.org/index.php/article-mainmenu-27/16-rohingya-article/3441-muslim-influence-in-the-kingdom-of-arakan.html.

BIBLIOGRAPHY

Islam, S. S. 2007. 'State Terrorism in Arakan', in A. T. H. Tan (ed.), *A Handbook of Terrorism and Insurgency in Southeast Asia*. Cheltenham: Edward Elgar, pp. 325–51.

Jamiatul-ulema. 1947. *Representation by the Muslims of North Arakan Claiming for an Autonomous State in the Buthidaung and Maungdaw Areas, 24 February 1947*. Juamiat-Ul Ulema [Muslim League] of North Arakan, record at the Government of Burma Home Department, available at www.burmalibrary. org/docs21/NM-1947–02–24-Jamiat-Ul_Ulema_of_N.Arakan-Representations_to_Mr_Bottomley-en.pdf.

Janus, T. 2009. 'Interventions and Conflict Incentives'. *Ethnopolitics* 8 (2): 191–208.

Jary, D., & J. Jary. 1991. 'Structure and Agency', in *Collins Dictionary of Sociology*. Glasgow: Harper Collins, p. 664.

Al Jazeera. 2015a. *Breaking Down Genocide in Myanmar*, 28 October. Distributed by Al Jazeera Investigates.

———— 2015b. *Genocide Agenda*. 28 October 2015. Distributed by Al Jazeera Investigates.

Jervis, R. 1976. *Perception and Misperception in International Politics*. Princeton: Princeton University Press.

Jervis, R. 1978. 'Cooperation under the Security Dilemma'. *World Politics* 40 (1): 167–214.

Jilani, A. F. K. 1999. *The Rohingyas of Arakan: Their Quest for Justice*. Dhaka: Ahmed Jilani.

———— 2001. *A Cultural History of Rohingya*. Dhaka: Ahmed Jilani.

Jones, L. 2017. 'A Better Political Economy of the Rohingya Crisis'. *New Mandala*, 26 September, available at http://www.newmandala.org/better-political-economy-rohingya-crisis/.

Jovchelovitch, S. 2012. 'Narrative, Memory and Social Representations: A Conversation between History and Social Psychology'. *Integrative Psychological & Behavioral Science* 46: 440–56.

Kaldor, M. 1999. *New and Old Wars: Organized Violence in a Global Era*. Cambridge: Polity Press.

Kalyvas, S. 2007. *The Logic of Violence in Civil War*. Cambridge: Cambridge University Press.

Karim, A. 2000. *The Rohingyas: A Short Account of their History and Culture*. Chittagong: Arakan Historical Society.

———— 2014. 'Some Muslim Ministers, Poets and Writers of the Royal Court of Arakan', in M. Siddiquee (ed.), *The Rohingyas of Arakan: History and Heritage*. Chittagong: Ali Publishing House, pp. 90–134.

Kaufman, S. 1996. 'An "International" Theory of Inter-Ethnic War'. *Review of International Studies* 22 (2): 149–71.

———— 2001. *Modern Hatreds: The Symbolic Politics of Ethnic War*. Ithaca: Cornell University Press.

BIBLIOGRAPHY

Keen, D. 2008. *Complex Emergencies*. Cambridge: Polity Press.

Khaing Myo Saung. 2012. *The Bad Colonial Heritage of Arakan and the Expansion of the Bengali Muslims of Chittagong* (in Burmese). Tokyo: Arakan Rakkhita Group.

Khan, A. M. 1992. 'The Arakanese in Bangladesh: A Socio-Cultural Study'. Ph.D. thesis, University of Calcutta, available at http://shodhganga.inflibnet.ac.in/handle/10603/165708.

Khan, M. S. 1937. 'Muslim Intercourse with Burma—Relations with Arakan'. *Islamic Culture* 11 (2): 248–66.

———— 1966. 'The Tragedy of Mrauk-U (1660–1661)'. *Journal of the Asiatic Society of Pakistan* 11 (2): 195–254.

Khin Maung Saw. 1994. 'The "Rohingyas", Who Are They? The Origin of the Name "Rohingya"', in U. Gärtner & J. Lorenz (eds.), *Tradition and Modernity in Myanmar: Proceedings of an International Conference Held in Berlin from May 7th to May 9th 1993*. Münster and Hamburg: LIT, pp. 89–100.

———— 2005. 'On the Evolution of Rohingya Problems in Rakhine State of Burma'. Self-published, available at www.networkmyanmar.org/.../ Illegal_Kular_Problem_in_Arakan.pdf.

———— 2011. 'Islamization of Burma through Chittagonian Bengalis as "Rohingya Refugees"'. Self-published, available at www.burmalibrary.org/ docs21/Khin-Maung-Saw-NM-2011–09-Islamanisation_of_Burma_ through_Chittagonian_Bengalis-en.pdf.

———— 2013. 'Analysis of Francis Buchanan's "Rooingas" and "Rossawns"'. Self-published, available at web.archive.org/web/20160429191925/www. networkmyanmar.org/images/stories/PDF17/Buchanan_New_Version. pdf.

———— 2014. 'Geopolitics of the Powers and the Bengali Problems in Burma'. Self-published, available at web.archive.org/web/201605060 53917/www.networkmyanmar.org/images/stories/PDF19/Corrected_ Version_Geopolitics.pdf.

———— 2015. *Arakan, a Neglected Land and her Voiceless People*. Yangon: U Htay Hlaing.

———— 2016. *Behind the Mask: The Truth Behind the Name 'Rohingya'*. Yangon: Taunggyi Printing.

King, C. 2004. 'The Micropolitics of Social Violence'. *World Politics* 25 (3): 431–55.

Kirichenko, A. 2009. 'From Ava to Mandalay: Toward Charting the Development of Burmese Yazawin Traditions'. *Journal of Burma Studies* 13: 1–75.

Klug, F. 2018. 'AP Finds Evidence for Graves, Rohingya Massacre in Myanmar'. AP News, 1 February, available at https://www.apnews.com/ ef46719c5d1d4bf98cfefcc4031a5434.

BIBLIOGRAPHY

Knafo, S., & B. Teschke. 2017. 'The Rules of Reproduction of Capitalism: A Historicist Critique'. Working Paper No. 12, Centre for Global Political Economy, University of Sussex, pp. 1–31.

Ko Pauk. 2012. 'Muslims Protest at Bengali Mosque in Rangoon against Murder of Muslims'. *Mizzima News*, 5 June, available at http://mizzimaenglish.blogspot.com.au/2012/06/muslims-protest-at-bengali-mosque-in.html.

Koenig, W. J. 1990. *The Burmese Polity, 1752–1819: Politics, Administration, and Social Organization in the Early Kon-Baung Period*. Michigan Papers on South and Southeast Asia 34. Ann Arbor: University of Michigan.

Koskenniemi, M. 2002. 'Between Impunity and Show Trials'. *Max Planck Yearbook of United Nations Law Online* 6 (1): 1–35.

Kramer, T. 2010. 'Ethnic Conflict in Burma: The Challenge of Unity in a Divided Country', in L. Dittmer (ed.), *Burma or Myanmar? The Struggle for National Identity*. Singapore: World Scientific Publishing Co., pp. 51–81.

Krasner, S. D. 1993. 'Westphalia and All That', in J. Goldstein & R. O. Keohane (eds.), *Ideas and Foreign Policy: Beliefs, Institutions and Political Change*. Ithaca: Cornell University Press, pp. 235–64.

———— 1995–6. 'Compromising Westphalia'. *International Security* 20 (3): 115–51.

Kriesberg, L. 1993. 'Intractable Conflict'. *Peace Review* 5: 417–21.

———— 1998. 'Intractable Conflicts', in E. Weiner (ed.), *The Handbook of Interethnic Coexistence*. New York: Continuum, pp. 332–42.

Kriesberg, L., T. A. Northrup, & S. J. Thorson (eds). 1989. *Intractable Conflicts and their Transformation*. Syracuse: Syracuse University Press.

Kuperman, A. J. 2005. 'Suicidal Rebellions and the Moral Hazard of Humanitarian Intervention'. *Ethnopolitics* 4 (2): 149–73.

———— 2008. 'The Moral Hazard of Humanitarian Intervention: Lessons from the Balkans'. *International Studies Quarterly* 52 (1): 49–80.

Kyaw Hla. 2010. 'Is There Any Hope of "Free and Fair" 2010 Elections in Burma?' *Kaladan News*, 2 February.

Kyaw San Wai. 2014. 'Myanmar's Religious Violence: A Buddhist "Siege Mentality" at Work'. Singapore: S. Rajaratnam School of International Studies [RSIS Commentaries], No. 037/2014, 20 February.

Kyaw Thu. 2017a. 'Myanmar Commission Prepares to Submit Report on Rakhine'. Radio Free Asia, 21 February.

———— 2017b. 'Myanmar Government to Conduct Investigation of Violence against Rohingya in Northern Rakhine State'. Radio Free Asia, 9 February.

Kyed, H. M., & M. Gravers. 2018. 'Representation and Citizenship in the Future Integration of Ethnic Armed Actors in Myanmar/Burma', in A. South & M. Lall (eds.), *Citizenship in Myanmar: Ways of Being In and From Burma*. Singapore: Chiang Mai University Press, pp. 59–86.

BIBLIOGRAPHY

Lake, D., & D. Rothchild 1996. 'Containing Fear: The Origins and Management of Ethnic Conflict'. *International Security* 21 (2): 41–75.

————— 2001. 'Political Decentralization and Civil War Settlements'. Paper presented at the Annual Meeting of the American Political Science Association, San Francisco, 30 August–2 September.

Laoutides, C. 2015. *Self-Determination and Collective Responsibility in the Secessionist Struggle*. London: Routledge.

Lall, M. 2016. *Understanding Reform in Myanmar: People and Society in the Wake of Military Rule*. London: Hurst.

Lawi Weng & Htet Naing Zaw. 2017. 'Tatmadaw Troops Killed and Wounded in Arakan Army Ambush'. *The Irrawaddy*. 9 November.

Leach, E. R. 1970 [1954]. *Political Systems of Highland Burma: A Study of Kachin Social Structure*. London: Athlone Press.

Le Billon, P. 2001. 'The Political Ecology of War'. *Political Geography* 20 (5): 561–84.

Lederach, J. P. 1995. *Preparing for Peace: Conflict Transformation across Cultures*. Syracuse: Syracuse University Press.

————— 1997. *Building Peace: Sustainable Reconciliation in Divided Societies*. Tokyo: United Nations University Press.

Lee, R. 2014. 'A Politician, Not an Icon: Aung San Suu Kyi's Silence on Myanmar's Muslim Rohingya'. *Islam and Christian–Muslim Relations* 25 (3): 321–33.

Lee, Y. 2017a. *End of Mission Statement by Special Rapporteur on the Situation of Human Rights in Myanmar*. Yangon: United Nations Human Rights, Office of the High Commissioner, 20 January.

————— 2017b. *Statement by Ms. Yanghee LEE, Special Rapporteur on the Situation of Human Rights in Myanmar at the 34th Session of the Human Rights Council*. Geneva: United Nations Human Rights, Office of the High Commissioner, 13 March.

Leider, J. 2002. 'On Arakanese Territorial Expansion: Origins, Context, Means and Practice', in J. Leider & J. Gommans (eds.), *The Maritime Frontier of Burma: Exploring Political, Cultural and Commercial Interaction in the Indian Ocean World, 1200–1800*. Amsterdam: Royal Netherlands Academy of Arts and Sciences, pp. 127–49.

————— 2004. *Le Royaume d'Arakan, Birmanie: son histoire politique entre le début du XVe et la fin du XVIIe siècle*. Paris: École Française d'Extrême-Orient (EFEO).

————— 2005. 'The Emergence of Rakhine Historiography: A Challenge for Myanmar Historical Research', in *Proceedings of the Myanmar Historical Commission Golden Jubilee International Conference*, 12–14 January 2004. Yangon: Ministry of Education, pp. 38–58.

————— 2014. 'Rohingya: The Name, the Movement, the Quest for Identity', in *Nation Building in Myanmar*. Yangon: Myanmar EGRESS and Myanmar Peace Center, pp. 204–55.

———— 2015. 'Competing Identities and the Hybridized History of the Rohingyas', in R. Egreteau & F. Robinne (eds.), *Metamorphosis: Studies in Social and Political Change in Myanmar*. Singapore: NUS Press, pp. 151–78.

———— 2017a. 'Transmutations of the Rohingya Movement in the Post-2012 Rakhine State Crisis', in O. K. Gin & V. Grabowsky (eds.), *Ethnic and Religious Identities and Integration in Southeast Asia*. Paris: École Française d'Extrême-Orient (EFEO)/Chiang Mai: Silkworm, pp. 191–239.

———— 2017b. 'Mapping Burma and Northern Thailand in 1795: Francis Hamilton's Critical Accounts of Native Maps', in P. Skilling & J. T. McDaniel (eds.), *Imagination and Narrative: Lexical and Cultural Translation in Buddhist Asia*. Chiang Mai: Silkworm, pp. 117–59.

———— 2018a. 'Conflict and Mass Violence in Arakan (Rakine State): The 1942 Events and Political Identity Formation', in A. South & M. Lall (eds), *Citizenship in Myanmar: Ways of Being In and From Burma*. Singapore: Chiang Mai University Press, pp. 193–221.

———— 2018b. 'History and Victimhood: Engaging with Rohingya Issues'. *Insight Turkey* 20 (1): 99–118.

Leider, J., & Kyaw Minn Htin. 2015. 'King Maṅḥ Co Mvan's Exile in Bengal: Legend, History, and Context'. *Journal of Burma Studies* 19 (2): 371–405.

Leuprecht, C. 2010. 'The Demographic Security Dilemma'. *Yale Journal of International Affairs* 5 (62): 60–74.

Lewa, C. 2009. 'North Arakan: An Open Prison for the Rohingya'. *Forced Migration Review* 32: 11.

Lieberman, V. 1978. 'Ethnic Politics in Eighteenth-Century Burma'. *Modern Asian Studies* 12 (3): 455–82.

———— 1986. 'How Reliable is U Kala's Burmese Chronicle? Some New Comparisons'. *Journal of Southeast Asian Studies* 17 (2): 236–55.

———— 2003. *Strange Parallels: Southeast Asia in Global Context, c. 800–1830*, vol. I: *Integration on the Mainland*. Cambridge: Cambridge University Press.

Lintner, B. 1999. *Burma in Revolt: Opium and Insurgency since 1948*. Chiang Mai: Silkworm.

Liu, J. H., & D. J. Hilton. 2005. 'How the Past Weighs on the Present: Social Representations of History and their Role in Identity Politics'. *British Journal of Social Psychology* 44: 537–56.

Luce, G. H. 1969. *Old Burma: Early Pagán*. New York: Artibus Asiae.

———— 1985. *Phases of Pre-Pagan Burma*, 2 vols. New York: Oxford University Press.

Lun Min Mang. 2015. 'National Reconciliation Top Priority and Toughest Challenge'. *Myanmar Times*, vol. 16, November.

Maje. 1991. *Our Journey: Voice from Arakan, Western Burma*. Cranford, NJ: Project Maje.

BIBLIOGRAPHY

Malesevic, S. 2004. *The Sociology of Ethnicity*. London: Sage.

Manrique, F. S. 1927. *Travels of Fray Sebastien Manrique 1629–1643* [a translation of *Itinerario de las missiones orientales*]. C. Eckford Luard (trans). London: Hakluyt Society.

Matisoff, James A. 2016. *The Sino-Tibetan Language Family*. Berkeley: University of California, available at http://stedt.berkeley.edu/about-st.

Maung Tha Hla. 2004. *The Rakhaing*. New York: Buddhist Rakhaing Cultural Association.

———— 2009. *The Rohingya Hoax*. New York: Buddhist Rakhaing Cultural Association.

Mann, M. 1993. *The Sources of Social Power*, vol. II: *The Rise of Classes and Nation-States, 1760–1914*. Cambridge: Cambridge University Press.

———— 2005. *The Dark Side of Democracy*. Cambridge: Cambridge University Press.

Mearsheimer, J. J. 2001. *The Tragedy of Great Power Politics*. New York: Norton.

Michael, M. S. 2007. 'The Cyprus Peace Talks: A Critical Appraisal'. *Journal of Peace Research* 44 (5): 587–604.

———— 2011. *Resolving the Cyprus Conflict: Negotiating History*, rev. edn. Basingstoke: Palgrave Macmillan.

Min Aung Hlaing. 2017a. 'Conspirators of Terrorist Attacks and Families Flee to Bangladesh'. Senior General Min Aung Hlaing, Facebook, 16 November, available at http://bit.ly/2muFJY4.

———— 2017b. 'Gallant Efforts to Defend the HQ against Terrorist Attacks and Brilliant Efforts to Restore Regional Peace, Security are Honoured'. Senior General Min Aung Hlaing, Facebook, 21 September, available at http://bit.ly/2hCQq9o.

Min Aung Khine. 2018. 'Four Rohingya Sentenced to Death for Deadly 2016 Attack in Rakhine'. *The Irrawaddy*, 23 February.

Min Min & Moe Aung 2015. 'The Welcome Migrants from Bangladesh'. *Frontier Myanmar*, 23 September, available at https://frontiermyanmar.net/en/features/welcome-migrants-from-bangladesh.

Min Thein Aung. 2017. 'Myo Farmers Dead and Missing in Myanmar's Volatile Maungdaw Township'. Radio Free Asia, 3 August.

Minye Kaungbon. 1994. *Our Three Main National Causes*. Rangoon: News & Periodicals Enterprise.

Mitchiner, M. 2000. *The Land of Water: Coinage and History of Bangladesh and Later Arakan circa 300 BC to the Present Day*. London: Hawkins.

Mizzima. 2012. 'Suu Kyi Discusses Racial Violence with Muslims'. *Mizzima*, 7 June.

MLC. 2014. *Myanmar–English Dictionary*. Yangon: Department of the Myanmar Language Commission, Ministry of Education, Union of Myanmar.

Moe Myint. 2017. 'Settling Scores in Northern Rakhine State'. *The Irrawaddy*, 14 December.

———— 2018a. 'Construction Plan for New Police Regimental Base Causes Rohingya to Flee'. *The Irrawaddy*, 16 February.

———— 2018b. 'Ninety Percent of Rohingya Population Ejected from Rakhine'. *The Irrawaddy*, 23 February.

MoHA. 2018. 'Bengalis Leaving Maungdaw Township for Bangladesh'. Ministry of Home Affairs Facebook feed [in Burmese], 18 February, available at www.facebook.com/officemohamyanmar/posts/2247724118586523.

Mole, R. 2001. *The Temple Bells are Calling: A Personal Record of the Last Years of British Rule in Burma*. Durham, Edinburgh, and Oxford: Pentland Press, available at www.networkmyanmar.org/images/stories/PDF12/robert-mole.pdf.

Moore, J. 2017. 'al-Qaeda Promises Jihad against Myanmar over Rohingya Crackdown'. *Newsweek*, 13 September.

MPM. 2012. 'Rakhine State Crisis Efforts'. Chiang Mai: Burma News International, available at http://www.mmpeacemonitor.org/peace-process/rakhine-state-crisis-efforts.

———— 2016. 'Conflicts Archive'. Chiang Mai: Burma News International, available at www.mmpeacemonitor.org/conflict/conflict-overview/conflicts-archive.

Mratt Kyaw Thu. 2016. 'IDP Numbers Rise in Rakhine as Forced Labour Allegations Fly'. *Frontier Myanmar*, 6 May.

———— 2017. 'Rakhine Govt to Sign Maungdaw Economic Zone MOU with Mysterious Consortium'. *Frontier Myanmar*, 11 September, available at https://frontiermyanmar.net/en/rakhine-govt-to-sign-maungdaw-economic-zone-mou-with-mysterious-consortium.

Mratt Kyaw Thu & S. Gleeson. 2016. 'Arakan Army Chief's Father-in-Law Appointed Rakhine Parliament Speaker'. *Frontier Myanmar*, 8 February.

MSF. 2017. 'MSF surveys estimate 6,700 Rohingya were killed in Myanmar'. Médecins Sans Frontières, 13 December, available at https://www.msf.org.za/stories-news/press-releases/msf-surveys-estimate-6700-rohingya-were-killed-myanmar.

Muller, E. N. & E. Weede. 1994. 'Theories of Rebellion, Relative Deprivation and Power Contention'. *Rationality and Society* 6 (1): 40–57.

Murer, J. S. 2012. 'Ethnic Conflict: An Overview of Analyzing and Framing Communal Conflicts from Comparative Perspectives'. *Terrorism and Political Violence* 24 (4): 561–80.

Murray, P. 1949. 'Secret' Correspondence (Perspective on the troubles in North Arakan). To Robert W. D. Fowler Commonwealth Relations Office, 26 January 1949, UK Foreign Office file SW1, F 1323/1015/79.

———— 1980. 'The British Military Administration of North Arakan 1942–43'. Private communication, available at www.burmalibrary.org.

BIBLIOGRAPHY

Murshid, N. 2013. *The Politics of Refugees in South Asia*. London: Routledge.

Myanmar Times. 2017. 'Rakhine to Construct Maungdaw Economic Zone'. *Myanmar Times*, 1 September.

Myo Pa Pa San. 2017. 'Rakhine Govt Forges on with Maungdaw Economic Zone'. *The Irrawaddy*, 13 September.

Narinjara. 2012. 'Arakan Public Meeting Successfully Concludes in Rathidaung'. Narinjara Independent Arakanese News Agency, 29 September, available at http://narinjara.com/arakan-public-meeting-successfully-concludes-in-rahindaung/.

Nay Yi [aka Ye Moe]. 2016. 'An Anti-Terrorism Military Operation in Western Border of Myanmar'. *Myanmar Review Journal*, 19 October, available at http://yehtunblog.blogspot.com/2016/10/operation-backdoor.html.

Nay San Lwin. 2012. 'Making Rohingya Statelessness'. *New Mandala*, 29 October, available at http://www.newmandala.org/making-rohingya-statelessness/.

NDPD. 2012. *In Respect of the Fact that the Muslim Inhabitants of Rakhine State are Natives by Race and Citizens of the Republic of the Union of Myanmar Under Law or by Natural Birth*. Yangon: National Democratic Party for Development, 7 April, report circulated to Naypyitaw cabinet ministers and MPs.

Nemoto, K. 2000. 'The Concepts of *Dobama* ("Our Burma") and *Thudo-Bama* ("Their Burma") in Burmese Nationalism, 1930–1948'. *Journal of Burma Studies* 5: 1–16.

New York Times. 2016a. 'Aung San Suu Kyi's Cowardly Stance on the Rohingya'. *New York Times*, editorial, 9 May.

———— 2016b. 'Kofi Annan, in Myanmar, Voices Concern over Reported Abuses of Rohingya'. *New York Times*, 6 December.

Nicholson, C. 2016. 'The Role of Historical Representations in Israeli–Palestinian Relations: Narratives from Abroad'. *Peace and Conflict: Journal of Peace Psychology* 22 (1): 5–11.

NLD. 2015. *2015 Election Manifesto*. Authorised translation, National League for Democracy, available at www.burmalibrary.org/docs21/NLD_2015_Election_Manifesto-en.pdf.

NLM. 2012a. '10 Muslims Killed in Bus Attack'. *New Light of Myanmar*, 5 June, p. 10.

———— 2012b. 'Three Murderers who Raped, Stabbed a Woman to Death to be Brought to Trial Soonest'. *New Light of Myanmar*, 5 June, p. 10.

Nyan Lynn Aung. 2016. 'Rakhine Chief Minister Says IDPs from All Communities Need Aid'. *Myanmar Times*, 28 April.

Nyan Hlaing Lynn. 2018. 'Inn Din Village Administrator Facing Investigation after Reuters Report on Massacre'. *Frontier Myanmar*, 12 February.

Nyein Nyein. 2012. 'Riot Claims Three Lives in Arakan State'. *The Irrawaddy*, 8 June.

BIBLIOGRAPHY

OCHA Myanmar. 2017. *Myanmar: Northern Rakhine State Flash Update No. 1 (as of 8 March 2017).* United Nations Office for the Coordination of Humanitarian Affairs, Myanmar, available at http://reliefweb.int/sites/reliefweb.int/files/resources/170308%20Myanmar%20Flash%20Update.pdf.

OHCHR. 2017. *Flash Report: Interviews with Rohingyas fleeing from Myanmar since 9 October 2016.* Yangon: Office of the High Commissioner, United Nations Human Rights, 3 February, available at www.ohchr.org/Documents/Countries/MM/FlashReport3Feb2017.pdf.

————— 2018. *37th Session of the Human Rights Council: Opening Statement by UN High Commissioner for Human Rights.* Office of the High Commissioner, United Nations Human Rights, available at www.ohchr.org/EN/NewsEvents/Pages/DisplayNews.aspx.

OIC. 2016. 'OIC Groups in Geneva and Brussels Hold Emergency Meetings on Crisis Situation Facing the Rohingya in Myanmar'. 23 December, available at www.oic-oci.org/topic/?t_id=12966&t_ref=5697&lan=en.

————— 2017. *Final Communique of the Extraordinary Session of the OIC Council of Foreign Ministers on the Situation of the Rohingya Muslim Minority in Myanmar.* Organization of Islamic Cooperation, Kuala Lumpur, 19 January, available at www.oic-oci.org/docdown/?docID=573&refID=64.

Paddock, R. C., E. Barry, & M. Ives. 2017. 'Persecuted Minority in Myanmar is Escalating its Armed Insurgency'. *New York Times*, 19 January.

Paton, C. 1826. *A Short Report on Arakan.* London: Colonial Office, available at https://www.scribd.com/document/143190474/Charles-Paton-s-a-Short-Report-on-Arakan.

Pe Maung Tin & G. H. Luce. 1923. *The Glass Palace: Chronicle of the Kings of Burma.* Translation of the first portions of the *Hmannan Maha Yazawindawgyi*, compiled by the Royal Historical Commission between 1829 and 1832. London: Oxford University Press.

Phayre, A. P. 1841. 'Account of Arakan'. *Journal of the Asiatic Society* 117 (33): 679–711.

————— 1844. 'On the History of Arakan'. *Journal of the Asiatic Society of Bengal* 1: 23–52.

PHR. 2013. *Massacre in Central Burma: Muslim Students Terrorized and Killed in Meiktila.* Cambridge, MA and Washington, DC: Physicians for Human Rights.

Ponnudurai, P. 2012. 'Monks March against Rohingya'. Radio Free Asia, 9 September.

Pope Francis. 2017. 'Pope Francis: Appeal for End to Violence against Rohingya'. Vatican Radio, 27 August, available at http://en.radiovaticana.va/news/2017/08/27/pope_francis_appeal_for_end_to_violence_against_rohingya/1333091.

BIBLIOGRAPHY

Posen, B. R. 1993. 'The Security Dilemma and Ethnic Conflict'. *Survival* 35: 27–47.

Psaltis, C. 2016. 'Collective Memory, Social Representations of Inter-communal Relations, and Conflict Transformation in Divided Cyprus'. *Peace and Conflict: Journal of Peace Psychology* 22 (1): 19–27.

Pugh, M., & N. Cooper, with J. Goodhand. 2004. *War Economies in a Regional Context: Challenges of Transformation*. Boulder and London: Lynne Rienner.

Rattansi, A. 1999. 'Racism, "Postmodernism", and Reflexive Multi-culturalism', in S. May (ed.), *Critical Multiculturalism: Rethinking Multicultural and Antiracist Education*. London: Falmer Press, pp. 77–111.

Renard, R. D. 1988. 'Minorities in Burmese History', in K. M. de Silva (ed.), *Ethnic Conflict in Buddhist Societies*. London: Pinter, pp. 78–91.

Reuters. 2012. 'Four Killed as Rohingya Muslims Riot in Myanmar: Government'. Reuters, 8 June, available at https://www.reuters.com/article/us-myanmar-violence/four-killed-as-rohingya-muslims-riot-in-myanmar-government-idUSBRE85714E20120608.

————— 2018. 'Bill Richardson Quits Myanmar's "Whitewash" Rohingya Crisis Panel'. Reuters, 24 January, available at https://www.reuters.com/article/us-myanmar-rohingya-richardson-exclusive/exclusive-richardson-quits-myanmars-whitewash-rohingya-crisis-panel-idUSKBN1FD2OJ.

RFA. 2017. 'Myanmar to Begin Taking Back Rohingya Refugees in January: Social Welfare Minister'. Radio Free Asia, 13 December.

Richardson, B. 2018a. Statement of Governor Bill Richardson. Press release, 24 January.

————— 2018b. 'How the West Can Help Fix the Rohingya Crisis'. *Time Magazine*, 15 February.

RNDP. 2012. *Criticizing the Historical Fabrication of Bengali who Assume themselves as Rohingya and Pretend themselves to be taing-yin-thar*. Sittwe: Rakhine Nationalities Development Party, May, report circulated to Naypyitaw cabinet ministers and MPs.

Robinson, G. 2016. 'Rakhine State Conflict Changes Myanmar's Game: International Outcry over Rohingya Crackdown Puts Fresh Pressure on Suu Kyi'. *Nikkei Asian Review*, 19 December.

————— 2017. 'The State Counsellor Daw Aung San Suu Kyi's Exclusive Interview with Nikkei Asian Review'. State Counsellor Office, Naypyitaw, 22 September, available at www.statecounsellor.gov.mm/en/node/1035.

Roe, P. 1999. 'The Intrastate Security Dilemma: Ethnic Conflict as a "Tragedy"?'. *Journal of Peace Research* 36 (2): 183–202.

————— 2005. *Ethnic Violence and the Societal Security Dilemma*. Abingdon: Routledge.

Romah, A. 2015. 'Indonesia: Aceh Wants Myanmar Punished for Rohingya Abuse'. Anadolu Agency, 29 June.

Ross, M. H. 1993. *The Management of Conflict: Interpretations and Interests in Comparative Perspective*. New Haven: Yale University Press.

———— 2007. *Cultural Contestation in Ethnic Conflict*. Cambridge: Cambridge University Press.

Rouhana, N. N., & D. Bar-Tal. 1998. 'Psychological Dynamics of Intractable Ethnonational Conflicts: The Israeli–Palestinian Case'. *American Psychologist* 53: 761–70.

Sadan, M. 2013. *Being and Becoming Kachin: Histories beyond the State in the Borderworlds of Burma*. Oxford: Oxford University Press.

Sagart, L. 2005. 'Tai-Kadai as a Subgroup of Austronesian', in L. Sagart et al. (eds.), *The Peopling of East Asia: Putting Together Archaeology, Linguistics and Genetics*. London: Routledge, pp. 177–81.

Sakhawat, A. 2017. '"We Will Fight Until the Last Drop of Blood"'. *Dhaka Tribune*, 10 January.

Sassen, S. 2008. *Territory, Authority, Rights: From Medieval to Global Assemblages*, 2nd rev. edn. Princeton: Princeton University Press.

———— 2013. 'Global Finance and its Institutional Spaces', in K. Knorr-Cetina & A. Preda (eds.), *The Oxford Handbook of the Sociology of Finance*. Oxford: Oxford University Press, pp. 13–32.

———— 2014. *Expulsions: Brutality and Complexity in the Global Economy*. Cambridge, MA: Belknap Press of Harvard University Press.

———— 2016. 'A Massive Loss of Habitat: New Drivers for Migration'. *Sociology of Development* 2 (2): 204–33.

———— 2017a. 'Is Rohingya Persecution Caused by Business Interests Rather Than Religion?'. *The Guardian*, 5 January.

———— 2017b. 'The Assault on the Rohingya is Not Only about Religion—It's Also about Land'. *Huffington Post*, 15 September.

Schissler, M., M. J. Walton, & Phyu Phyu Thi. 2015. 'The Roots of Religious Conflict in Myanmar'. *The Diplomat*, 6 August.

Scott, J. C. 2009. *The Art of Not Being Governed*. New Haven: Yale University Press.

Seit Twe Maung. 1960. 'Rohengya Affairs'. *Rakhine Tanzaung Magazine* 2 (9).

Selth, A. 2002. *Burma's Armed Forces: Power without Glory*. Norwalk, CT: Eastbridge.

———— 2003. *Burma's Muslims: Terrorists or Terrorised?*. Canberra: Strategic and Defence Studies Centre, ANU.

———— 2004. 'Burma's Muslims and the War on Terror'. *Studies in Conflict and Terrorism* 27 (2): 107–26.

———— 2013. 'Burma's Muslims: A Primer'. *The Interpreter*, Lowy Institute for International Policy, 27 March.

Sen, A. K. 1999. *Development as Freedom*. Oxford: Oxford University Press.

———— 2006. *Identity and Violence*. New York: Norton.

BIBLIOGRAPHY

Seppings, E. H. L. 1925. 'Arakan: A Hundred Years Ago, and Fifty Years After'. *Journal of the Burma Research Society* 15 (1): 53–72.

Serajuddin, A. M. 1986. 'Muslim Influence in Arakan and the Muslim Names of Arakanese Kings: A Reassessment'. *Journal of the Asiatic Society of Bangladesh* 31 (1): 17–23.

Schissler, M., M. J. Walton, & Phyu Phyu Thi. 2015. 'Threat and Virtuous Defence: Listening to Narratives of Religious Conflict in Six Myanmar Cities'. Working Paper 1:1, Myanmar Media and Society (MMAS).

Sherman, J. 2003. 'Burma: Lessons from the Ceasefires', in K. Ballentine and J. Sherman (eds.), *The Political Economy of Armed Conflict: Beyond Greed and Grievance*. Boulder: Lynne Rienner, pp. 225–55.

Shwe Zan. 2005. 'Study of Muslim Infiltration into Rakhine State', in Shwe Zan & Aye Chan (eds.), *Influx Viruses: The Illegal Muslims in Akrakan*. New York: Arakanes in United States, pp. 3–20.

Shwe Zan & Aye Chan (eds.). 2005. *Influx Viruses: The Illegal Muslims in Arakan*. New York: Arakanes in United States.

Siddiquee, M. M. (ed.). 2014. *The Rohingyas of Arakan: History and Heritage*. Chittagong: Ali Publishing House.

Siddiqui, H. 2008. *The Forgotten Rohingya: Their Struggle for Human Rights in Burma*. Amazon Digital Services.

——— 2012. 'Letter from America: The Rohingya Question—Parts 1–6'. *Asian Tribune*, 25 November, 2, 9, 16, and 23 December 2012 and 2 January 2013.

——— 2014. 'Rohingya: The Forgotten People '. *Kaladan Press*, 27 June.

Singer, N. F. 2008. *Vaishali and the Indianization of Arakan*. New Delhi: APA Publishing.

Sithu Aung Myint. 2016. 'A Lesson in Defusing Tensions'. *Frontier Myanmar*, 22 May.

Sithu Lwin. 2012. 'Mandalay Residents, Monks Protest Rakhine Violence'. *Myanmar Times*, 10 September.

Slim, H. 2014. *Expert Opinion on Humanitarian Strategy in Rakhine State: A Report for UNOCHA Myanmar*. Oxford: Institute of Ethics, Law and Armed Conflict, University of Oxford.

Slodkowski, A. 2016. 'Myanmar Army Says 86 Killed in Fighting in Northwest'. Reuters, 15 November.

Smart, R. B. 1917. 'Akyab District', in *Burma Gazetteer*. Rangoon: Government Printing, vol. A.

Smith, A. D. 1986. *The Ethnic Origins of Nations*. Oxford: Basil Blackwell.

——— 1999. *Myths and Memories of the Nation*. Oxford: Oxford University Press.

Smith, M. 1989. 'Burma and World War II'. *Cultural Survival Quarterly* 13 (4), available at https://www.culturalsurvival.org/publications/cultural-survival-quarterly/13-4-burma-search-peace.

———— 1991. *Burma: Insurgency and the Politics of Ethnicity*. London: Zed.

———— 1994. *Ethnic Groups in Burma: Development, Democracy and Human Rights*. London: Anti-Slavery International.

———— 1995. 'The Muslim "Rohingya" of Burma'. Conference paper, Burma Centrum Nederland, Amsterdam, 11 December, available at www.kaladan-press.org/scholar-column-mainmenu-36/36-rohingya/194-the-muslim-rohingya-of-burma.

———— 1999. *Burma: Insurgency and the Politics of Ethnicity*, 2nd edn. London: Zed.

———— 2007. 'Ethnic Conflicts in Burma: From Separatism to Federalism', in A. T. H. Tan (ed.), *A Handbook of Terrorism and Insurgency in Southeast Asia*. Cheltenham: Edward Elgar, pp. 293–321.

———— 2018. 'Ethnic Politics and Citizenship in History', in A. South & M. Lall (eds.), *Citizenship in Myanmar: Ways of Being In and From Burma*. Singapore: Chiang Mai University Press, pp. 26–58.

Snow, D. A., & R. D. Benford. 1992. 'Master Frames and Cycles of Protest', in A. D. Morris & C. M. Mueller (eds.), *Frontiers in Social Movement Theory*. New Haven: Yale University Press, pp. 135–55.

Snyder, R. 2006. 'Does Lootable Wealth Breed Disorder? A Political Economy of Extraction Framework'. *Comparative Political Studies* 39 (8): 943–68.

Soe Lin Aung. 2017. 'Three Theses on the Crisis in Rakhine'. *Tea Circle: An Oxford Forum for New Perspectives on Burma/Myanmar*, 27 September 27.

Solnit, D. B., & F. K. Li. 2007. 'Tai Languages'. *Encyclopaedia Britannica*, available at https://www.britannica.com/topic/Tai-languages.

South, A. 2008. *Ethnic Politics in Burma: States of Conflict*. Abingdon: Routledge.

South, A., & M. Lall. (eds). 2018. *Citizenship in Myanmar: Ways of Being In and From Burma*. Singapore: Chiang Mai University Press.

Steinberg, D. I. 2006. *Turmoil in Burma*. Norwalk, CT: Eastbridge.

Stewart, F. 2000. 'Crisis Prevention: Tackling Horizontal Inequalities'. *Oxford Development Studies* 28 (3): 245–62.

———— 2008. *Horizontal Inequalities and Conflict*. Basingstoke: Palgrave.

Swan Ye Htut. 2016. 'Parliament Approves Urgent Debate on Rakhine Fighting'. *Myanmar Times*, 3 May.

Tahir, M. A. 1998 [1963]. *A Short History of Rohingya and Kamans of Burma*. Ahmed F. K. Jilani (trans). Chittagong: Institute of Arakan Studies; 1st edn Myitkyina: United Rohingya National League, 1963.

Tajfel, H. 1981. *Human Groups and Social Categories*. Cambridge: Cambridge University Press.

Tarrow, S. 1994. *Power in Movement: Social Movements, Collective Action and Politics*. Cambridge: Cambridge University Press.

———— 1998. *Power in Movement: Social Movements and Contentious Politics*, 2nd edn. Cambridge: Cambridge University Press.

Taylor, D. M., & F. M. Moghaddam. 1987. *Theories of Intergroup Relations: International Social Psychological Perspectives*, 2nd edn. Westport: Praeger.

Taylor, R. H. 1982. 'Perceptions of Ethnicity in the Politics of Burma'. *Southeast Asian Journal of Social Sciences* 10 (1): 7–22.

———— 2007. 'British Policy towards Myanmar and the Creation of the "Burma Problem"', in N. Ganesan & Kyaw Yin Hlaing (eds.), *Myanmar: State, Society and Ethnicity*. Singapore: Institute of Southeast Asian Studies, pp. 70–95.

———— 2009. *The State in Myanmar*. London: Hurst.

———— 2015. 'Refighting Old Battles, Compounding Misconceptions: The Politics of Ethnicity in Myanmar Today'. *ISEAS Perspective* 12: 1–16.

Teschke, B. 2003. *The Myth of 1648: Class, Geopolitics and the Making of Modern International Relations*. London: Verso.

———— 2016. 'Rethinking International Relations: An Interview with Benno Teschke'. *Viewpoint Magazine*, 18 August.

Than Tun (ed.). 1983a. *The Royal Orders of Burma, AD 1598–1885*, part 1: *AD 1598–1648*. Kyoto: Center for Southeast Asian Studies, Kyoto University.

———— (ed.). 1983b. *The Royal Orders of Burma, AD 1598–1885*, part 2: *AD 1649–1750*. Kyoto: Center for Southeast Asian Studies, Kyoto University.

Thant Myint-U. 2001. *The Making of Modern Burma*. Cambridge: Cambridge University Press.

———— 2006. *The River of Lost Footsteps: A Personal History of Burma*. New York: Farrar, Straus & Giroux.

Thaw Kaung. 2000. 'Ayedawbon Kyan, an Important Myanmar Literary Genre Recording Historical Events'. *Journal of the Siam Society* 88 (1–2): 21–33.

———— 2010. *Aspects of Myanmar History and Culture*. Yangon: Loka Ahlinn Publishing.

Thawnghmung, A. M. 2012. *The 'Other' Karen in Myanmar: Ethnic Minorities and the Struggle without Arms*. New York: Lexington Books.

———— 2016. 'The Politics of Indigeneity in Myanmar: Competing Narratives in Rakhine State'. *Asian Ethnicity* 17 (4): 527–47.

The Star. 2016. 'Putrajaya: Rohingya Issue Has Become an International Matter'. *The Star (online)*, 3 December.

Tibbetts, G. R. 1979. *A Study of the Arabic Texts Containing Material on South-East Asia*. Leiden: Brill for the Royal Asiatic Society.

Tilly, C. 1993. 'National Self-Determination as a Problem for All of Us'. *Daedalus* 122 (3): 29–36.

———— 1998. *Durable Inequality*. Los Angeles: University of California Press.

Titchen, A., & D. Hobson. 2005. 'Phenomenology', in B. Somekh & C. Lewin (eds.), *Research Methods in the Social Sciences*. London: Sage, pp. 121–30.

TNI. 2014. *Ethnicity without Meaning, Data without Context: The 2014 Census,*

Identity and Citizenship in Burma/Myanmar. Amsterdam: Trans-National Institute (TNI) Burma Policy Briefing 15.

Toft, M. 2006. *The Geography of Ethnic Violence*. Princeton: Princeton University Press.

Tomuschat, C. 2006. 'Secession and Self-Determination', in M. G. Cohen (ed.), *Secession: International Law Perspectives*. Cambridge: Cambridge University Press, pp. 23–45.

Tonkin, D. 2014a. 'The "Rohingya" Identity: British Experience in Arakan 1826–1948'. Network Myanmar, 9 April, available at www.networkmyanmar.org/images/stories/PDF17/Rohingya-Identity-rev.pdf.

———— 2014b. 'The "Rohingya" Identity: Further Thoughts'. Network Myanmar, 19 April, available at www.networkmyanmar.org/images/stories/PDF17/Rohingya-Identity-II.pdf.

———— 2018. 'Exploring the Issue of Citizenship in Rakhine State', in A. South & M. Lall (eds.), *Citizenship in Myanmar:Ways of Being In and From Burma*. Singapore: Chiang Mai University Press, pp. 222–63.

Turner, A. J. 2014. *Saving Buddhism: The Impermanence of Religion in Colonial Burma*. Honolulu: Hawaii University Press.

Ullah, Aman. 2017. 'The Rohingya and their Right to Self-Identification'. 4 May, The Stateless Rohingya, available at http://www.thestateless.com/2017/05/the-rohingya-and-their-right-to-self-identification.html.

UNHCR. 2011. *States of Denial: A Review of UNHCR's Response to the Protracted Situation of Stateless Rohingya Refugees in Bangladesh*. Geneva: United Nations High Commissioner for Refugees.

———— 2016. *UNHCR Bangladesh Fact Sheet: March 2016*. UNHCR Bangladesh, available at http://reporting.unhcr.org/sites/default/files/UNHCR%20Bangladesh%20Factsheet%20-%20MAR16.pdf.

———— 2017. *Mixed Movements in South-East Asia*. Bangkok: UNHCR Regional Office for South-East Asia, available at http://reporting.unhcr.org/sites/default/files/UNHCR%20-%20Mixed%20Movements%20in%20South-East%20Asia%20-%202016%20—%20April%202017_0.pdf.

UNOCHA. 2013. *Rakhine Response Plan (Myanmar) July 2012–December 2013*. Yangon: United Nations Office for the Coordination of Humanitarian Affairs; revised 12 August, available at http://reliefweb.int/report/myanmar/rakhine-response-plan-myanmar-july-2012-%E2%80%93-december-2013.

UoB. 1973. *1973 Population Census: Rakhine State* (in Burmese). Rangoon: Department of Population, Ministry of Home and Religious Affairs, The Socialist Republic of the Union of Burma, available at www.dop.gov.mm/moip/index.php?route=product/product&path=54_56&product_id=174.

———— 1983. *1983 Population Census: Rakhine State*. Rangoon: Department of Population, Ministry of Home and Religious Affairs, The Socialist Republic of the Union of Burma, available at www.dop.gov.mm/moip/index.php?route=product/product&path=54_55&product_id=198.

UoM. 2013. *Final Report of Inquiry Commission on Sectarian Violence in Rakhine State.* Yangon: Republic of the Union of Myanmar, 8 July.

———— 2015. *The 2014 Myanmar Population and Housing Census, Rakhine State Report, Census Report Volume 3–K.* Nay Pyi Taw: Ministry of Immigration and Population, Union of Myanmar.

———— 2016. *The 2014 Myanmar Population and Housing Census, The Union Report: Religion, Census Report Volume 2-C.* Nay Pyi Taw: Ministry of Immigration and Population, Union of Myanmar.

———— 2017a. '42 Weapons Still Lost in Maungtaw Following 9 October Attack'. President's Office, The Republic of the Union of Myanmar, March, available at www.president-office.gov.mm/en/?q=issues/rakhine-state-affairs/id-7385.

———— 2017b. '163 Killed, 91 Missing from 9 Oct to 26 Sept in N-Rakhine 254 Total Casualty under ARSA Terrorist Attack'. State Counsellor Office Information Committee, The Republic of the Union of Myanmar, 27 September, available at www.statecounsellor.gov.mm/en/node/1042.

———— 2017c. 'Amphetamine Tablets Seized in Maungtaw'. President's Office, The Republic of the Union of Myanmar, 20 February, available at www.president-office.gov.mm/en/?q=issues/rakhine-state-affairs/id-7309.

———— 2017d. 'ARSA Burns Down Villages'. President's Office, The Republic of the Union of Myanmar, 4 September, available at www.president-office.gov.mm/en/?q=issues/rakhine-state-affairs/id-7648.

———— 2017e. 'ARSA Extremists Burn Down Houses in Maungtaw'. President's Office, The Republic of the Union of Myanmar, 6 September, available at www.president-office.gov.mm/en/?q=issues/rakhine-state-affairs/id-7664.

———— 2017f. 'Breaking News-29: ARSA Extremist Terrorists Open Fire at Security Forces, Torch Homes'. State Counsellor Office Information Committee, The Republic of the Union of Myanmar, 4 September, available at www.statecounsellor.gov.mm/en/node/993.

———— 2017g. 'Breaking News-32: Humanitarian Aid Provided to Displaced People Without Segregation'. State Counsellor Office Information Committee, The Republic of the Union of Myanmar, 5 September, available at www.statecounsellor.gov.mm/en/node/995.

———— 2017h. 'More than 190,000 Amphetamine Pills Seized in Sittway'. President's Office, The Republic of the Union of Myanmar, 19 February, available at www.president-office.gov.mm/en/?q=issues/rakhine-state-affairs/id-7295.

BIBLIOGRAPHY

———— 2017i. 'Tatmataw Ends Area Clearance Operations in Northern Rakhine State'. President's Office, The Republic of the Union of Myanmar, 16 February, available at www.president-office.gov.mm/en/?q=issues/rakhine-state-affairs/id-7288.

van Galen, S. E. A. 2008. 'Arakan and Bengal: The Rise and Decline of the Mrauk U Kingdom (Burma) from the Fifteenth to the Seventeeth Century AD'. Doctoral thesis, Universiteit Leiden.

van Schendel, W. (ed.). 1992. *Francis Buchanan in Southeast Bengal*. Reprint of Buchanan's 'An account of a journey undertaken by Order of the Board of Trade through the provinces of Chittagong and Tiperah, in order to look out for the places most proper for the cultivation of spices' (1798). Dhaka: Dhaka University Press.

Vandenbrink, R. 2012. 'Call to Put Rohingya in Refugee Camps'. Radio Free Asia, 12 July.

Verkuyten, M. 2005. *The Social Psychology of Ethnic Identity*. Hove and New York: Psychology Press.

VOA. 2018. 'Bangladesh Prepares to Mend Border Fence'. Voice of America–Burmese. 5 February.

Voice. 2017. 'India–Myanmar Neh-saq-twin ISIS a-kyan-peq-aphweq-mya kho-aung-ne-hu ye-daq-pweq tha-din-ya-shi' [ISIS terrorist group hides at the India–Myanmar border: police]. *The Voice*, 25 October.

Volkan, V. 1988. *The Need to Have Enemies and Allies: From Clinical Practice to International Relationships*. Northvale, NJ: Aronson.

Vrieze, P. 2013. 'Experts Reject Claims of "Rohingya Mujahideen" Insurgency'. *The Irrawaddy*, 15 July.

Wade, F. 2015. 'West Bank of the East: Burma's Social Engineering Project'. *Los Angeles Review of Books*, 7 November.

———— 2017. *Myanmar's Enemy Within: Buddhist Violence and the Making of a Muslim 'Other'*. London: Zed.

Wa Lone & Thu Thu Aung. 2016. 'Tatmadaw Rejects Arakan Army Offer of Talks'. *Myanmar Times*, 11 January.

Wa Lone, Kyaw Soe Oo, S. Lewis, & A. Slodkowski. 2018. 'Massacre in Myanmar: How Myanmar Forces Burned, Looted and Killed in a Remote Village'. Reuters Investigates, 8 February, available at https://www.reuters.com/article/us-myanmar-rakhine-events-specialreport/special-report-how-myanmar-forces-burned-looted-and-killed-in-a-remote-village-idUSKBN1FS3BH.

Walter, B. 1999a. 'Introduction', in B. F. Walter & J. Snyder (eds.), *Civil Wars, Insecurity and Intervention*. New York: Columbia University Press, pp. 1–12.

———— 1999b. 'Designing Transitions from Civil War: Demobilization, Democratization, and Commitments to Peace'. *International Security* 24 (1): 127–55.

Walton, M. J. 2013. 'The "Wages of Burman-ness": Ethnicity and Burman Privilege in Contemporary Myanmar'. *Journal of Contemporary Asia* 43 (1): 1–27.

———— 2018. 'National Political Dialogue and Practices of Citizenship in Myanmar', in A. South & M. Lall (eds.), *Citizenship in Myanmar:Ways of Being In and From Burma*. Singapore: Chiang Mai University Press, pp. 95–112.

Waltz, K. 1979. *Theory of International Politics*. New York: McGraw Hill.

Ware, A. 2015. 'Secessionist Aspects to the Buddhist–Muslim Sectarian Conflict in Rakhine State, Myanmar', in D. Kingsbury & C. Laoutides (eds.), *Territorial Separatism and Global Politics*. London: Routledge, pp. 153–68.

Webb, C. M. 1912. *Census of India, 1911*, vol. IX. Rangoon: Office of the Superintendent, Government Printing, available at www.networkmyanmar.org/images/stories/PDF17/1911-Extract.pdf.

Webb, K. 1995. *An Introduction to Problems in the Philosophy of Social Sciences*. London and New York: Pinter.

Welsh, B., & K. P. Huang. 2016. *Myanmar's Political Aspirations & Perceptions: 2015 Asian Barometer Survey Report*. Center for East Asia Democratic Studies, National Taiwan University.

Wertsch, J. V. 2002. *Voices of Collective Remembering*. Cambridge: Cambridge University Press.

———— 2008. 'The Narrative Organization of Collective Memory'. *Ethos* 36: 120–35.

Westcott, B., & K. Smith. 2017. 'Rohingya Violence a "Textbook Example of Ethnic Cleansing", UN Rights Chief Says'. CNN Edition (Updated 14:18 GMT), 11 September, available at http://edition.cnn.com/2017/09/11/asia/rohingya-un-ethnic-cleansing/index.html.

Wolf, E. 1969. *Peasant Wars of the Twentieth Century*. New York: Harper & Row.

Wolf, S. O. 2015. 'Myanmar's Rohingya Conflict "More Economic than Religious"'. Deutsche Welle, 4 June, available at http://www.dw.com/en/myanmars-rohingya-conflict-more-economic-than-religious/a-18496206.

Wolff, S. 2006. *Ethnic Conflict: A Global Perspective*. Oxford: Oxford University Press.

Woods, K. 2011. 'Ceasefire Capitalism: Military–Private Partnerships, Resource Concessions and Military–State Building in the Burma–China Borderlands'. *Journal of Peasant Studies* 38 (4): 747–70.

World Bank. 1990. 'Problems and Issues in Structural Adjustment'. Development Committee No. 23. Washington, DC: World Bank.

———— 2015. *Data:Wealth Ranking World Bank*. Yangon: Myanmar Information Management Unit (MIMU), available at www.themimu.info/search/node/World%20Bank%20Wealth%20Ranking.

Yale Law School. 2015. 'Persecution of the Rohingya Muslims: Is Genocide

Occurring in Myanmar's Rakhine State? A Legal Analysis'. Prepared for Fortify Rights by Allard K Lowenstein International Human Rights Clinic, Yale Law School.

Ye Mon. 2015. 'Rakhine Chief Minister Hits Out at Army over Fighting'. *Myanmar Times*, 1 May.

Ye Mon & Thu Thu Aung. 2016. 'Tatmadaw Pledges to "Eliminate" Arakan Army in Rakhine Fighting'. *Myanmar Times*, 8 January.

Yegar, M. 1972. *The Muslims of Burma: A Study of a Minority Group*. Wiesbaden: Otto Harrassowitz.

———— 2002. *Between Integration and Secession: The Muslim Communities of the Southern Philippines, Southern Thailand, and Western Burma / Myanmar*. New York: Lexington.

Yule, H. 1882. 'Notes on the Oldest Records of the Sea-Route to China from Western Asia'. *Proceedings of the Royal Geographical Society and Monthly Record of Geography* 4 (11): 649–60.

Yunus, M. 1994. *A History of Arakan (Past & Present)*. Chittagong: Magenta Colour.

Zarni, M., & A. Cowley. 2014. 'The Slow-Burning Genocide of Myanmar's Rohingya'. *Pacific Rim Law & Policy Journal* 23 (3): 681–752.

Zaw Lynn Aung. 2009. 'A Brief Study of the Three Manuscripts Deposited in the British Library'. *Universities Research Journal* 2 (8): 261–71.

———— 2010. 'Introduction to Rakhine Razawin Nge Palm-Leaf Manuscript'. *Journal of the Myanmar Academy of Arts and Science* 9 (8): 1–12.

———— 2013. 'Two Rakhine Manuscripts in the Early Colonial Period (1824–1885)'. *Journal of the Myanmar Academy of Arts and Science* 11 (9): 1–12.

Zaw Min Htut. 2001. *The Union of Burma and Ethnic Rohingyas*. Tokyo: Burmese Rohingya Association in Japan.

Zaw, N. 2015. 'Union Parliament Passes Population Control Bill'. *The Irrawaddy*, 27 April.

Zul Nurain. 2009. *Rohingya History: Myth and Reality*. Ovi Project: self-published.

INDEX

INDEX

INDEX

INDEX

INDEX

INDEX